MW00584535

Putting It
All Together

Putting It All Together

The New Orthomolecular Nutrition

Abram Hoffer, M.D., Ph.D.
& Morton Walker, D.P.M.

 Keats Publishing, Inc., New Canaan, Connecticut

Putting It All Together: The New Orthomolecular Nutrition Copyright © 1996 by Abram Hoffer and Morton Walker

This book is a complete revision and expansion of *Orthomolecular Nutrition*, copyright © 1978 by A. Hoffer and Morton Walker

Library of Congress Cataloging-in-Publication Data
Hoffer, Abram, 1917–
    Putting it all together : the new othomolecular nutrition / Abram Hoffer & Morton Walker.
        p.   cm.
    Rev. ed. of: Orthomolecular nutrition / Abram Hoffer and Morton Walker, New Canaan, Conn. : Keats Pub., c1978.
    Includes bibliographical references and index.
    ISBN 978-0-07-183959-4
    1. Orthomolecular therapy. 2. Vitamin therapy. 3. Nutrition. I. Walker, Morton. II. Hoffer, Abram, 1917–   Orthomolecular nutrition. III. Title.
RM217.H58   1996
615.5'3—dc20   96-14298
                                                                                      CIP

Printed in the United States of America

Keats Publishing, Inc.
27 Pine Street Box 876
New Canaan, Connecticut 06840-0876

        12 13 14   DSH/DSH   0 1 0

Contents

Introduction

Great control over many infectious diseases was achieved about fifty-five years ago. A principal factor in their control was the development of the sulfa drugs and of penicillin and other antibiotics. Many diseases, including cancer, cardiovascular disease and mental disease, have resisted the efforts toward control, and have continued to constitute a serious cause of human suffering.

Vaccines, antisera, and antibiotics have not been the only factors involved in controlling the infectious diseases. Over one hundred years ago tuberculosis was a great scourge. It began to diminish in significance before the antibiotics were developed, and it is likely that the control of tuberculosis was achieved largely through the development of better living conditions, including improved nutrition.

The importance of good nutrition to the preservation of health and prevention of disease, especially with respect to the question of the optimum intake of vitamins, has been almost entirely ignored by the authorities in the field of nutrition and of medicine and public health. During the period from about 1935 to 1945, when many vitamins became available in pure form and at reasonably low price, there was considerable interest in the question of whether or not an increased intake of vitamins could be used to prevent or cure various diseases. Positive results were reported by many investigators for many different diseases. Interest in the vitamins then died out. The reason for the decreased interest in vitamins is not clear, but it is likely that the development of the sulfa drugs and antibiotics was mainly responsible. Only during the last few years has the field of orthomolecular medicine attracted much attention. Dr. Abram Hoffer and his former collaborator Dr. Humphry Osmond deserve major credit for initiating the present era of great activity in the megavitamin and orthomolecular field through their discovery of the value of large doses of niacin or niacinamide in the control of schizophrenia.

I believe that a really great improvement in health can be achieved through the ingestion of the optimum amounts of vitamins and other nutrients, as described in this book by Hoffer and Walker on orthomolecular nutrition. The available evidence indicates that through improved nutrition the age-specific incidence of disease and mortality from disease can be decreased to one quarter of the present value and that other health measures taken in conjunction with these could lead to a further decrease. The length of the period of well-being of men and women might well be increased by sixteen to twenty-four years through improved nutrition and other health measures. Additional research is needed to determine with reliability the amounts of various nutrients that lead to the best of health. Dr. Hoffer has had extensive experience in the field of orthomolecular medicine, and I have trust in his judgment and recommendations.

Linus Pauling
Linus Pauling Institute of
Science and Medicine
Menlo Park, California

Preface to the First Edition

In 1950, I had completed my education as a physician and was ready to begin my second career. Before becoming a medical student, I had been a research biochemist working in a vitamin control laboratory for a flour mill, and was strongly interested in nutrition. By the time I had interned for a few months at City Hospital, Saskatoon, Saskatchewan, Canada, I had no further interest in nutrition but was very excited by the newer ideas in psychiatry. I found, to my chagrin, that having an M.D. degree had not prepared me for dealing with a large number of patients who were ill without any definite organic syndrome. Psychosomatic medicine became the vogue.

After a few years of intensive study and work in the new psychiatry (analytic and psychosomatic theory), I became convinced that these were not going to improve our understanding or our treatment results. Gradually my earlier interest in human nutrition, which had been so effectively quenched by four years as a medical student, began to return. By a direct route from our double-blind controlled experiments in 1952, which showed that vitamin B3 was an effective therapy for early schizophrenics, to investigations of carbohydrate metabolism (relative hypoglycemia) in 1966, I came to realize that there was no single chemotherapeutic substance—no single magic bullet. The secret of optimum health lay in the whole broad concept of nutrition, as developed by a large number of pioneer nutritionists. I have come full circle, back to my interest in nutrition—but now in clinical nutrition. My main contribution has been to help introduce the concepts developed by these scientists into psychiatry and, more recently, into general medicine.

It is sad to think that, had I remained at the same level of nutritional knowledge which I considered adequate, even advanced, in 1945, I could now be a standard modern nutritionist, a professor of nutrition, a hospital nutritionist, or an advisor to departments of public health, without learning anything beyond a few more details.

ABRAM HOFFER, M.D., Ph.D.

Twenty-seven years ago, I turned from the delivery of highly specialized foot treatment to writing about the entire structure of health care: disease prevention, obesity, genetics, emotional disturbances, nutrition, medical education, sexuality and more. I evolved into a full-time freelance medical writer and found the rewards of medical journalism stretching beyond money. Like medicine, it is a helpful and invaluable craft, steeped in the intrigue of techniques and the drama of human beings. Medical journalism has the staying power of service and curiosity. Besides, my writing offers other benefits. I gain personally from the information I disseminate and from the dedicated, intelligent people who supply this information.

Orthomolecular nutrition and its inventor, Dr. Abram Hoffer, are typical of what I mean. Here is a concept, which when put into daily practice, may allow the full span of 120 years of life human beings are allotted by nature. They will be healthy years, and happiness often accompanies good health. Dr. Abram Hoffer is a living testimonial to the nutritional concept he has developed.

It is our hope that people who read this book will follow the nutritional pathway in order to achieve the best good health their genetic structure will permit. This is important for everyone, but especially for professional people who are in a much better position to influence the health of many others. We hope it will help nutritionists regain their interest in and enthusiasm for understanding the relationship between good nutrition and good health. For, if they fail to rebuild nutrition as a modern progressive science, they will be bypassed by others who will.

Unless our society adopts the concepts of orthomolecular nutrition, there can be no halt in the progression of chronic physical and mental disease. Bad nutrition has destroyed whole societies, as it is today destroying primitive peoples exposed to "civilized" diets. Perhaps historians of disappearing cultures should be examining the role of technological development in food production. Did Rome deteriorate because the Romans switched from whole grain bread to a whiter bread and used water transported through lead pipes? Bad nutrition, like bad money, drives out the good.

MORTON WALKER, D.P.M.

Preface to This Edition

Since this book was first published in 1978 there has been a major paradigm shift in the way the medical profession views the use of vitamins. For many years the vitamin-as-prevention paradigm had held the field and was supported by all the healing professions. According to this viewpoint, vitamins were needed in very small amounts only for known vitamin deficiency diseases, such as scurvy or pellagra. It therefore made no sense to use doses larger than those recommended and enshrined in the nutrition standards promulgated by governments, nor to use vitamins in any dose for conditions not recognized as deficiencies. It was also considered unethical for physicians to use vitamins in this way and several lost their licenses to practice as a result.

In 1955 my colleagues and I published our finding that very large doses of nicotinic acid lowered total cholesterol levels. This vitamin is now considered one of the best and safest substances for lowering cholesterol and at the same time increasing high density lipoprotein cholesterol. Our report is considered the beginning of the new vitamin paradigm, the vitamin-as-treatment approach, because it broke the main tenets of the earlier paradigm. Earlier studies with vitamin E and vitamin C had broken the old, erroneous beliefs, but it was easier to reproduce chemical assays of cholesterol levels as proof of nicotinic acid's efficacy than to run corroborative clinical sudies on the two antioxidant vitamins.

It required about 40 years, not unusual in the history of medical discovery, before this new paradigm began to take over, and today it is moving at a rapid pace into modern medicine—but unfortunately not yet into psychiatry. The modern paradigm's main tenets are that one must use optimum doses of vitamins, which may be large or small, and that they may be very helpful for conditions which are not deficiency diseases of the classical type.

The best measure of this rapid new development is the existence of the Office of Alternative Medicine in the National Institutes of Health in Washington, D.C., and the recent introduction of alternative medicine into major medical schools such as Harvard, Columbia and others. Recently a series of seminars were devoted to this topic at Harvard Medical School. Orthomolecular medicine should, however, not be considered alternative medicine. It is really a major component of standard medicine and represents a return to our earlier roots in the 1930s when nutrition was a much more basic medical science.

I am very happy that this book, written by Dr. Morton Walker and myself and now revised, has made a major contribution to this healthy change of an outdated paradigm to the new one which is more accurate and will help many more patients. The benefits to people following the nutritional principles described in this book are not experienced as widely as they should be, but if physicians and other health professionals do not follow these principles, they will eventually lose their practices and may even be subject to sanctions. There is no better way to lower health costs than to help patients get well. This is what orthomolecular nutrition and this book are all about.

A. HOFFER, M.D., Ph.D.

Putting It All Together

Current Health Crises

POISONS EVERYWHERE AROUND US

A man, forty-six years old, a prominent West Coast executive, suffered from obscure complaints. They included headaches, backaches, episodes of weakness and tremulousness. His problem was diagnosed as "nerves—business tensions, you know!" He was treated for anxiety-depression by psychotherapists—first with antidepressant drugs and, when they didn't work, with shock treatment, which also didn't work. The depression and other nervous symptoms didn't leave. Later, drifting from one physician's care to another, the man happened to be referred to a doctor who practiced orthomolecular medicine. Among a variety of laboratory tests taken, hair analysis revealed that the patient suffered from mercury poisoning. The poor man had been made miserable almost as much from incorrect treatment rendered without a true diagnosis as he had from the invasion of his body by mercury.

A fourteen-year-old was diagnosed as schizophrenic. He was shy to an extreme. His behavior more often than not was erratic. Lacking coordination, items dropped from his hands recurrently, and he cried without provocation. He was given to talking to himself and to withdrawing into himself. Frequently he did not sleep for days at a stretch. When he did sleep he often awoke so wet with perspiration that his bed clothes had to be changed. This child was eventually institutionalized when conventional methods failed to solve his problem. Even hospitalization did nothing except alleviate his symptoms. It appeared that this young man would be lost to society as a perpetually unproductive adult. However, his parents persisted and explored every avenue of care. They brought him finally to an orthomolecular psychiatrist, who treated him with megavitamins and other dietary measures. On the basis of a "no-junk" diet, dietary supplements and no other treatment, the child became a bright, happy and active young man and grew into a well-functioning adult.

What initially caused this child's medical problem and prolonged it until the age of fourteen? The answer may seem oversimplified, but is inescapable: overwhelming changes in our food supply. No pharmaceutical company can introduce a new medicine until it has been shown to be nontoxic for humans when used as recommended. But anyone can do anything to food components and market the product with no requirement that it must at least match the nutritional quality of the agricultural products from which it was made. Even more dangerous, nutritionists are not remotely aware of the dangers of these products. Sugar is added to most processed foods, and this child had been undergoing allergic reactions to sugar. His condition was caused completely and solely by the foods he ate.

NUTRITIONAL SCIENCE LACKS RESOURCES

Almost half the population of the United States and Canada is more or less steadily subject to a variety of physical or mental ills. These recurrently sick people fall heir to chronic diseases ranging from learning and behavioral disorders of children to chronic arthritides of aging. Life seems more or less a continuous struggle against disabling conditions until irreversible senility or death frees the sufferer from his burden.

In spite of amazing technological advances over the past 45 years and a huge expenditure of resources, we are experiencing a steady rise in the incidence of degenerative diseases. Medicine, practiced in the traditional sense, has not done much to alter *infiltration degeneration*, the changes that arise from the deposit of abnormal matter within the tissue. Why is this so? Why is there technological pollution of our food supply?

Deterioration has been forced on our population by the creation of artificial foods lacking in natural vitamins and minerals. Processed food manufacturers have dissipated and distorted nature's quality control by removing nutrients and adding artificial substances and flavorings—most notably, and most detrimentally, sugar. Why is this continuing? Don't we know enough about the poisons in our foods or the processing out of natural nutrients?

The answers to these questions are clear and simple. Nutrition science lacks intellectual resources. Very little brain power is concentrated in this branch of knowledge. The medical profession too often confuses nutrition with dietetics. It does not concern itself sufficiently with the possibility that inadequate nutrition leads to health problems. Only an infinitesimal amount of systematized learning has been gathered about nutritional disease. As a result, a rapidly expanding pandemic of chronic degenerative diseases is occurring, but since the diseases are of a variety, too little alarm has been generated.

Every fourth person in North America is the victim of one or more of these degenerative conditions. Surely, if one-quarter of our population suffered from *one* disease, diabetes for example, there would be a massive public effort to discover the reasons and to develop an effective cure. But when the sick population includes sufferers from senility, cardiovascular conditions, arthritis, schizophrenia, learning and behavioral disorders, cancer of the colon, peptic ulcer and many other individual problems, society seems not to add them together as one major problem.

Food technologists look upon agricultural produce as a source of raw material from which artifact components are extracted and recombined into foods they can persuade the public to like and eat. The fact that these products are deficient in essential nutrients does not concern them. For example, the technological change from home ground whole wheat flour to the commercial white loaf removed a wholesome food, able by itself to sustain life. The nutritionally valuable bread was replaced with an easily marketable, palatable product designed to be "taste tempting," not to maintain health by providing sound nutrition. Food technologists may then replace only a few of the multinutritional substances removed and label their product "enriched." This is the same as being held up at gunpoint on a dark street and ordered to strip naked. The thief takes clothes and valuables, notices your shivering embarrassment, then returns your underwear and $1.50 to take the bus home. Do you then feel enriched?

Costs of relieving degenerative disease symptoms have risen at an astronomical rate. Every decade a larger share of the gross national product is devoted to health care. Even so, the more health-care expenditure, the unhealthier our people are. Why? The real villain, the catastrophic deterioration in the quality of our food, is ignored. As long as food processing continues to strip out essential nutrients, there will be no letup in the creation of chronic ill health. In 1940 about 20 percent of the food consumed in this country was processed. Today it is close to 75 percent. We consume the elements of our own destruction, with our excessive intake of sugar and unsaturated fats, loss of bulk or fiber, elimination of vitamins and minerals, and the pollution of food with chemicals never demonstrated to be safe.

Throughout the course of evolution there has been a dance between living organisms and their environment. Life cannot exist unless living creatures constantly adapt to environmental changes. Most often these changes are slow, occurring over thousands of years; occasionally they are very rapid. Humanity still has not adapted fully or successfully to changes that started 10,000 years ago when agriculture, farming and herding began.

One of the major evolutionary adaptations required is to the food supply. The same harmony is required between the nutritional needs of the body and the food which is consumed as there is between the needs of a finely tuned motor and the fuel it runs on. The failure to adapt is usually because changes in the environment occur too quickly. As humans, we still have the nutritional physiology of the past 50,000 years, but there has been a remarkable change in the nature of our food in the last 100 years. This "maladaption" is the source of most of the major chronic illnesses current today. One of the best ways of describing the changes in our food supply is to compare the diet we have been adapting to with the one in use today.

Characteristics of foods we have been adapting to:

1. Alive: All nutrients are present, and there is little deterioration due to spoilage and contamination. Meat and fish have been recently alive, and edible seeds which can still germinate are alive.
2. Fresh: Our ancestors could not store most foods very long. The disadvantages were hunger and famine, but not of the subtle malnutritional type we have today.
3. Whole: Since animals in the wild eat whole seeds and all edible parts of their prey, including their internal organs, this ensured that humans consumed the entire range of essential available nutrients.
4. Nontoxic: Toxic foods were selected out very simply: they killed or made the consumer sick, so people quickly learned not to use them anymore.

5. Endogenous: Animals and plants living on the same soil and under similar environmental conditions are more in tune with each other. This is especially true about essential fatty acids (see Chapter 8). Since cold-climate species have more of these essential fatty acids, a person living in the north does better consuming food which is also grown in the north.

6. Varied: Because it was impossible to store foods, people gathered a wide variety depending upon the time of day and the season. A variety of foods decreases the development of allergies.

7. Scarce: Because storage was impossible, there was no accumulation of staples. Animals and people either ate enough or went without, but seldom were they able to overconsume and become obese the way we can today.

8. Naturally flavored: Condiments, sweets and other additives were unknown. The fortification of foods with sugars and other additives is one of the factors that creates cravings for foods.

9. Simple: Many modern recipes require up to a dozen ingredients, while primitive foods tend to be simple. This can create havoc for people who are allergic to some of them but are not aware of their presence.

Characteristic foods in the high-tech diet developed over the past 100 years:

1. Dead: Modern storage in cold, dry places only partially prevents the slow destruction of foods kept a long time.

2. Stale: The ideal of processed foods is that they are made to remain stable. But in order to achieve this, much of the nutritive quality of the food is sacrificed. Stale food has lost many of its most valuable nutrients.

3. Artifact: Some isolated components of foods such as sugar, pure carbohydrates, fats, oils and protein powders are of low nutritional quality. Other artifacts such as vitamins and minerals can be used as supplements to improve the quality of the diet. Two examples of the first type of prepared foods are caviar that is not fish eggs and tomato soup that contains no tomatoes.

4. Toxic: High-tech foods contain any number of a very large list of chemicals which are used to grow, prepare and manufacture them into artifacts. The usual toxicity tests are inad-

equate, since they have not been employed long term and healthy animals are only tested with one chemical at a time. However, a major toxicity trial is taking place continuously on our total population, and these human guinea pigs aren't doing very well.

5. Exogenous: Food grown in climatic regions far removed from the people who are eating it provides more variety, but in most cases people are less adapted to such foods.

6. Monotonous: Modern high-tech diets usually depend very heavily on a few staples. Thus one can eat bread three times each day for a lifetime. People develop sensitivities or allergies to these staples, and the worst of these is to sugar, followed by dairy products and grains. Allergies can be avoided by a rotation diet or varying the food supply.

7. Overabundant: One result is obesity, which afflicts up to 25 percent of the population. Overabundance is one of the main factors causing the saccharine disease.

8. Artificially flavored: For many years herbs and other plant products were used to disguise the awful taste of food that could not be stored and had gone off or bad. Modern high-tech foods contain synthetic flavoring compounds which add nothing to the nutritional quality of the foods, except they make them too attractive, thus adding to the problem of obesity and other eating disorders. They also increase the additive burden that the body must bear.

THE FOSSILIZED NUTRITIONISTS

It may seem hard to believe, but I have treated no less than three nutritionists for depression and anxiety arising from *relative hypoglycemia*—a nutritional condition which should have been well within their own competence to deal with. Unhappily, academic nutritionists generally remain fossilized in their thinking at the 1950 level. Government and hospital nutritionists, who are primarily dietitians, seem more interested in the cosmetic aspects of food than in its nutritional quality. The most advanced understanding of clinical nutrition is held by a few far-seeing clinicians and biochemists.

Dr. Roger Williams is one of these productive nutritional biochemists. His work, from 1950 on, has shown that individuality, in all animal life, including the human, is impossible without variability—that is, that genetics, the psychosocial environment and the biophysical environment are equally important in contributing to individuality. We inherit certain determined characteristics from our ancestors. That is *genetics*. A child with a special talent will gravitate or may be encouraged by his family to pursue this talent. That is the *psychosocial environment*. You continually interact with and are shaped by such factors as food, air, heat, toxic chemicals, viruses or bacteria, light and physical trauma. That is the *biophysical environment*.

The range of variation among individuals is enormous. Some people become violently ill from ingesting foods that are nutritious for others. This truth explodes the myth of the minimum daily requirements (MDR) and recommended dietary allowances (RDA) so loved by government agencies. The need for nutrients will vary by many hundred percent. With sick people the range of need is many times greater. Those who require very large quantities of vitamins are *vitamin dependent*. The fossilized nutritionists tend to disregard this essential variability among people, and stick with the old and useless MDRs and RDAs.

Individuality means that the requirement for nutrients varies much more than most nutritionists believe. It can vary by a factor of a thousand. For example, normally 0.001 milligram (1 microgram) per day of vitamin B12 is sufficient, but a few subjects require 1 milligram per day by injection. When a person requires an amount of vitamin normally present in a good diet and instead pursues a diet deficient in that vitamin, he will develop a deficiency disease such as pellagra, scurvy, beriberi, or rickets. If, however, the individual is vitamin-dependent, his requirement for a particular vitamin is much greater; and even a good diet will be nutritionally inadequate. There will be a relative deficiency which will cause metabolic havoc in his body. Dependency is ignored by conventionally minded physicians and nutritionists alike, who fail to realize that each person must be given the right nutrition, in food and supplements, to meet his needs, whether they are high or low.

RDAs have been like the holy writ for many years, in spite of the fact that they were designed to provide guidelines for only the healthy part of the population. They are of no value to individuals who are not averages—or 50 percent of the total population. Orthomolecular therapists have consistently argued against the use of RDAs and have ignored them in their practices. Recently, David Mark Hegsted, professor emeritus of nutrition appointed to Harvard's New England Regional Primate Research Center in Southborough, Mass., recommended that RDAs be abolished. He said that the system is unworkable—it's based on estimates using healthy young males, the group in the population least likely to have nutritional deficiencies— and no one knows how to use it. Characterizing the RDA committee as "hopelessly outdated," Dr. J. Blumberg, professor of nutrition at Tufts University, told J. Challem, "The RDA committee is locked into the old paradigm of nutrition—how much is needed to prevent deficiency disease. It has not shifted gears to where medicine is today."

NO NUTRIENT WORKS ALONE

Every biochemist interested in nutrition knows that transformation reactions in the body essential for the production of energy and metabolism require a number of enzymes working either together or in sequence. If a reaction requires three vitamins, one is not more important than the other; all are needed. If one is lacking, *it* becomes the important one therapeutically. No nutrient works alone.

Nutrients work together as does an orchestra, to use Dr. Roger Williams' way of putting it. Like instruments playing in harmony, all the nutrients must be available in their optimum amounts. Optimum quantities may be different for each nutrient. Fortunately, we have adapted to a variety of foods which provide nearly optimum nutritional quantities and which are not harmful. They contain protein, fat and carbohydrate combined with vitamins and minerals packed in complicated living structures—animals and plants used for human consumption.

Human metabolism has not adapted to food artifacts recombined into products designed only to please the palate. The producers of modern foods ignore the fundamental orchestra principle suggested by Williams. Processed foods provide discord in the metabolic harmony: a missing nutrient is like a fiddle with a broken string. This is one of the major objections to many processed foods.

A second objection to synthetic foods is that other accessory factors in unprocessed food are not yet identified. Being unknown, they cannot be used in synthetic processing, and the diet therefore lacks them. Until we can be certain that *every* natural nutrient has been identified and incorporated in processed foods, it would be very imprudent—even hazardous—to depend solely on such foods.

Finally, processed foods contain additives of various sorts. These are included not to enhance the nutritional quality but rather to increase the palatability and storage properties. Additives are part of the poisons that assault us. Some additives have been proven to be downright dangerous to health—even to cause cancer.

Thus modern clinical nutrition must be built around two main concepts: the individuality and variability of human beings and the orchestra-like function of nutrients acting in harmony. Until this is. done, modern academic nutrition will continue to drift, completely separated from and unrelated to what is happening to people. The incidence of degenerative diseases will continue to rise. From our current level of 25 percent of the population suffering from them, we will see damaging effects occur among most of us. Predicting this, practitioners of orthomolecular medicine have taken a very considerable departure from the route of conventional medicine. According to a rapidly growing body of reports, orthomolecular nutrition is benefiting tens of thousands—even millions—suffering from varied physical, mental and behavioral disturbances, including many unhelped by other methods. Orthomolecular medicine's very heavy emphasis—often sole emphasis—on nutrition as therapy places it far away from what has been until now the mainstream of professional medical therapeutics.

Over the past 40 years I have seen a marked change in medical opinion of nutrition and the use of nutrients as supplements. In 1950 when I first began to practice medicine, it was generally believed that nutrition played a very minor, if any, role in the practice of medicine. Nutrition was not taught in medical schools, and physicians allowed nonclinical nutritionists and dietitians to take over the whole field. In 1955 the first paper was published which introduced the concept that large doses of vitamins could be used therapeutically for treating conditions not known to be vitamin-deficiency diseases. The decade 1970 to 1980 marked the beginning of the megavitamin decade. The 1980s saw the introduction of mineral supplements on a larger scale and an enormous rise of interest in essential fatty acids (EFAs) and oils and the roles they play in a large number of diseases. This includes the study of cardiovascular disease, the connection to cholesterol and other fats and a large number of the chronic diseases, including cancer and digestive disorders. The practice of orthomolecular medicine for individual patient benefit is the subject of our next chapter.

2

What Is Orthomolecular Medicine?

THE HONG KONG VETERAN RECOVERS

In 1960, I was investigating what effects nicotinic acid (vitamin B3) would have in the prevention of senility. My studies took me to a nursing home rendering special care for the elderly, where the home's director agreed to cooperate. Each patient's private physician gave permission as well. A few weeks after the investigation had begun, the director approached me and asked, "Dr. Hoffer, would it be O.K. if I were to take nicotinic acid?"

I wondered why!

He said, "As I hand out nicotinic acid to my elderly patients, I want to be prepared for questions about side effects, if any. Therefore, I want to take it to see what happens."

I answered that it would not harm him and nicotinic acid could be taken if he liked. Remember, he was not my patient, only a colleague in another field.

A few months later the supervisor reported his findings to me. "First, let me tell you my story," he said. "I was a physical education instructor in the Canadian Army in 1939. Along with 2,500 other Canadian soldiers I was sent to Hong Kong to battle against the advance of the Japanese. All of us were promptly captured and spent forty-four months in prisoner-of-war camps. Our food was inadequate in calories, quality and essential nutrients. We suffered stress not only from the poor diet but from chronic infections and psycho-social trauma. The treatment under the Japanese was exceedingly harsh and brutal. Twenty-five percent of my group died. Those who were finally rescued had lost approximately one-third of their body weight. I went from superb health as a 195-pound teacher of athletics to a weak and diminished bag of bones weighing

120 pounds. We suffered from multiple vitamin deficiencies—beri-beri, scurvy, pellagra and associated symptoms—diarrhea, infections and other problems.

"Our rescue brought us hospital care with high doses of vitamins in the form of rice polishings extract. The pure vitamins were not yet available. We seemed to recover and were discharged. Within a few days my fellow veterans and I broke down physically and mentally. We remained chronically ill with a variety of physical or psychiatric problems or both. We formed our own Hong Kong Veterans Association and pleaded for government help out of an inability to earn a living."

Eventually the Canadian government did a study of Hong Kong veterans and their brothers who had served in Europe. The Hong Kong veterans proved to be much sicker with degenerative conditions such as arthritis, cardiovascular disease, blindness and psychiatric diseases. Their death rate was higher. Finally they won a 90 percent disability pension for the rest of their lives.

The nursing home supervisor told the rest of his story. "From the time of my incarceration to now I have suffered constant pain from severely crippling arthritis. My wife had to help each morning to get me out of bed. I could not lift my arms over my shoulders or tolerate cold. I underwent anxiety, tension, and had many irrational fears. To treat these emotional problems, I entered a psychiatric ward in Winnipeg for several weeks. I took barbiturates in quantity at evening time to get sleep, and amphetamines during the day to keep awake. My physicians prescribed them. Psychiatrists said I was neurotic. Thus I became reconciled to a life of pain, infirmity, depression, and anxiety.

"To my astonishment," the supervisor continued, "two weeks after taking one gram of nicotinic acid three times a day merely to experience any side effects that other people in this nursing home might have, I have felt no more pain. It has gone entirely. I can move my joints freely. I feel relaxed and at ease too. I am a normal person again. I intend to take nicotinic acid the rest of my life!"

The man later tested the efficacy of nicotinic acid, albeit accidentally, when he went on a two-week camping trip in the Canadian Rocky mountains. His symptoms returned because he forgot to bring along his nicotinic acid pills. He is resolved never to do that again.

The man whose story you have just read is George Porteous, the past Lieutenant Governor of the Province of Saskatchewan, Canada.

THE AREA ORTHOMOLECULAR MEDICINE ENCOMPASSES

Lieutenant Governor George Porteous helped himself by using orthomolecular medicine, the science and art of healing with nutrition therapy. Dr. Linus Pauling, the late Professor of Chemistry at Stanford University and twice winner of the Nobel Prize, coined the term *orthomolecular* and published it in his now-famous report on "Orthomolecular Psychiatry," in *Science*, the journal of the American Association for the Advancement of Science. "Ortho" means *to straighten*. Pauling wanted to convey the basic idea that many mental illnesses could be corrected by straightening out, in effect, the concentrations of specific molecules in the brain so as to provide the optimum molecular environment for the mind.

Pauling's principles include this: *Orthomolecular therapy consisting of the provision for the individual person of the optimum concentration of important normal constituents of the brain may be the preferred treatment for many mentally ill patients.*

Non-traditionally-oriented scientists are adopting that concept and have gone even further with Pauling's principles. They are employing nutrition to combat and prevent many physical illnesses as well. Practitioners of orthomolecular medicine use orthomolecular nutrition, specific diets and food supplements for treatment, which can vary greatly from patient to patient, depending upon individual problems and needs, and use a considerable battery of laboratory tests to help make their diagnoses.

Special tests with which to make evaluations include those for thyroid function, sugar handling, insulin levels, blood levels of vitamins, hair analysis for trace minerals and others. Orthomolecular doctors look sharply at dietary habits. They take careful histories of any allergic manifestations and of exposure to environmental chemicals. For example, a patient may be tested for cerebral allergy if psychiatric symptoms have developed. Doctors look for a sensitivity to any food, inhalant or environmental chemical or other poisons or pollutants. During treatment, more laboratory and behavioral tests are taken in order to monitor the results of therapy.

Large doses of vitamins are commonly prescribed. Typically, a daily dosage schedule may include four grams of B3, four grams of C, 800 milligrams of B6, 1,000 International Units of E and other vitamins indicated by the test results. Minerals prescribed may be zinc and manganese and others, depending on what laboratory tests have shown. It is not uncommon to have hormones used when deficiencies are found. Special diets form the real basis of therapy.

Nutrition therapy is not the practice of food faddism. If anything is faddist, it is the current way Americans and Canadians eat. Dr. Richard O. Brennan, Chairman of the Board of Trustees, the International Academy of Preventive Medicine, says, "Most of the food in America today will support life but it won't sustain health." The area of interest of orthomolecular medical practitioners leads them to alter a junk food diet and change it into one less stimulating to body malfunctionings. Most informed people are moving in that direction.

"Stamp Out Food Faddism," an editorial in *Nutrition Action,* a newsletter of the Center for Science in the Public Interest, Washington, D.C., and reprinted in *Science,* stated:

> Food faddism is indeed a serious problem. But we have to recognize that the guru of food faddism is not Adelle Davis, but Betty Crocker. The true food faddists are not those who eat raw broccoli, wheat germ, and yogurt, but those who start the day on Breakfast Squares, gulp down bottle after bottle of soda pop, and snack on candy and Twinkies.
>
> Food faddism is promoted from birth. Sugar is a major ingredient in baby food desserts. Then come the artificially flavored and colored breakfast cereals, loaded with sugar, followed by soda pop and hot dogs. Meat marbled with fat and alcoholic beverages dominate the diets of many middle-aged people. And, of course, white bread is standard fare throughout life.
>
> This diet—high in fat, sugar, cholesterol, and refined grains—is the prescription for illness; it can contribute to obesity, tooth decay, heart disease, intestinal cancer, and diabetes. And these diseases are, in fact, America's major health problems. So if any diet should be considered faddist, it is the standard one. Our far out diet—almost 20 percent refined sugar and 45 percent fat—is new to human experience and foreign to all other animal life. . . .
>
> It is incredible that people who eat a junk food diet constitute the norm, while individuals whose diets resemble those of our great-grandparents are labeled deviants. . . .

THE NUTRITIONAL NEEDS OF THE BODY AND MIND

A growing segment of our population has learned it can become master of its own health. Through use of orthomolecular medical principles, providing themselves with the proper biochemical environment, people are building upon their own naturally strong genetic code. They are changing from a way of life that promotes improper eating to a new total life pattern of optimum nutrition.

Every living cell in your body requires a number of chemical nutrients in its immediate environment—the extracellular fluid. Your body's organs, tissues and cells have two main functions: (1) growth and repair and (2) their specific assignment. For example, the kidney helps rid the blood of chemicals not required; the adrenal gland secretes hormones; the skin repels foreign organisms and excretes wastes; the brain receives impulses, relays them to other portions of the body and initiates activity. Your brain also perceives, thinks, feels and controls behavior. Poor nutrition will slow down or stop the functions of these organs, tissues and cells.

Multicellular animals such as human beings have bodies designed to carry essential nutrients derived from ingested foods to individual cells and to remove the waste products. This is different from plants, which synthesize their own proteins, fats, carbohydrates, vitamins, enzymes and all other needed chemicals. However, much energy is required for plants to meet their own requirements and no energy is left over for movement as seen in animals. It is more economical for animals to eat than to make nutrients.

For humans, about forty to forty-five nutrients essential to life must be taken in our diet because our bodies do not make them naturally. Vitamin C, for example, is absolutely necessary for life, but we must ingest it because we cannot synthesize it within our bodies.

Your body and mind need vitamins and minerals. They facilitate thousands of essential reactions but are not themselves sources of energy. You need proteins present in meat, fish, poultry and many vegetable sources. Proteins possess more than twenty amino acids, of which eight are essential. The body can synthesize the remaining twelve from other amino acids. If one of the eight essential amino acids is missing, the others cannot be used efficiently.

You need fats for calories and to form structural elements. Carbohydrates in food consist of starches and sugars used by the body primarily for energy. Small quantities of carbohydrate are used in building tissue as glycoproteins. After a meal rich in carbohydrates there is rapid increase in tryptophan in the brain followed by an increase in serotonin. Serotonin is one of the hormones used by the brain to control functions. By a proper mixture of food, you can elevate, maintain or lower brain serotonin levels to adjust brain functions including perception, thinking, feeling and generalized activity.

A balanced diet will provide all the essential nutrients in optimum quantity including minerals such as calcium required in much larger dosage than the ordinary trace elements. A balanced diet delivers nutrients to cells in a steady flow, but an unbalanced diet provides too much or too little of these nutrients.

One does not require extensive nutritional knowledge to obtain a good balanced diet. Humans have evolved and adapted to a small number of foods including grain, vegetables, fruits, fish, meat and poultry. As long as these foods are not tampered with, you and I will find our diet balanced.

However, the processed foods so widely available—indeed, almost unavoidable—permit us to avoid starvation, even to feel well fed and grow fat, while we suffer from malnutrition. The manufacturers of food have become quite skillful. They have developed palatable food substitutes such as soft drinks that provide water, carbon dioxide and harmful synthetics but no protein, fat, carbohydrate, minerals or vitamins. Millers have taken apart the wholeness of grains. They separate the endosperm of wheat (white flour) from the germ and bran. Sugar manufacturers give us pure sucrose from beets and sugar cane. Soft drinks, white flour bread and white sugar are examples of the many foods that provide malnutrition in the form of naked or empty calories.

Empty-calorie foods are deficient in nutrients. They cannot be used in the body without vitamins and minerals and other foodstuffs. If the nutrient factors do not accompany naked-calorie foods, they must be taken from other food. This means that a diet heavy in sugar or other naked calories must inevitably lead to multiple vitamin and mineral deficiencies. Orthomolecular medical scientists know this to be the case.

Over the past three centuries, for instance, the consumption of sugar in this country has increased from five pounds to about one hundred twenty-five pounds per person each year. Excessive sugar consumption leads to an excessive drain on the pancreas for insulin. This is a main factor in the cause of hypoglycemia, one of the members of the master disease caused by refined foods, the *saccharine disease*.

Food manufacturers add an enormous amount of food additives designed to stabilize, color and increase palatability. They consider nutritional quality minor. Thus too much sugar, salt, coloring and other chemicals are fed to us in processed foods.

Orthomolecular medicine is concerned with the consequences of eating the typical American and Canadian junk diet, the Western form of malnutrition. The basic treatment consists of removing from a patient's diet food artifacts and synthetics, and restoring to his diet those natural foods which are rich in all the nutritional elements. Although individuals vary enormously in their needs for the specific substances required to sustain optimum health, the balanced diet could supply those substances if we let it. Deficiencies exist but orthomolecular nutrition can overcome them.

The next chapter will explain what happens when natural laws of proper eating are disobeyed and what you can do to restructure yourself to follow those laws. Our aim is to help you keep your natural good health and perhaps bring it up to a state of superhealth.

3

How Orthomolecular Therapy Works

Some years ago a woman was admitted to City Hospital, Saskatoon, Saskatchewan, with a diagnosis of self-induced skin gouges, a supposed psychiatric problem. Her immediate history included a broken love affair—which was generally considered the reason why this woman, a nurse, was tearing at her own skin. Invariably I include a nutritional history as part of any patient's entry under my care, and I learned that she had suffered severe malnutrition long ago as a prisoner of a concentration camp in Europe. Now she had a resultant vitamin dependency. Additionally, she was eating a highly processed carbohydrate diet routinely. This was a combination debilitating to her mental health.

This nurse was gouging out portions of herself because of a severe state of anxiety-depression. I treated her psychiatric problem with orthomolecular nutrition (which consisted primarily of a nonrefined carbohydrate diet and vitamins) and she became well enough to be discharged from the hospital within two weeks. Her skin damage had ceased altogether. Any other orthodox medical treatment would have placed her under long-term, detailed psychotherapy—perhaps once a week for the next five years. It could not possibly have helped. Her malnutrition of thirty years before had finally caught up with her and caused mental derangement—which was relieved through nutrition according to the principles of orthomolecular therapy.

THE CONSEQUENCES OF CONSUMING A JUNK DIET

Overconsumption of refined food causes the *saccharine disease*. Organ changes from the saccharine disease result in diabetes, peptic ulcer, constipation (and its effects such as varicose veins, hemorrhoids and cancer of the bowel) and other debilitations. Consequently, an orthomolecular therapist will direct primary attention toward changing the patient's diet.

Associated with the saccharine disease, and especially with mental and emotional problems resulting from it, is the condition known as *relative hypoglycemia*. In reality, relative hypoglycemia is not a clinical entity in itself, being a term used to denote a laboratory test result in which a person's blood sugar level decreases more than 20 milligrams per 100 milliliters after being given a "challenge dose" of 100 grams of glucose, constituting a six-hour sugar tolerance test. One can only guess at the proportion of our population who have relative hypoglycemia, but assuredly it is large—perhaps close to a majority.

Of 500 alcoholics that my colleagues and I have tested, almost all suffered a decrease of 20 milligrams or more in blood sugar. About 10 percent of any adult population consumes excessive quantities of alcohol, and it is likely this group suffers from the saccharine disease. And as two-thirds of all neurotics and people with depression have the condition, we may assume that at least 35 to 50 percent of our entire population is victimized by its mental and physical manifestations. It is a result of the average North American ingesting a junk diet.

A JUNK DIET IS:

A junk diet supplies poor quality eating—foods which contain sugar, white flour or polished rice, alcohol and items processed by manufacturers from whole foods. People are allergic to certain foods, and consumption of them can result in disease.

In effect, a junk diet is a disease, especially resulting in the so-called degenerative diseases of civilization such as heart problems, and forms of cancer, arthritis and diabetes. Junk foods are artifacts derived from living organisms, either plant or animal. The major plant material which comprises living natural food is the seed of wheat, corn and rice. Seeds are the plant's future progeny. When a wheat kernel is formed, it contains the amount of protein, carbohydrate, fat, vitamins and minerals necessary to launch a new plant. These components must also be present in adequate amounts in the human diet to support a person's nutrition. In processed foods such components are not present. On the other hand, seeds and nuts, which are capable of growing new plants, are nutritious packets of food for us.

The flesh and organs of animals are even closer in composition to our bodies. When they are consumed they provide most of our requirements, provided we do not eat damaged goods of devitalized quality altered during the journey from the animal to our plates.

The components of food in nature's packets are combined in a very intricate relationship. Protein, fat and carbohydrate interlaced with vitamins and minerals must be present. When natural food is consumed, all its components are provided at the same time. The elemental nutrients such as the amino acids, simple sugars and other items, will be delivered via the circulated blood to all the cells together. All the essential amino acids must be present about the same time. It does not help the cell to be supplied half the essential amino acids and then to receive the other half twelve hours later. If all the components are not present simultaneously, the cell functions poorly.

People are surprised when they discover that our present diets are generally inferior to the diets of our ancestors. They point to the tremendous advances in the science of nutrition and to our present food technology. It is hard for them to believe that modern foods, which taste so palatable, are so attractively packaged, and are so easy to warm up in a twentieth-century kitchen, can be as harmful as they are. Not uncommonly, people who are burying themselves with their teeth look upon those who are disturbed by our modern diets as food faddists or freaks.

Patients who have recovered from disease by eliminating sugar from their diet sometimes force a test of their eating programs upon themselves. Very often they will expose themselves to several relapses by reverting to the diet that originally made them ill. They then return to orthomolecular physicians for care, while knowing full well what has gone wrong. Although they could overcome recurrence of their symptoms by halting their intake of processed and high-sugar foods, they return for treatment because they need the doctor's reassurance and confirmation that their eating lifestyle is valid, to offset the negative opinions of ignorant consumers of highly refined foods.

THE RESULTS OF EATING JUNK FOOD

Artifact or "junk" foods include such items as white bread, commercial french-fried potatoes, non-dairy creams made of chemicals and all the foods to which sugar has been added. Pies, pastry, cakes, chocolate, candy, most desserts, jello and many canned goods such as soups, contain added sugar.

Most children like sweets, and often sugared foods form a staple of their diet. When fed a diet free of processed junk, these children may feel deprived. However, not uncommonly after six months the sugar addiction will be lost, and they can adapt to the various healthier foods substituted. If sugar addiction actually manifests itself as allergy, junk food will produce disease symptoms which become uncomfortable. Any tissue or organ of the body may react.

Allergy to sugar and other components of processed food may react to the skin in the form of hives, rashes, itch, swelling, redness, decreased ability to move because of skin rubbing and tautness, and pain. The urinary bladder may shrink and cause bed wetting. The central nervous system can react, causing a variety of unpleasant symptoms such as tension, anxiety, depression, hallucinations, thought disorder and changes in behavior. The neuroses or psychoneuroses are psychiatric diseases that mainly alter mood. They will be discussed in detail in Chapter Five. Psychosomatic conditions also fall into this category.

Malnutrition resulting from excessive consumption of processed food in the form of refined carbohydrates is also the major cause of a broad group of neuroses and physical illnesses. Until recently these were looked upon as unrelated diseases with no known etiology, but now the root cause, nutritive deficiency, has become apparent. It may help many people who suffer from these diseases to embrace principles of proper eating. They will become aware immediately, from the reduction of their symptoms, of the reasons why they have been ill.

The mass indictment of refined carbohydrates as the cause of many of the ills of Westernized countries today was advanced by Surgeon-Captain T. L. Cleave, M. R. C. P., formerly director of medical research of the Institute of Naval Medicine, Great Britain. In 1956, he designated "the saccharine disease" as the master disease, incorporating diabetes, coronary disease, obesity, peptic ulcer, constipation, hemorrhoids, varicose veins; *Escherichia coli* infections such as appendicitis, cholecystitis, pyelitis and diverticulitis; renal calculus, many skin conditions and dental caries.

The master disorder which is the saccharine disease produces a variety of physical and mental manifestations that derive from the excessive consumption of refined or processed carbohydrates. Primarily, these are sugar and white flour. Highly processed products of this type cause specific physical and psychiatric changes sometimes labeled *psychosomatic* and sometimes considered *idiopathic*. To distinguish them, however, and separate them from "thinking" diseases that arise from an influence of the mind or "unknown" diseases that come from no apparent extrinsic cause, the doctor merely needs to perform a six-hour glucose tolerance test on his patient.

A hypoglycemic curve will result that is just an expression of the disturbance in carbohydrate metabolism. The physical symptoms include peptic ulcer, diabetes, colitis and other troubles. We will discuss these physical manifestations of the saccharine disease in this chapter in the paragraphs that follow. The psychiatric symptoms include headache, depression, nervousness, anxiety, tension, palpitations and other problems. We will discuss these psychiatric manifestations of the saccharine disease in Chapter Five under the subtitle "Psychoneuroses from Improper Nutrition."

Often the diagnosis of the saccharine disease, whether physical or psychiatric, depends upon the orientation of the attending physician. If he is interested only in ulcers, for instance, he is liable to ignore the psychiatric changes and diagnose only peptic ulcer. But all these various changes are aspects of the same disease.

PHYSICAL MANIFESTATIONS OF THE SACCHARINE DISEASE

When normal quantities of fiber (bulk) are consumed, the normal transit time of feces is about twenty-four to forty-eight hours. People who live on low-fiber diets have a feces transit time forty-eight to ninety-six hours. Today, constipation among populations of the Westernized countries is quite common. In Britain, up to 15 percent of the population regularly take laxatives. Malabsorption is the result. Laxative use and malabsorption among the elderly, who have had more time to damage their bowels from defective nutrition, are most common.

Two serious consequences arise from the constipation: diverticulosis and diverticulitis. *Diverticulosis* is a term used to describe the presence of a number of internal pouches or sacs opening from the intestine. It is commonly an occurrence of middle age. Cleave suggests that the slow passage of the colon's contents leads to increased absorption of water from feces and consequently greater viscosity of the contents, necessitating excessive contraction of the bowel. There is a clear association between constipation or diverticulosis, and absence of a diet containing adequate quantities of fiber. *Diverticulitis* is an inflammation of such a pouch or sac opening in the gut. It is ascribed to a combination of the constipation due to the lack of fiber and the deleterious effect of the high sugar intake which accompanies it. There is a pathological effect on the bacterial population of the gut due to the surplus of sugar. Effects may take up to forty years before they are fully manifest.

Another manifestation of the saccharine disease is the irritated colon (simple colitis). Irritable colon is closely related to mood disorders. It is rare to be free of depression, tension and anxiety when the condition is present. In fact, ulcerative colitis, a disease characterized by ulceration of the colon and rectum with bleeding, mucosal crypt abscesses and inflammatory pseudopolyps, has been considered one of the classic psychosomatic conditions. Ulcerative colitis frequently causes anemia, hypoproteinemia and electrolyte imbalance, and is less frequently complicated by perforation or carcinoma of the colon. Elimination of sugar and an increased intake of fibrous foods can cure the constipated patient and suddenly dispel his anal-retentive characteristics.

Refined food intake leads to unnatural concentration of carbohydrates which deceive the palate and cause overconsumption. This is the sole immediate cause of obesity. Obesity is not the result of a large appetite nor a dislike of exercise. For example, it would be highly unusual for anyone to consume six apples in five minutes. The bulk of this natural food prevents it from happening. It is not unusual, however, to consume an equivalent amount of calories as that in six apples in the form of sugar and one's tea, coffee or soft drink. The large number of so-called diabetics, especially the adult maturity type associated with obesity, do not really have diabetes but one of the variants of relative hypoglycemia.

A patient who does not require insulin probably does not suffer from true diabetes.

Peptic ulcer occurs in the alimentary mucosa, usually in the stomach or duodenum, and is exposed to acid gastric secretions. When food reaches the stomach, gastric juices containing hydrochloric acid are secreted to help digest protein, which ordinarily makes up 99 percent of the quantity of human's natural food. Before processed foods were developed, there was no surplus amount of acid lying around the stomach and its inner lining. The mucosa remained intact. Protein buffered the acid's contact with the stomach wall. In today's way of eating, food is very often consumed that contains less protein than in natural diets, and may in fact contain no protein at all. When you drink a bottle of soda pop, you fool the stomach with what appears to be food. There will be the same increased excretion of stomach acid but no protein present to work on. The acid remains free in the stomach. The only protein to buffer the acid is the stomach mucosa itself, and the protein exudates on its surface. Peptic ulcer thus becomes another of those classic psychosomatic diseases incorrectly treated by psychoanalysis.

A patient with peptic ulcer could soon cure his condition and perhaps his personality problems as well. What he must do is add fiber and remove refined carbohydrates from his diet.

4

Orthomolecular Psychiatry

Every tissue of the body is affected by nutrition. Under conditions of poor nutrition the kidney stops filtering, the stomach stops digesting, the adrenals stop secreting, and other organs follow suit. Unfortunately, some psychiatrists labor under the false belief that somehow brain function is completely unaffected by nutrition.

Since Dr. Humphry Osmond and I established that the addition of megadoses of vitamin B3 to a therapeutic program for treatment of the mentally ill is beneficial, I have been continually amazed at the violence of attack from traditionalists in psychiatry. It seems that many psychiatrists and their parapsychiatric colleagues such as psychologists and social workers consider that the brain is not an organ of the body that needs nourishment.

Another, and growing, body of psychiatrists, however, realizes the overwhelming importance of proper cellular metabolism. Foremost among these doctors are the members of the Academy of Orthomolecular Medicine. They are becoming members of the International Academy of Orthomolecular Medicine with major representation from the present orthomolecular societies in Brazil, Canada, Italy and the United States. They have taken a very considerable departure from conventional psychiatry—and, according to a rapidly growing body of reports, it is benefiting tens of thousands with varied mental illnesses and behavioral disturbances, including many unassisted by other methods.

Orthomolecular psychiatry involves medical scientists who are interested in nutrition, altered metabolic states, defects in brain chemistry, molecular biology, genetics, research in brain enzymes and psychiatric treatment based upon altering molecular levels and concentrations of essential substances for optimum brain functioning. It is of particular interest also to scientists concerned with altered states of consciousness.

The unifying concept of orthomolecular psychiatry was formulated by Professor Linus Pauling, who defined it as "the treatment of mental disorders by the provision of the optimum molecular environment for the mind, especially the optimum concentrations of substances normally present in the body."

The purpose of the Academies of Orthomolecular Medicine is to further and increase scientific knowledge in psychiatry and to serve as a meeting ground for interested professionals so as to extend knowledge in this field. It seeks to make clinical application of orthomolecular psychiatry for the alleviation of mental disorders and to study ways in which optimal mental functioning can be achieved for all citizens, including those without mental disorders.

In the course of their studies of human biochemistry a growing number of research scientists have uncovered evidence that mental illness and other degenerative diseases may be linked by similar metabolic processes dependent upon nutrition. Their investigations have opened the door to discoveries that could help to alleviate widespread suffering and result in the general improvement of health for all humankind.

The Journal of Orthomolecular Medicine and the Canadian Schizophrenia Foundation believe that we are now on the brink of a biological revolution that can be hastened by the development of orthomolecular medicine. An increasing number of doctors are currently treating schizophrenia, learning disabilities, drug addiction, pellagra, alcoholism and memory loss successfully with varying combinations of megavitamins, drugs and carefully controlled diet. By providing the optimum biochemical and nutritional environment for *every* person, the attainment of individual potential and social betterment can be maximized.

MY HISTORY WITH ORTHOMOLECULAR PSYCHIATRY

During 1951-1952 I was given the task of organizing a research program in psychiatry for the Department of Public Health, Psychiatric Services Branch, Saskatchewan, Canada. As a result of my contact with Humphry Osmond, M.R.C.S., D.P.M., who joined us as clinical director of the Saskatchewan Hospital, Weyburn, I became interested in the causes and treatment of schizophrenia.

The treatment of schizophrenia in 1952 was in poor shape. Standard treatments consisted of insulin coma and electroconvulsive therapy. Insulin coma was coming into disfavor because of difficulty of administration and high relapse rate. Electroconvulsive therapy (ECT) fell out of favor some time later. Only barbiturates used in large quantities and the morphine derivatives were reasonably effective as emergency sedatives. Generally, we were reluctant to diagnose schizophrenia, not because this was difficult but because a schizophrenic would have to be committed to one of the old mental hospitals——in effect, sentenced to a living death. The inadequacy of the existing therapeutic approach to schizophrenia was a challenge that impelled us to undertake our research program.

As a result of observing similarities between the effects of hallucinogen use among normal subjects and the schizophrenic experience, we turned our attention to the biochemistry of schizophrenia. We developed the *adrenochrome hypothesis* with use of water soluble vitamins, vitamin B3 being the most significant. We established that there might be an excessive conversion of adrenalin into adrenochrome in the schizophrenic body. This was the basis of the major research program that we developed over the years. It then occurred to us that if we could reverse this change, that perhaps we might have a therapy for schizophrenics. This was one of the reasons we began to look at vitamin B3. Theoretically, it could cut down the conversion of noradrenaline into adrenaline. In this way, it would cut down the production of adrenochrome. There are a number of ways vitamin B3 can be therapeutic:

1. It eliminates an important vitamin deficiency.
2. It has a cerebrovascular effect.
3. It has a mass action effect on cellular metabolism.
4. It furnishes a psychological placebo effect.
5. It restores acetylcholine esterase activity.
6. It inhibits NADase activity.
7. It accelerates the destruction of and acts as a direct antagonist to schizophrenic toxin.
8. It has an anti-allergy effect for some schizophrenics.

However, the most violent criticism of the adrenochrome hypothesis of schizophrenia came from scientists who claimed that adrenochrome was not made in the body. This was in spite of our rejoinder that all the conditions were there and that in time it would be shown to be present. Adrenochrome is made from adren-

aline and noradrenaline, and the body has enzymes and other catalysts which could convert those substances to adrenochrome and
noradrenochrome. But the critics were adamant. Until today psychiatrists have been so impressed with these criticisms that there are
no psychiatric institutes anywhere doing research with the oxidized
derivatives of these powerful chemicals. However, other medical
scientists have not been so adverse. Now it has been proven that
the body makes adrenochrome and methods have been developed
for measuring it in the blood. For several years Dr. R. E. Beamish,
emeritus professor at the University of Manitoba School of Medicine, and his group have been developing evidence that the heart
muscle soaks up adrenaline where 80 percent can be converted
into adrenochrome. Excess adrenochrome may cause damage to
the heart muscle and distort the rhythm of the heart, leading to
fibrillation and death.

PILOT STUDIES

Osmond and I undertook studies of vitamin B3 in the form of
nicotinic acid in the spring of 1952. The study function was to
determine a dose range that would not be toxic and would have
an effect. The first eight acute or subacute patients treated showed
a prompt and sustained response to 3 grams of nicotinic acid per
day given over a one-month period.

The Saskatchewan Committee on Schizophrenia Research received Osmond's and my report June 30, 1962. Eight patients with
acute and subacute cases had been treated with excellent or good
results. Four cases are as follows:

1. P. B. was committed to Saskatchewan Hospital diagnosed
as suffering from Alzheimer's disease but with behavior more
like catatonic schizophrenia. He was prescribed nicotinamide,
one gram per day. He was well four days later and remained
well six weeks later by maintaining his program, as did all of the
following patients.

2. A twenty-five-year-old woman became psychotic following the
birth of her baby. She responded temporarily to a series of ECT
but showed no response to 60 insulin comas. However, within two
weeks she was well after taking 5 grams daily of nicotinic acid and
ascorbic acid.

3. A severely psychotic man was well on the fourth day after starting 10 grams per day of nicotinic acid and ascorbic acid.

4. Miss G., middle-aged, had failed to respond to several series of ECT and was advancing into chronic schizophrenia. We started her on nicotinic acid, 1 gram per day, later increased to 3 grams per day. She recovered. Over the next five years she discontinued the vitamin B3 intake on three occasions and each time relapsed within two weeks. When she again took her vitamins she recovered. In 1957, she discontinued taking the vitamin and is still well today.

THE FIRST DOUBLE-BLIND EXPERIMENTS IN THE TREATMENT OF SCHIZOPHRENIA

My group, in the fall of 1952, was the first to undertake double-blind experiments in schizophrenia. Our pioneering use of this double-blind technique does not mean that I still look upon the technique as the only valid approach. In truth, I consider double-blind experiments inferior, expensive and tedious. A double-blind study has a limited role in good clinical research.

Having thus disavowed the value of double-blind techniques, I had better explain what they are. Most patients with disease want to get better, and most investigators have some sort of prejudice about any given drug—usually in wanting to come up with successful results, but at times in the opposite direction. This enthusiasm (or lack of enthusiasm, such as the prejudice displayed by the American Psychiatric Association Task Force in its study "Megavitamins and Orthomolecular Therapy in Psychiatry") should be allowed to diffuse itself as equally as possible over the medications under study, which is usually accomplished by the "blind" technique. Usually this is "double blind," with the patient and observer both unaware of the nature of a particular medication. At times, a "single-blind" technique suffices, if the end point to be determined (such as death) is not particularly amenable to overstatement or understatement, or if the patient records the data himself under circumstances in which the experimenter cannot influence him.

Whether the treatments being compared are active drugs or active drugs and placebos (indifferent substances, in the form of a medicine, given for the suggestive effect), it is necessary for successful deception to have tablets or capsules or injections that are as indistinguishable in physical appearance as possible. The medications are then designated by code letters or numbers (preferably a different one for each patient) and the code is known only to certain individuals not directly concerned with the performance of the trial.

The double blind, which we originally designated the "double dummy method," works best when it is least needed. Our first experiment had to do with the study of a nucleotide preparation, which turned out to be ineffective. Then we undertook a second double-blind study that was a comparison of nicotinic acid, nicotinamide and a placebo. Our placebo was an inert compound, identical in appearance with the material being tested, and the patient and the physician did not know which was which. Thirty patients were divided by random selection into three groups. One group was given the placebo; the second group was given nicotinamide, which was a hidden control since it did not produce the characteristic nicotinic acid flush; the third group was given nicotinic acid, which would be known, since patients regularly flush when they first start on the vitamin.

This second double-blind study indicated that schizophrenic patients evaluated by their own therapists, treated with or without ECT, placed on nicotinic acid for thirty-three days, reevaluated and discharged, after reevaluation two years later, *doubled the two-year recovery rate*. The reevaluating worker was not aware of the double-blind code. But by year's end the placebo group had one-third of its patients well and the two vitamin groups, nicotinamide and nicotinic acid, had two-thirds of its patients well.

We ran a third double-blind study, the second with nicotinic acid, among eighty-two patients. It did not include nicotinamide control, but we covered for this by informing the staff that it was the same design as the one just completed. The results were the same as our second study. Nicotinic acid added to standard ECT (which about 50 percent of our study patients received) was responsible for the vast improvement of most of these patients.

ORTHOMOLECULAR PSYCHIATRIC CARE TODAY

Our major contribution to orthomolecular therapy was to establish vitamin B3 as an important ingredient of schizophrenia treatment. However, present treatment is much more elegant, sophisticated and effective. It resembles the 1952-1953 psychiatric treatment program about as much as a present-day Ford Motors product resembles a Model T Ford. Both run, but few would prefer the Model T for everyday use. It's just a collector's item.

The basic or fundamental rule of orthomolecular psychiatric care today is to depend on optimum doses of nutrients most likely to help the patient recover. All the other components of modern standard psychiatry are used also. Treatment is individually tailored for each patient. The treatment program is continually modified according to the patient's progress. The aim for every patient is recovery even though not every patient will recover. Mental disease is too serious to take lightly and unless the therapist aims at a complete recovery, he or she will not work hard enough and patiently enough, and the patient may be deprived of a chance for improvement or recovery.

Unfortunately, many traditional psychiatrists do not believe schizophrenics can recover. Some psychiatrists are content merely to achieve a permanent improved state for the people they treat. Their objectives include discharge from hospital and reduction of symptoms to a tolerable behavior pattern but not necessarily recovery.

Why is this archaic thinking persistent in traditional psychiatric concepts? There are a few reasons. First, the work of Sigmund Freud dominated psychiatric thinking in the United States, although not in Europe, throughout much of this century. Many influential intellectuals themselves were psychoanalyzed and in the heyday of analysis, talking of one's own experience on the couch was very much a staple of cocktail party chitchat.

Analysis was never a particularly effective form of treatment. It is viewed by many as an educational and research tool today. But formerly, its protagonists applied it hopefully in the treatment of varied and multiple disorders. Freud himself said that psychoanalysis was not suitable for such diseases as schizophrenia and postulated that the cause eventually would be found to be biochemical and that successful treatment would have to deal with that. Still, many analysts tried to treat schizophrenia, alcoholism and other serious problems, with scant success.

Second, American medicine is drug-oriented—make a diagnosis and prescribe a drug to treat it. The concept seems to be: one disease, one drug or series of drugs. Biologically oriented psychia-

trists increased markedly in the mid-1950s with the advent of tranquilizers. Tranquilizers did help to reduce the number of mentally
ill patients in hospitals. They were able to vegetate in a euphoric
state at home without being a state burden.

Then, in addition to major and minor tranquilizers, anti-depressant
drugs became available. The pharmaceutical companies spend millions of dollars annually to encourage prescription and dispensing
of thousands of drugs, tranquilizers and antidepressants among
them. Drug manufacturers have persuaded doctors that what is
good for one of them is good for both—and for the health of
the community. Physicians, prescribing psychiatrists included, are
intensely bombarded with pharmaceutical industry propaganda.
This does not absolve psychiatrists of their responsibility, but it
does explain something of how they have been conditioned to make
use of new drugs, dispense samples, try this or that chemical, and
write more prescriptions. The drug industry makes next to no
money on vitamins, minerals, no-junk diets and various food supplements, compared to the billions it makes on its pharmaceuticals.
Orthomolecular psychiatrists use ingredients which mainly are not
chemicals, but foods.

In 1993 A.H. initiated a study of 27 chronic schizophrenic patients. This series of schizophrenic patients was not a randomly
selected sample from a larger population of schizophrenics. They
were selected using the following criteria: (1) They had been under
treatment at least ten years. (2) With a couple of exceptions, they
had been ill an average of seven years before they came for treatment, and their average age was 40. (3) They had not been respon-
sive to any previous treatment.

From this group of 27 patients treated over ten years, I concluded that 18 are now well, 3 are much improved, 5 are improved
and 1, who did not follow the program upon returning home, is
the same as he was at the beginning of the study. None is worse.
This does not mean that they will no longer see psychiatrists at
regular intervals. If they are on medication, it is mandatory that
they be followed to ensure they come to no harm from the drugs.
In addition problems arise now and then as they do with any group
of patients who have a chronic disease.

The second major conclusion is that orthomolecular treatment is
safe when used over ten years. The third conclusion is that no
major side effects are caused by the smallish doses of tranquilizers
that many of these patients will require. The program does not

produce tranquilizer psychosis. The final conclusion is that schizophrenic patients find the program palatable and will remain compliant. They are able to look forward to continuing improvement. I expect that if I did another followup in ten more years with the same group the results would be even better.

In general chronic patients respond very slowly to orthomolecular treatment, and in this series there was little change during the first half of the followup period. This slow response is a major disadvantage since few psychiatrists in private practice are willing to work that long with their patients. Too often in mental hospitals discharged patients are not followed long enough by the same psychiatrist. In my opinion followup must be done by physicians who can change medications and nutrients as needed.

Only in the past five to seven years have I seen a steady and enduring improvement. This cannot be ascribed to the use of new and improved tranquilizers since this is not the usual response with these drugs alone. However, it is possible that the newer tranquilizers may have become more effective when combined with the nutrients. Another factor might be the use of antidepressants, especially clomipramine. I have found this to be very useful in reducing and eliminating paranoid ideas. I consider recurrent paranoid ideas equivalent to obsessive/compulsive ideas. I began to use antidepressants when I realized I had never seen cheerful paranoids. It occurred to me that if I could remove their depression, they might find it easier to let go of their paranoid ideas.

There is undoubtedly some bias in this chronic population, but 26 were willing to stay compliant for this period of time. (All others were excluded from the study.) In my opinion compliance is much less of a problem when orthomolecular treatment is used, since the dose of tranquilizers is much less and there is less incentive for patients to go off the program.

Because of all these factors one cannot generalize beyond the parameters of this study. However, it does show that chronic patients who are compliant over enough years do improve substantially. To deprive them of this chance for recovery and improvement is to me the height of irresponsibility. Double blind purists will dismiss this conclusion because it is not a prospective double blind controlled study. However, such a study, even if I thought it scientifically valid, would be impossible to carry out. I cannot visualize any substantial body of schizophrenic patients taking placebos for this length of time. Nor would it be ethical to expose them to such a charade. Those who demand double blinds are simply using this procedure as a weapon against this particular treatment.

Of course, there is a way of rebutting this data. That is for any skeptical psychiatrist to select from his other caseload a similar group of patients who have only been on tranquilizers and show that they have done equally well. I would be delighted to see such a series, since in my clinical experience going back from the time tranquilizers were first introduced in 1955, I have not been able to find such patients and such responses only with the use of drugs.

There is one possible comparison with a study reporting the course and outcome of 34 early schizophrenic patients. They had one episode or admission and were classed as early (acute) patients. They were the best group to treat from a prognostic point of view because they had had only one episode and came from intact nuclear biologic families who were informed about their diagnosis. They were followed for five years. Sixty percent were still living at home and 82 percent were involved in followup. Half were on antipsychotic drugs, with only one not on medication. Forty-five percent who had been working at the onset were still working, but worktime was often reduced to part-time for extended periods.

Thus, with the best possible group of patients given good and dedicated care by professionals and their warm and supporting parents, only 40 percent were able to work part- or full-time. With these kinds of patients orthomolecular treatment over two years would have yielded at least 90 percent full recovery. With the use of the best possible ancillary treatment including only drugs, this group has not done as well as the chronic group described in my report. Nor is it likely that the early group will do much better over the next five years, since, as I have shown, it is not possible to get well on tranquilizers alone. The authors ended their report: "only time will tell whether this cohort is able to work and love in their adult years."

The onus is now on orthodox psychiatry to demonstrate by their own research that there is a major fault with the conclusions from my study. It is not good enough to assume that the results are all due to a series of unproven assumptions such as a placebo effect, faith or even some monstrous conspiracy to show something works when it does not. Will the profession adopt the stance of a California psychiatrist who testified for 15 minutes before a judge that one of the patients was psychotic because she believed that vitamins had been helpful to her? World psychiatry experienced similar types of reasoning and conclusions from Russian psychiatrists who labeled dissidents psychotic simply because they were dissidents.

TURNING AWAY FROM THE MAINSTREAM

Even though the predominant belief, and one still held by many psychiatrists, was that tranquilizers merely made amenable psychotherapy patients who previously had been unapproachable, the tranquilizer era aroused a new interest in brain biochemistry. In 1968, Linus Pauling defined orthomolecular psychiatric therapy as "the treatment of mental disease by the provision of the optimum molecular environment for the mind, especially the optimum concentrations of substances normally present in the human body.... The brain provides the molecular environment of the mind. "I use the word *mind*," said Pauling, "as a convenient synonym for the functioning of the brain. The word *ortho-molecular* may be criticized as a Greek-Latin hybrid. I have not, however, found any other word that expresses as well the idea of the right molecules in the right amounts."

This definition and the scientific reasoning behind it have initiated a new direction in psychiatry and in medicine. It signals a turning away from the mainstream, an exclusive preoccupation with tranquilizers, antidepressants and other psychoactive chemicals for the treatment of mental illnesses. It emphasizes the idea which has been slowly developing over the past century that mental symptoms are the product of central nervous system disorders. In turn, these disorders arise from a variety of metabolic faults such as genetic defects or the inadequate concentration of molecules native to the body. Mental illness arises when the requirement—the right molecules in the right amounts—is not met.

Mental illness does not arise from a deficiency of chlorpromazine or amitriptyline. These are useful drug molecules that do something to restore a more normal brain metabolism, but they are not naturally present in the body or the brain. They are unnatural substances which require an unnatural body and brain reaction.

A TEST FOR MEASURING WHETHER VITAMIN B3 AND/OR VITAMIN B6 IS NEEDED

Thirty-five years ago Drs. H. Osmond and A. Hoffer began to look for psychological tests to help us diagnose schizophrenia and decide when patients were improving or getting worse and by how much. This was in preparation for initiating the first prospective double blind therapeutic trials in world psychiatry and the first in all clinical medicine in North America. The only tests then available were useless, including the Rorschach test and several others.

After several years of investigation (and 50,000 vintage-1955 dollars later), the chief psychologist where we worked informed us that no such tests were available and could never be developed because psychiatrists could not agree on the criteria for making diagnoses. This made us question exactly what one did in making a diagnosis. It occurred to us that a medical diagnosis is a binary problem. One simply asks the right question which is answered yes or no. The configuration of the yes answers helps determine what the disease is. For instance, the answer yes to the following two questions indicates one is dealing with pneumonia: (1) Do you have pain in your chest that is worse with breathing? (2) Do you have fever? We then examined in detail the world as experienced by schizophrenic patients by reading their autobiographies, by talking to hundreds of patients and by studying the experiences induced by hallucinogens including LSD. From these studies we made up 145 questions, which became the basis for the Hoffer-Osmond Diagnostic Test (HOD).

The 145 questions were placed on individual cards. Each card had its own number on the back from 1 to 145. To conduct the test, the cards are randomized, shuffled and given to the person being tested. The subject is told that this is a symptom checklist which is helpful in making a diagnosis. The person is asked to place each card in either a true box or a false box if the question can be answered true or false. If they cannot answer it or are not sure, they are instructed to place the card in the false box. All the cards from the true box are recorded on special scoring sheets. From these scores individual scores are developed. A rating system of scores was based upon analysis of thousands of records from patients and normal volunteers.

This simple test provided the research group with a useful diagnosis. Normal people have very low scores, usually under 20, schizophrenic patients have very high scores, averaging around 65. The higher the test score the greater the probability the patient is schizophrenic. HOD scores are also high in subjects who have taken hallucinogenic drugs such as LSD or mescaline, in subjects high on street drugs and in subjects suffering from delirium of any type. High scores induced by drugs quickly become normal when the drug effect is gone. Schizophrenic scores do not come down unless there has been improvement, which usually takes a very long time. Total scores begin to go up if the patient begins to relapse. Scores are also related to age, being higher in early adolescence and in premenstrual women. It was also found that schizophrenic patients excreting kryptopyrrole (kp) had high scores. They were also deficient in vitamin B6 and zinc.

Many subjects have elevated scores no matter what the psychiatric diagnosis is. They include patients with alcoholism, depression and so on. They were not schizophrenic, but they had enough perceptual disturbances to elevate their scores. They have recovered when treated with vitamins B3 and B6. Since these vitamins decreased their elevated scores at the same time they recovered, one can conclude that these elevated scores are also a measure of the need for optimum doses of these two vitamins. The HOD test is also helpful in determining whether any individual would benefit from taking these vitamins. The earliest symptoms and signs of vitamin B3 and B6 deficiencies are changes in perception, usually illusions, but often patients develop hallucinations. In the opinion of A.H. perceptual distortions and illusions are the earliest evidence of the presence of vitamin B3 and B6 deficiencies and will probably show up long before the classical changes found in these deficiencies develop and long before laboratory tests give the same information.

The HOD test is used by a relatively small number of practitioners, psychologists and chiropractors. Physicians have found it very helpful in drawing attention to perceptual disorders which are so characteristic of the schizophrenic patient. Using the HOD test, they are able to start their patients on the right vitamins. For example, Dr. D. Hawkins, a pioneer orthomolecular psychiatrist, used it in association with a church-sponsored outpatient clinic. Practitioners there found that diagnoses were so accelerated that waiting lists they had had to contend with for years were eliminated in one year, and the clinic went from a deficit into the black. More importantly, they could provide their clients service when they needed it, not many months later. I have not heard of any practitioners who have given up this test once they tried it.

The HOD test kit is available from Behavior Science Press, 3710 Resource Drive, Tuscaloosa, AL 35401-7059; (205) 758-2885. It includes the manual, the book by Hoffer, Kelm and Osmond, *The Hoffer-Osmond Diagnostic Test*, which describes the test in detail, the templates for scoring, the scoring sheets and the cards. A software program has been developed for IBM compatible PCs. The questions can be printed, the answers recorded and the scores obtained immediately. It can be ordered from Soft Tac Enterprises, 1181 Union Road, Victoria, BC Canada V8P 2J2. For information via the World Wide Web: http://www.islandnet.com/Members Mall/ Health and Medication/Soft Tac Ent HOD.

5

Poor Nutrition and Mental Disease

CRITERIA OF MENTAL HEALTH

Disappointment and annoyance are emotions I feel at the number of psychiatrists who remain content to keep their schizophrenic patients heavily and permanently tranquilized. Those patients are perfect consumers of services, support and every other community resource, but never again are they able to be productive citizens of society. They are being given cruel, ignorant and inhumane treatment. Keeping them tranquilized holds them in a state of abnormality not reconcilable with the precepts of morality—the science of the good and the nature of the right.

By my criteria, a patient is well or recovered from mental disease as soon as he is free of all signs and symptoms. He returns, or is able to return, to his former occupation or, if he had never worked before, now acquires a useful occupation. He gets on well with his family and with the community.

The basic treatment for mental disease in orthomolecular medicine is the overcoming of the effects of poor nutrition with corrective nutritional therapy. Yet a measure of ignorance of many medical critics of this care is that they hardly ever take nutritional histories of their patients. The most enthusiastic exponents of treatment of mental disease with nutrition are physicians who have themselves suffered with psychological manifestations of the saccharine disease. There is nothing as convincing as a personal cure, especially when every other treatment has been ineffective.

An example of what I mean is the result of my treatment of four general physicians who became severely psychotic before entering the study of medicine or who became ill after being in practice. They are now normal and practicing successfully. Two other medical students recovered from mental ills under my care and now are completing their medical training. Medical study, calling for stringent concentration as it does, points up these recoveries as remarkable. I am unaware of other physicians able to recover from psychosis and practice medicine after being treated with standard tranquilizer therapy.

PSYCHONEUROSES FROM IMPROPER NUTRITION

In Chapter Three we described the physical manifestations of the saccharine disease described by T. L. Cleave in *The Saccharine Disease*. Even more common are mood alterations among people from the same cause, an excessive consumption of refined carbohydrates. These changes are quantitatively different from mood changes that are part of people's normal reactions. They are psychiatric diseases classified as neuroses or psychoneuroses. They manifest no perceptual illusions and hallucinations—no thought disorder. Therefore they are not schizophrenic.

We determine the presence of early perceptual changes by the use of perceptual tests. Also, neuroses must be distinguished from the *psychotic depressions:* differences between reactive depression and endogenous depression. A *reactive depression* is present when the feeling of sadness is appropriate to the psychosocial environment. Thus mourning is normal following bereavement. An *endogenous depression* occurs independent of the environment. It is a subjective judgment made by the diagnosing psychiatrist who decides whether he or she might react to a similar event or series of events. The tendency is to believe depressed patients who find some psychosocial explanation for their depression. They may find ample reason to be depressed even though there is no relationship whatever.

Anxiety and depression may coexist in varying proportions. Depression can be the primary symptom with anxiety super-imposing, or vice versa.

Neuroses are distinguished from psychopathic disorders by behavioral changes. *Psychopaths* are behaviorally inappropriate. They have (1) a failure to learn how to give and take love; (2) an inability to form stable interpersonal relationships; (3) a failure to develop a normal conscience—guilt and remorse may be absent. Psycho-paths are very impulsive, overreact emotionally and often engage in antisocial behavior. Neurotics don't suffer these symptoms. Or-thomolecular psychiatry treats the biochemical aspects of both neu-roses and psychoses. A main cause of neuroses and psychoneuroses is malnutrition derived from faulty nutrition.

The two most common forms of malnutrition causing anxiety relate to a deficiency of some of the B vitamins and to the excessive consumption of processed and refined foods. Although any vitamin deficiency will produce some form of ill health, the B vitamins seem more closely related to anxiety. B vitamin neuroses will be discussed in Chapter Nine.

The saccharine disease provides a metabolic environment for the carbohydrate neuroses. It is rare to find patients with the physical expression of the saccharine disease who do not also suffer from many of the mood changes typically found in the neuroses. In fact, it is common to find serious mood disorders *without* the physical components. Patients with physical symptoms receive somatic treat-ment. Patients with psychiatric symptoms may wind up in the tradi-tional psychiatrist's office—where the last thing considered will be a physical cause such as malnutrition.

PSYCHOLOGICAL MANIFESTATIONS OF THE SACCHARINE DISEASE

I have identified relative hypoglycemia (functional insulinism) as a psychological component of the saccharine disease. The basic prob-lems arise from the excessive consumption of refined carbohydrates, chiefly sugar and white flour. In 1924, about one year after insulin came into general use for the treatment of diabetes, Seale Harris, M.D., Professor of Medicine at the University of Alabama, noted that many non-diabetics experienced some symptoms of insulin overdosage, *insulin shock*. He suggested that in some people "hy-perinsulinism" occurred; that is, the pancreas overreacted with se-cretion of too much insulin. Dr. Harris developed the six-hour glucose tolerance test to determine its presence.

However, today relative hypoglycemia is uniformly rejected by the majority of physicians as a valid disease entity or even as the end result of a diagnostic laboratory test. It remains one of the diseases *not* taught in medical schools. Not uncommonly, a 50- to 75-year gap will occur between medical discovery and application of its knowledge. For example, it took 50 years before the Royal Navy adopted Sir James Lind's discovery that citrus fruits would cure and prevent scurvy. Nevertheless, more than 90 years have passed since Dr. Harris developed his glucose tolerance test and there still remains a reluctance to accept it on the part of medical traditionalists. Reading about relative hypoglycemia here, *you* now know that low blood sugar is responsible for a great deal of mental illness. When the sugar content of the blood goes too low all the tissues of the body have alternative sources of energy except the brain. Brain tissue depends primarily upon glucose for its energy.

A consistent association prevails between neuroses and relative hypoglycemia. Symptoms may include depression, insomnia, anxiety, irritability, crying spells, phobias, lack of concentration and confusion. Accompanying these neurotic symptoms may be physical ones: fatigue, sweating, rapid heartbeat, diminished appetite and chronic indigestion. Other main neurologic symptoms may be headache, dizziness, tremor, muscle pain and backache. Hypoglycemic people do have the typical neurotic symptoms. Possibly one-third of people visiting their physicians for various symptoms suffer from this condition. It is one of the most common causes of neuropsychiatric illness, and it occurs because of the poor dietary habits of Western civilization.

How might we conquer relative hypoglycemia? That is one topic discussed in Chapter Seven, *Orthomolecular Nutrition: Part I, The Optimum Diet*. For now it is sufficient to know that we should come as close to the diet of primitive man as possible. He ate the meat of small animals, fish and fowl, robbed nests of eggs, dug roots and picked leafy vegetables, nuts, fruits and berries.

At all costs you should avoid high-carbohydrate drinks containing caffeine and sugar. Don't eat white bread, white crystalline and powdered sugar, cakes, cookies, candy, syrups, jams, jellies and a host of other processed items. Primitive man did not have these modern-day poisons falsely called food. Invariably they elevate the blood sugar level temporarily to give a lift. Then they drop you down suddenly into hypoglycemic despair. These overprocessed items produce disease.

Dr. Seale Harris deduced that his patients were suffering from the effects of too much insulin produced in the body as a reaction to the consumption of sugar. He outlined the concept of low blood sugar or high insulin blood content and reported that modification of the diet removed the condition. The diet he recommended was a sugar-free, frequent-feeding diet. Recent nutritional research has again demonstrated that frequent eating of small meals is generally healthier than eating one or two meals per day.

SYMPTOMATIC SIMILARITIES BETWEEN NEUROSES AND THE SACCHARINE DISEASE

The relationship between neuroses and the group of diseases known as the saccharine disease becomes even clearer when we examine some of the symptoms which are frequently found in both.

Dizziness: Low blood sugar is found often among patients complaining of dizziness; and conversely dizziness appears regularly among those known to have low blood sugar. My experience has been that a large number of patients with hypoglycemia will now and then suffer so severely from dizziness that they will even lose their balance and fall down. The reason? Low sugar levels in the blood prevent transfer of adequate quantities of glucose into the brain. A constant supply of sugar is needed since the brain uses it as a primary source of energy.

Migraine and Related Vascular Headaches: Of 421 patients suffering from severe migraine and other vascular headaches who had failed to gain relief from standard treatment, relative hypoglycemia was found in 226 when tested by Roberts with the glucose tolerance test. Another 155 had clinical evidence for hypoglycemia but did not demonstrate it by the sugar test. Clinical symptoms of these patients included (1) typical hypoglycemic attacks occurring two to five hours after eating and (2) their prompt alleviation of attack by ingestion of food or sugar. From this large series Dr. Roberts uncovered the following associated conditions:

Narcolepsy was present in 380 patients (90 percent). The narcoleptic condition was indicated by irresistible drowsiness and pathologic or inappropriate sleep. The patients also experienced hypnagogic hallucination, sleep paralysis, a family history of these problems, electroencephalographic evidence and a dramatic response to the drugs methylphenidate or pipradol. Consequently, a conclusion may be drawn that low blood sugar can cause pathological drowsiness.

Peripheral neuropathy showed up among 136 of Roberts' patients (32 percent). Peripheral neuropathy is a variety of symptoms affecting the terminal areas of the nerves, such as numbness and tingling in the fingers and toes.

Spontaneous muscle cramps and restless legs troubled 297 (49 percent) of these patients with low blood sugar.

Obesity was apparent among 204 (46 percent). Obesity occurred from too much sugar consumption, forced feeding of only one or two meals a day, narcoleptic hypokinesia (the sudden uncontrollable disposition to sleep occurring at irregular intervals, with or without obvious predisposing or exciting cause) and the lipogenic (fat-producing) action of excessive insulin.

Swelling of a recurrent edema type took place in 234 patients (56 percent).

Angina pectoris and cardiac arrythmia was found in 65 (15 percent).

Peptic ulcer affected 52 (12 percent).

Alcoholism was present in 30 patients (7 percent). It is my experience that almost every alcoholic has relative hypoglycemia.

Psychiatric features, especially anxiety, depression or both were found among 117 of Roberts' patients (28 percent). The patients' various typical symptoms could be aggravated merely by bringing on a hypoglycemic attack. Previous psychiatric treatment for these patients had been unsuccessful, including the use of psychotropic drugs and ECT. After their relative hypoglycemia was treated, psychiatric treatment results were often quite impressive.

In his paper, Dr. Roberts referred to another paper by Minot, who wrote: "I wish to emphasize to you that there occurs a group of patients with periodic headaches and some with chronic persistent headaches in which gastrointestinal symptoms may be absent, slight, or marked, who are benefited by reduction particularly of carbohydrate and occasionally of protein. . . . The ultimate criterion to decide whether carbohydrate is associated with the production of headache rests with the therapeutic effect of diet properly administered and likewise with the production of the symptoms following the intake of a known, excessive amount of carbohydrates." Dr. Minot won the Nobel prize for his work with pernicious anemia. His valuable observation of the relationship between headache and carbohydrate seems to have been overlooked by most physicians.

Thus it is clear that the symptoms that occur so frequently in neuroses also occur as frequently with patients known to have relative hypoglycemia. You can reproduce these symptoms more or less at will. All it takes is the challenge of the involved person's physiology with high doses of sugar or with easily and rapidly hydrolyzed starchy foods. Logically, the medical challenger must conclude that in most cases the dietary pattern is the cause of this typical symptomatology. It has diurnal rhythm and a blood glucose pattern of relative hypoglycemia.

The hypoglycemic experience is an event which can be studied while the person who experiences it will always be aware of its existence. It is perfectly fair to ask: Why does it happen? Why do hypoglycemic symptoms come on?

THE PHYSIOLOGICAL MECHANISM OF HYPOGLYCEMIA

Drs. Buckley and Gellhorn proposed a central mechanism to account for the total hypoglycemic syndrome. The researchers outlined two quite different physiological mechanisms, one having to do with the blood supply and the other with the experience of hypoglycemia itself.

When the blood supply is reduced to an area of the body, the imposition of either hypoglycemia or hypoxia (a decrease in the normal levels of oxygen in the blood or tissues) will cause effects that are similar to those of a further decrease in blood supply. Hypoglycemic symptoms are the result. For example, the patient with coronary artery disease can develop angina pectoris at rest when he experiences a hypoglycemic episode. Yet he may be capable of moderate activity right after a meal. Exercise that is comfortable at sea level may induce angina in the mountains.

The second mechanism of hypoglycemia is the result of the inhibition of the glucoreceptors in the central area of the hypothalamus (an endocrine gland involved in the functions of the autonomic nervous system). Slow inhibition takes place by food deprivation and rapid inhibition occurs from hypoglycemic episodes. In other words, starvation cuts down slowly on involuntary nervous function but elevation of the blood sugar activates this center. When the glucoreceptor area is inhibited by a fall in blood sugar it will release the posterior hypothalamus and activate the sympathetic nervous system. The hypoglycemic experience can best be understood at two levels. First, it can be measured physiologically. Second, it is existential and can be experienced. The measurement and the experience represent different levels of abstraction. You can study hypoglycemia and observe the symptoms in a person, but you have to experience the symptoms to appreciate their subtle discomfort.

6

Psychosomatic Conditions Resulting from Improper Diet

STOMACH SURGERY PERFORMED WITHOUT CAUSE

Some years ago I was asked to examine an emaciated middle-aged man in the hospital. He was losing weight rapidly as he could not eat or retain the food he managed to get down. He weighed only 75 pounds and could not have lost much more without dying. He had suffered from severe ulcer-like pain that had not responded to conservative dietary treatment. A gastric cancer was suspected, and his stomach was scheduled to be removed. At the operation, only half the stomach was taken out, a portion that contained a suspicious thickening of the stomach wall. However, the final pathological examination showed he had not had cancer at all.

He did feel better for two weeks while he recuperated from the surgery. Then his old problem of severe ulcer-like pain returned. Now he could retain no solid food and lived only on milk shakes. When I visited him the man was very weak, tired, depressed and unable even to chew.

My psychiatric examination included an observation of perceptual symptoms, but his thinking was clear. Looking further at the pattern of his symptoms, I concluded that his condition initially came from relative hypoglycemia. Stomach surgery performed without cause now had the patient in a severe state of inanition due to malnutrition. He was critically ill—potentially on his deathbed—and there was no time to do a five- or six-hour glucose tolerance test. Instead I started him on a liquid food mixture made from milk, bananas and eggs, homogenized together, and a few of the B and C vitamins. My orders were to give him one ounce of the mixture every hour he was awake.

The program of nourishment worked. His weight loss stopped and soon he regained enough strength to chew food. After a week, he was gaining one pound a day. On discharge he was placed on the sugar-free hypoglycemic diet this book recommends, and he required no further hospital admission.

Nevertheless, the intern in charge of following my orders, a product typical of present inadequate teaching of nutrition in our medical schools, blurted out, "Why are you depriving him of sugar? We are trying to get him to gain weight!" He was convinced that sugar was an energy food. The intern thought, and almost spoke the words, that I would accelerate the patient's slide downhill by the diet I had prescribed. That unlucky intern was almost totally ignorant of clinical nutrition.

The patient's physicians and surgical team lacked knowledge of clinical nutrition too. They took out his stomach without cause, simply in response to the man's psychosomatic symptoms as a reaction to hypoglycemia. They lacked that certain "degree of suspicion" that relative hypoglycemia might cause psychosomatic stomach pain. A great deal of psychosomatic mental and physical illness derives from chronic low blood sugar levels prevailing among patients.

I have alluded before to the fact that the brain requires sugar and cannot develop energy from protein or fats as can other tissues. Therefore the brain is the first organ to suffer from a lack of blood sugar and reacts most severely. Permanent brain damage can occur if the hypoglycemia is severe and prolonged. In a scholarly publication, Halfken, Leichter and Reich described two patients who suffered progressive mental deterioration because of hypoglycemia following removal of their stomachs. These three authors wrote: "We suggest that clinicians consider alimentary hypoglycemia as a possible cause of seizures, coma, acute confusional states and dementia in patients who have had partial gastrectomies." Often called "dumping syndrome," it has been my misfortune to observe other patients who have fallen into hypoglycemia following gastrectomy (stomach surgery).

I would suggest even more strongly that this hypoglycemic condition be examined for in each patient prior to performing any gastric surgery. Look for low blood sugar. A lot of stomachs may be saved from removal that way. Some studies have shown that 16 to 65 percent (an average of 40 percent) of all cases of peptic ulcers come from hypoglycemia. Peptic ulcers also have been labeled as derived from psychosomatic causes. We should put cause and effect together.

WHAT IS PSYCHOSOMATIC DISEASE?

The original term *psychosomatic* referred to the interrelation between the psyche and the soma—between the mind and the body. It was coined in an attempt to bridge the gap in thinking between two types of scientist, the pure somaticist and the pure psychologist. Psychosomatic disease works both ways. Pathology in the body can cause mental symptoms and problems in the mind can cause physical symptoms.

In practice, the term was soon taken over by the psychodynamic or psychological school. Psychologists believe that it is the psyche that predominates for a series of psychosomatic conditions such as peptic ulcer, ulcerative colitis, hyperthyroidism, arthritis and other conditions. Gradually, *psychosomatic* has become a one-way term. The role of physiological factors in producing disease of the mind is being almost totally ignored in favor of a series of psychological ideas based primarily upon psychoanalytic theory in one form or another.

Over time, the term is falling into disuse. Now it serves no practical purpose because it no longer has any real meaning. This is unfortunate, since hypoglycemia is a fine example of psychosomatic disease in which the main problem is in the individual's nutrition. The soma causes a resultant reaction of the psyche.

What we have said here about neuroses and neurotic symptoms applies equally well to the psychosomatic conditions. Perhaps if the psychoanalysts of 40 years ago had been aware of the relationship of food to disease, they might have had more luck defining a characteristic personality profile for each psychosomatic condition. An astonishing amount of research went to this problem but very little has been published. There is no characteristic profile.

Years ago, I visited Dr. F. Alexander's analytic institute in Chicago. He invited me to participate during one of the luncheon research meetings at the institute. The training residents and staff had been given a verbatim recording of an interview with a patient who was possessed of one of seven psychosomatic conditions. Any reference to the disease was deleted. From listening to the interview, each participant had to guess which condition it was. That day, out of twenty professional people present, *none* was correct in diagnosing the patient's condition. Even by chance, one of the seven psychosomatic conditions should have been chosen, but it was not. My conclusion from this and many other observations is that the chance of accurately predicting psychosomatic disease by such methods is virtually nil.

One of the psychological components in psychosomatic disease is being ignored. Diseases such as peptic ulcer and ulcerative colitis are related to a certain type of saccharine disease. Relative hypoglycemia is a definite component. Dynamic psychological explorations for psychosomatic disease so common 25 years ago deserve very low priority now.

Even the Bible, Genesis 25:29-33, knew better about nutrition having something to do with behavior. Esau is the first recorded case of psychosomatic disease and personality disorder from relative hypoglycemia:

> And Jacob sod pottage: and Esau came from the field and he was faint: And Esau said to Jacob, Feed me, I pray thee, with that same red pottage; for I am faint. . . .: And Jacob said, Sell me this day thy birthright. And Esau said, Behold I am at the point to die; and what profit shall this birthright do to me? . . . and he sold his birthright unto Jacob.
>
> Then Jacob gave Esau bread and pottage of lentiles; and he did eat and drink and rose up and went his way. Thus Esau despised his birthright.

OUR PSYCHOSOCIAL COMPUTER PERSONALITY

Esau probably suffered from severe hypoglycemia and knew that a protein-rich soup made from lentils (beans) would restore him to health. His feeling that he would die was motive enough to force him to sell his birthright. He wanted to live. This is an excellent account of the powerful drive in people, when they have hypoglycemia, to consume what will elevate their blood sugar levels.

Indeed, psychosomatic disease is a product of our biochemical environment. Few people seem to be aware of this fact; our psychosocial environment seems to overshadow in importance consideration of our biophysical environment. The relationship of the individual to the psychosocial environment—prenatal influences, interaction with parents, family and community, social and economic class, education and life experiences—produces a personality which can instructively be compared to a computer.

A computer has four basic functions: to (1) receive information or input; (2) do something with that information—get at it when necessary—use it; (3) receive orders about what it should do with the information (the *program*); (4) display the results of the operation. A person—any living animal—has the same four basic functions. Your input comes to you via the sensory apparatus. Our eyes, ears, nose, taste, sense of touch obtain information for us about the environment. Complexity of input varies with animal species, and humans are very complex. Even a one-celled animal can sense the presence of an undesirable chemical. Input in animals is called *perception,* and there are two major types: *exteroception* deals with the relationship between individual and environment; *interoception* relates to the brain's reception of essential information from muscles, bones, joints, organs and other tissues. The brain is intimately connected to the rest of the body by motor and sensory nerves. In fact, the brain is part of the body and becomes affected by anything that causes change in the body.

The brain carries on "thinking" that depends upon memory and one's ability to learn. Your thinking is analogous to the operation of the computer, but infinitely more complex. Reasoning is the most complex human function, something computers have not yet been able to do, even though the ability not to repeat errors is being built into them.

People are programmed by life instead of by a detailed set of instructions or software. Life experiences are our software, with the term *education* denoting those experiences. Our education begins at birth and never ceases. If you gain new ideas or change concepts from reading this book, the book will have *reprogrammed* you. You will have been reeducated.

Personality, the way we react to events or ideas, is a result of a given genetic program molded by the psychosocial environment.

This molding determines why we react to our perception the way we do. The end result of the programming will be motor or speech activity.

INSANITY OR COMPUTER MISPERCEPTION

However, a computer may be defective. It may react incorrectly. Theoretically, errors are possible in each of its various functions. Perhaps the input is wrong or it may respond at random. Or its circuits may be disarranged. A society of computers would judge this computer to be different—insane or criminal—sick or willfully bad. It would need to be sent to a computer physician to determine what is wrong.

In the same way, the *human* computer may be incorrect. Error may arise from any one or more of the four functions. John Conolly, M.D., an English physician practicing 165 years ago, gave this sort of explanation for strange or psychotic behavior. Of course, he knew nothing about computers then, but he defined insanity as a disease of perception combined with an inability to tell whether these misperceptions were real or not. This extremely important concept for modern psychiatry is slowly coming back into vogue. It had been submerged for nearly 85 years by the popularity of psychoanalysis.

Human computer misperception occurred to a highly respected and moral man years ago. He was brought to the psychiatric ward against his will because he suddenly began to chase a young woman along the street. When I examined him he told me that God suddenly appeared out of the heavens and told him to chase the woman. He had been brought up to believe in God and to obey Him. Therefore, he began to chase the girl. His reaction, racing after the girl, was the end result of the misperception, his judgment of it and his response. The problem was that he suffered from two major perceptual changes, a visual and an auditory hallucination. Two senses reported something that happened. He saw God emerge from heaven and heard Him speak. Not knowing that he had been schizophrenic for some time, he thought the perceptual phenomena were real. Thus he behaved in a way he thought appropriate. To his surprise the man found himself locked into a psychiatric ward.

The perception was *real* to my patient. Had he decided he had seen and heard an hallucination, he would not have behaved in a way that society judged abnormal. I placed the man on nicotinic acid, 1 gram three times per day, and he recovered. Luckily, tranquilizers had not as yet come into use at that time. Now, 30 years later, the man is still well and has been promoted to high office in his organization.

Had my patient experienced only a visual hallucination or had he only heard a voice, it is doubtful that he would have run after the girl, for he is a moral person. What he believed to be an urgent message from God made him do what he did. Any perceptual distortion can produce an unusual reaction. As opposed to an illusion where an object is seen in the usual way, an hallucination causes the person to see an object as others do not see it. Hallucinations can affect all the senses. They may be judged real by the hallucinator if they are present for a long time. If more than one of the senses provides coherent information, it is even more difficult to ignore the hallucination as unreal. A few strong-willed persons may mistrust the evidence from two senses, but it is highly unlikely that evidence from three senses would be so judged and not acted upon. If a person had a visual hallucination of an angel, heard him speak and felt his hand upon his shoulder (visual, auditory and touch senses), he would undoubtedly conclude this was a real angel and not a three-dimensional apparition who could speak.

Imagine yourself having a variety of perceptual changes and decide how you would react if you decided these changes were true, or if you believed them false. The exercise will amaze you.

PSYCHOSOMATIC REACTION TO ENVIRONMENT

Psychosomaticism is a reaction between the person and his psychosocial or biophysical environment. If the senses are normal and only have minor variations in interpretation of what is experienced, that individual will react in a normal way with the environment. Nevertheless, a person with a normal sensory apparatus (input) may react abnormally to his environment. His program may be faulty. If a person is brought up in a culture where it is considered normal to be hostile, to rob and steal, and if he is transported into another psychosocial environment where this sort of behavior is not tolerated, he will behave abnormally until he is reprogrammed.

Also, a person's muscular apparatus—lack of coordination—may make it impossible for him to behave in a normal way. Thus, if your speech is garbled and distorted by a muscular abnormality, you would have great difficulty behaving normally. You would be unable to communicate with others.

The interaction between the biophysical environment and the individual is equally complex. We react directly to our environment. We react differently in the dark than we do in daylight, for example. Even more subtle is the impact of this environment on our perception of the psychosocial environment.

Chronic malnutrition and cerebral allergy are producers of misperception. They alter perception and thinking. Consequently, the relationship of an individual to the psychosocial environment will change. My patient who chased the girl suffered from perceptual changes owing to his need for extra quantities of nicotinic acid, vitamin B3. Giving him the needed vitamin cured his perceptual changes; a change in nutrition restored his previously normal behavior.

All of us react to two environments: psychosocial and biophysical. Our response to the psychosocial environment is mediated by the senses. The biophysical environment is both a cause and an effect. It influences our reaction to both environments.

If disease, ill health or discomfort arise out of any cause relating to psychosocial environmental factors—in other words, from a disharmony between the physically normal individual and the environment—they must be dealt with by psychosocial techniques. Biochemical treatment won't work. Conversely, if the error is in the biochemistry of the brain, there is little point in trying to correct it by psychosocial techniques alone. The correct treatment is to restore the normal biochemistry.

To return to the computer analogy, if the computer is defective because of a problem in the hardware, no amount of software tinkering will correct its operation. If the error is in the software, no amount of hardware tinkering will correct the error. So it is with human beings. Their psychosomatic ills arise from one of two environments. Treatment and cure of them will take place by finding the error in either software or hardware: programming or physical malfunction. The next chapter describes orthomolecular treatment for the latter.

7

ORTHOMOLECULAR NUTRITION—PART I
The Optimum Diet

ORTHOMOLECULAR NUTRITION DEFINED

You will enjoy super good health when you are in harmony with the environment. Then you sense the surroundings, perceive them as most normal people do, experience clear thinking, act alert, feel in tune with the general thought of the day (but not necessarily in agreement with it), show a normally cheerful mood, sometimes feel appropriately depressed and sometimes ecstatic and can perform desired physical activities with adequate energy and enthusiasm. Not every person will reach this state of superhealth. Everyone should try for it, however. A large number of people will be happily surprised if they do make the effort. Will you be one of them?

Super good health can be reached through the application of orthomolecular nutrition. *Orthomolecular nutrition is the ingestion of the optimum level of each nutrient for each individual.* Its concept is founded upon the recognition that no living organism lives within a perfect environment. For example, if yeast cells, which grow exceedingly rapidly, were supplied with the ideal environment, they would in a short period use up all the nutrients on Earth. Nature has evolved a complicated set of checks and balances so that such a quick-growing organism runs into the reality of a limited environment.

If rabbits find too perfect an environment, they will overpopulate. Eventually there will be so much rabbit meat available for their predators that the predators will in turn multiply. Then the rabbit population will be brought into balance. A perfect environment for one species not only is impossible, it would be intolerable for other species and eventually for the one species temporarily enjoying that environment. Dr. Roger Williams has been instrumental in making us aware of these factors. They apply as well to the cells of a multicellular animal. The environment of every animal is imperfect. It follows that the cells within the animal also must live in an imperfect environment.

Each cell in the body is surrounded by a thin layer of water which contains the nutrients, hormones, waste products and other substances essential for its function. Ideally, all the forty-five nutrients required by the cell should be present in optimum quantities which must vary from time to time. In actuality, this hardly ever occurs, as the cells must compete with others for their share of the limited supply of nutrients. There is an enormous range in need.

For example, the range in need for lysine is 700 percent from subjects requiring the least amount to those requiring the most for optimum function. The need for vitamins is even greater if the range is considered for those who are vitamin-dependent individuals. *Orthomolecular nutrition is nutrition which strives to provide these optimum quantities for the cells of the body and takes into account the enormous individuality of persons and the variations caused by time and stress.*

Orthomolecular nutrition offers a program for each of the following categories of individuals:

(1) People who are very healthy now but would like to increase the probability that they will remain the rest of their lives in super good health.

(2) People who need to change their pattern of living and eating in order to gain a much better state of health—good health.

(3) People who are already in the throes of serious physical and psychiatric disability.

People in category 3 will use orthomolecular nutrition as a treatment program. Categories 1 and 2 are preventive and maintenance programs.

NUTRITIOUS FOODS

The best foods are whole foods to which human beings have adapted in the course of their evolution. They are the opposite of junk foods. They contain the protein, fat and carbohydrate fractions of the food in combination with the vitamins and minerals.

When the wheat kernel is growing, the vitamins and minerals used in synthesizing its chemical components are deposited and left there. Following the milky stage, when the green kernel is full of a milk-like liquid, the kernel begins to harden. Once it is full, little additional material is made and the water present is lost from the kernel by evaporation through the bran. The movement of the liquid through the brain translocates some of the vitamins and minerals toward the outer coats. The important part of the kernel, the germ, which will grow into a new plant, is for this reason very rich in all the nutrients essential for growth. If all the vital nutrients of the kernel were isolated and fed simultaneously, this would be as nutritious as eating the whole kernel, provided that in the process of extracting all these nutrients they remained undamaged by the chemical process used—which is not possible. In addition, we cannot assume that every essential nutrient has already been identified; surely others remain to be discovered. For these reasons, given our present state of technology, *there is no way to process a food into as nutritious a product as the original food.*

The kernel is fractioned by current bakery technologists into white flour (called endosperm), germ and bran. Then only the white flour is fed to people as loaves of bread. The people, as a result, are being cheated of proper nutrition. They are being deprived of most of the vitamins and minerals used by the plant to make its own food. Plants manufacture food with which to feed themselves; people do not. People eat and digest food to release essential nutrients and make them available to the body. The body, in turn, metabolizes the food into energy or into structural components. In the absence of nutrient-rich components, there is an immediate imbalance in the human body. White flour cannot be metabolized unless vitamins and minerals are present. When white flour fails to carry the correct amount of nutrients, the body must get them from other food stuffs.

In modern society you are being robbed of nutrients by use of junk foods. These are packaged parasites, the sneak thieves of essential micronutrients from all other foods you eat. By eating them, you are participating in the food technology conspiracy to line manufacturers' pocket with your silver at the expense of your bodily and mental health.

None of the processed foods carry their optimum quota of essential micronutrients, but some are much worse and more lacking then others. There is only one safe rule to follow. USE WHOLE FOODS WHENEVER POSSIBLE. Eat an orange rather than its juice—whole wheat and not white flour—brown rice instead of polished rice—an entire potato in place of instant mashed potatoes. Furthermore, whole foods provide one other major health advantage. They are packaged by nature in fibrous material which provides bulk to the body. Digestion without bulk becomes very difficult. Another excellent rule: IF MANUFACTURED, DON'T EAT IT!

Perhaps someday, food manufacturers really will enrich our good foods to provide nutrients that are in short supply. After all, seeds are originally designed to grow new plants and not to provide us with food. The needs of growing plants are not identical with ours, but seeds are to date the finest natural food that farming manufacturers can provide.

RAW FOODS

Since cooking involves altering the nutrient characteristics of foods through the action of heat or the dissolving effect of water, it is wise to eat uncooked or raw food whenever possible. Certain foods must be cooked in order for us to digest them or to protect ourselves from bacterial or parasitic invasion. Foods like pork and poultry should be cooked well. Some others such as fish may be cooked lightly. Various vegetables like carrots, turnips and celery might best be consumed raw. No vitamins and minerals will be wasted in this way. Of course, clean your food of chemicals first. Chemical contamination in no way enhances its nutritional quality and may even make it unsafe to eat. Insecticides, parasiticides and other pesticides are often poisonous to people.

Some foods eaten raw are said to pack purifying properties. They

act as antidotes against poisonous additives if inadvertently ingested.
A list of these foods follows:

Alfalfa tea	Dandelion root	Herbs including—
Apples	& leaves	Angelica
Apricots	Grapefruit	Borage
Asparagus	Horseradish	Fennel
Beet tops	Lemons	Horehound
Blackberries	Oranges	Juniper
Blueberries	Mustard greens	Marjoram
Carrot juice	Peaches	Rue
Cauliflower	Raspberries	Sarsaparilla
Celery juice	Turnip tops	Slippery elm
Clover	Watercress	Southernwood
Cranberries		

NOTE: Vitamin C (ascorbic acid) is known as "the anti-pollution
vitamin" and protects in part against toxic poisons and gamma rays.

Bone meal contains calcium, which influences an individual's immunity to cancer and acts as a protection against radiation.

BALANCED NUTRITION

"Balanced meal" has been a favorite term used by nutritionists for
many years. It means that the optimum proportion (a balance) of
all the food components is provided—an excellent idea in theory.
But the term has come to mean something else too. In the name
of a balanced meal, many nutritionists have compromised their
knowledge and accepted that even large quantities of sucrose in a
meal are fine provided that it is balanced against some protein, fat
and the essential vitamins and minerals. This has led to the prepos-
terous statement that junk cereal and milk are nutritious whereas
in reality that cereal has diluted the nutritional quality of the milk.

Some nutritionists have said that the super doughnut made from
white flour, oil and sugar, plus a tiny quantity of added vitamins,
is a good food. They suggest that a balanced meal is provided by
eating a couple of super doughnuts and drinking a glass of milk.
How nonsensical! Yet there has even been backup by the United
States Department of Agriculture for this kind of suggestion. Of

course, white flour and milk are agricultural products, which suggests an inappropriate bias on the part of the government agency.

The concept of balance thus was useful originally, but it has been corrupted by the industries devoted to food technology, and no longer serves any valid purpose. Since no better description of proper eating exists though, we will continue to use "balance" here—in its original sense. In effect, "balanced nutrition" and "orthomolecular nutrition" are similar terms because they both denote *the importance of using optimum quantities of all the essential nutrients.* This is best achieved by obtaining these nutrients from a variety of foods. Variety is more apt to satisfy our needs than is dependence upon any one food.

Of itself, food should be balanced for each meal and over an entire day. The best way to ensure such balance is to use whole foods that nature has already balanced. Eat several items from different groups such as meats, fresh vegetables, fresh fruits, fresh fish, poultry, dairy products, nuts and seeds. Ensure total daily balance by attempting orthomolecular nutrition every time you eat. Snacks may not be included in this admonition since they seldom are made from a variety of foods and comprise only a minor component of our diet. Even so, it is very important to make sure that snacks are whole foods and not of the refined carbohydrate type such as doughnuts, chips, pretzels, chocolate bars and other junk. This junk steals the good out of the meal balancing and leaves you with empty calories.

Balanced nutrition demands that you follow a series of dietary rules. Primitive humans followed them naturally without realizing they were rules for healthy living. They did what came naturally, making use of what was available. All they had was healthy food.

SPECIFIC DIETARY RULES

Following a set of general rules will ensure an adequate diet for most people. Yet the individuality of people suggested by Dr. Williams does mean that some will have widely varying requirements. Consequently, a few special rules offered here are designed to meet those individual requirements. Follow them and you will be doing what is best for your body and mind.

A. *Eat an optimum amount of protein,* either vegetable, animal or both. You will have to determine what amount is optimum for you. The best way to accomplish that is by trial and error. First start with a lower level of intake, then increase it slowly while you judge what effect your form of eating is having.

Use of the word *protein* here refers to protein-rich foods, not to any protein powder or other protein supplement. You may feel a sense of well-being as your protein intake increases; assume then that more is a better level. Don't push onto others what you find is an optimum level for yourself. People, being individual, have different optimum requirements. "Do your thing" and let others do theirs. If they ask for advice, give it, of course.

While testing yourself for optimum protein intake, keep the fat and carbohydrate levels about the same as usual. Otherwise you may find it difficult to decide what makes you feel better. This is a therapeutic preventive and maintenance program being recommended for those described in categories 1 and 2 set out at the beginning of this chapter. Finding the correct levels of protein, fat and carbohydrate is a course designed for people who are healthy now and wish to stay that way or who desire super good health. Also this method will help those who have let themselves deteriorate and need to change their pattern of living to gain a somewhat healthier state. If this is to be achieved, the type of protein consumed should have enough of the essential amino acids.

B. *Eat an optimum amount of fat (lipids).* Proceed to work out what this is the same way you did with protein.

C. *Eat an optimum amount of unprocessed carbohydrates.* These should be from fresh vegetables and fruits. We've already discovered that the optimum quantity of processed or refined carbohydrates such as sugar, white flour, alcohol, polished rice and some other edibles is zero. Every increment above zero of these ultra-refined food artifacts decreases the quality of your diet. In other words, the more you eat of these zero edibles, the more you are stealing nutrient value from good foodstuffs. You dilute your intake of nutrition that way and detract from your overall health. Why accept anything less than the optimum diet when it is available?

THE OPTIMUM DIET

A diet that provides orthomolecular nutrition, *the optimum diet,* will consist of the necessary protein, fat and carbohydrates increments from natural foods. Over thousands of years humankind has adapted to these during evolution. These elements are mingled with each other and with other essential nutrient factors such as vitamins and minerals. Extra supplementation may be required by certain people whose optimum requirements can't be met by even the best program of nutrition. Self-experimentation with vitamins and minerals is something you can engage in to determine whether or not you need this supplementation program. Chapter Nine discusses vitamin supplementation. Chapter Ten explains about mineral nutrients.

Keep in mind that vitamins are not drugs; they are foods. Many physicians do not look at vitamins and minerals that way. They put this form of food supplementation in the same category as tranquilizers and other unnatural synthetics. They believe that food supplements should remain under prescription control as are antibiotics or other potent medication. Why do they hold this erroneous belief? Because physicians are trained to recognize deficiency diseases, and they are taught that in modern society the majority of people are not suffering from any deficiency. This is true in the sense that patients are not dropping on the streets with disease symptoms. But that is the only truth that doctors are taught about vitamin deficiency.

Physicians enter practice trained in the germ theory of disease, they look for illness arising from that cause and not from the lack of vitamin and mineral nutrition, and therefore, they take for granted that people should not need any more minerals and vitamins. Doctors recognize that some of their patients do require supplementation, especially when specific deficiency diseases are present. They do administer vitamin B12 for pernicious anemia, vitamin D for rickets and other therapeutic vitamins for other individual problems that appear. They equate vitamins used in this way with drug treatment, which often involves the possibility of serious toxic reaction. Physicians bolster this position with dire warnings. Doctors are correct when they point out that it requires medical expertise to recognize the deficiency diseases. But considering that vitamins and minerals properly should be classed as nutrients, the situation becomes altogether different.

Let's face it! The typical deficiency diseases are uncommon. They can be identified easily by any person interested in nutrition. Many people, possibly you among them, are very keen to learn all they can about nutrition and the diseases proper nutrition prevents. People want to know how to keep themselves healthy. The popular literature is well endowed with this information, but it seems difficult for medical students and some doctors to find it. They insist on remaining disease- and illness-oriented rather than becoming person- and health-oriented. Doctors *treat* crises and tend not to prevent them.

Knowing what is the optimum diet for yourself is of great advantage. To find that out does take experimentation of a controlled nature. The concept of controlled experiments in nutrition is not very novel, either. You can and should do it for yourself. However, nutrition scientists would prefer to hold onto the reins of research themselves. Some modern research workers would have us believe that controlled clinical experiments are difficult and very recent, going back perhaps four or five decades. Yet in the Bible, *The Book of Daniel*, Chapter 1 verses 3 to 16, we find the following account of what may have been one of the earliest recorded controlled clinical experiments.

> Then the king [Nebuchadnezzar] commended Ashpenaz, his chief Eunuch, to bring some of the people of Israel, both of the royal family of the nobility, youths without blemish, handsome and skillful in all wisdom, endowed with knowledge, understanding, learning, and competent to serve in the king's palace, and to teach them the letters and language of the Chaldeans. The king assigned them a daily portion of the rich food which the king ate, and of the wine which he drank. They were to be educated for three years, and at the end of that time they were to stand before the king. Among these were Daniel. . . .

> But Daniel resolved that he would not defile himself with the king's food, or with the wine which he drank, and therefore he asked the chief of the Eunuchs to allow him not to defile himself. And God gave Daniel favor and compassion in the sight of the chief of the Eunuchs, and the chief of the Eunuchs said to Daniel: "I fear lest my lord the king, who appointed your food and your drink should see that you were in poorer condition than the youths who are of your own age. So you would endanger my head with the king."

> Then Daniel said to the steward:

"Test your servants for ten days. Let us be given pulse to eat and water to drink. Then let our appearance, the appearance of the youths who eat of the king's rich food be observed by you, and according to what you see deal with your servants."

So he harkened to them in this matter, and tested them for ten days. At the end of ten days it was seen that they were in better appearance and fatter in flesh than all the youths who ate of the king's rich food. So the steward took away the rich food and wine they were to drink, and gave them pulse.

ANTI-ALLERGY NUTRITION

An anxious and depressed man consulted me in 1967. He had been following a typical high-carbohydrate, processed-food program of eating and had the usual diurnal rhythm of symptoms in response. My treatment included his adoption of the hypoglycemic diet with inclusion of plenty of protein. He returned two years later with assurances that he had followed my recommendations faithfully and seriously for months. He ate beef at each meal and avoided all junk food. Yet, he became steadily worse, more depressed than ever. Eventually he found his way to an allergist who discovered that the man was allergic to beef. When he eliminated beef from his diet, he promptly recovered from all mental symptoms. My recommendation had worsened him by increasing his consumption of a food to which he was allergic.

This points up the very real existence of nutritional allergies. Many people are allergic to some of the protein-rich foods. Neither they nor their doctors are aware of this. Increasing the intake of these allergy foods may make mental and/or physical symptoms come on even stronger. When I first began to diagnose and treat relative hypoglycemia, I placed all patients on the usual high protein, sugar- and processed-carbohydrate-free, frequent feeding program. This was very effective for a large proportion of patients, but eventually I discovered that some who had been well for up to a year noted the return of severe depression, anxiety and other symptoms, as had been the case with this patient allergic to beef.

You may gather from this that the main nutritional problems are not single-vitamin deficiencies. Rather, they are usually multiple subclinical deficiencies or allergies. This means that the symptoms are vague and diffuse. A sick person will no doubt have something wrong, but there is little specificity about what it is. It is only before death is likely to occur that the fully developed symptoms appear. There is no guide to what is wrong with a person possessed of a nutritional problem. Even with their medical expertise, physicians are not more skillful in concluding which subclinical deficiency or allergy is present. The intelligent lay person is just as adept at detecting the source of the problem.

However, physicians do have access to laboratory tests and know better how to use them and how to interpret them. A physician knowledgeable about nutrition is a desirable individual to know and consult. When such a physician can't be found, you, the lay person, will have to go ahead alone.

What should you do to help yourself or someone you love? Since symptoms are not too helpful, except that they indicate something definitely is wrong, there is no alternative to trial and response techniques.

Seek out anti-allergy nutrition. Don't accept symptoms as being psychosomatic or allow yourself to be branded as neurotic simply because the complaints do not fit in with any well-known physical problem. A physician may not be able to find anything wrong. All his tests could well be negative. I have seen ailing people undergo dozens of tests, receive over a thousand dollars worth of investigatory examinations and end with being labeled "neurotic." Yet, for these so-called neurotics, nutritional tests or allergy tests were prominent by their absence from the whole battery of those administered. Neuroses must never be diagnosed simply by excluding well-known syndromes.

One more bit of knowledge you should have: there are two basic reasons for organic pathology: (1) anatomical and/or histological changes in the body such as actual wounds, tumors, blockages and other such physical difficulties; (2) biochemical physiological changes which may not show as anatomical-histological changes, at least in the beginning. The second type of changes probably won't be readily diagnosed by physical examination or even by the usual laboratory tests. The first type of changes produces easily recognized diseases such as pneumonia, heart disease, jaundice and the like. The second kind produces equally serious illnesses, but not other physical changes.

Both symptoms and signs will be apparent in the first set of conditions, but not in the second set—only symptoms, as the physician seldom is experienced enough to recognize biochemical signs. Note that *a symptom is the patient's complaint; a sign is evidence of malfunction elicited by the physician either in the history or by appropriate laboratory tests.* Nobody should accept the diagnosis of neurosis (that it's all in your mind; you're imagining it; you have psychological problems) unless certain conditions have been fulfilled first. There should be clear evidence that psychological problems or conflicts prevailed which *preceded* the illness, or there should have been a complete examination, including a nutritional investigation, allergy test and a six-hour glucose tolerance test.

THE DIETARY TREATMENT FOR HYPOGLYCEMIA

Hypoglycemia treatment is primarily dietary. For allergy-free people who suffer from low blood sugar, the diet should exclude all junk. The uncompromising rule: all foods which contain added sugar, are highly refined and/or are vigorously processed should be considered so much packaged garbage.

The pattern of eating may be variable for some hypoglycemics. A three-meals-a-day pattern will be suitable for most, but others do require additional snacks between meals. Even though these people are free of allergies, an allergy could develop, and it should be watched for. To reduce the chance of triggering an allergic response, it is best not to rely too much on eating any one food. Vary the diet as much as possible. Leave a gap of several days for a repeat consumption of the same edible.

If you or a member of your family is allergic and hypoglycemic at the same time—hypoglycemic because of the allergy, or whose hypoglycemia is aggravated by the allergy—rigorously avoid those allergy foods. If the allergy is a *fixed* one, it will *always* produce the allergic response and should not be excited by eating what brings it on. Otherwise, after six months to a year, the foods you have omitted from your diet may be reintroduced in small quantities at infrequent intervals.

If you are hypoglycemic and allergic simultaneously, there may be some foods that cause an allergic response and should not be eaten. If that is the case, you may find it impossible to avoid them.

Then your diet may have to be one of rotation, going from one such food to another. If other allergies are present, such as allergy to dust, pollen or fumes, these should be eliminated from the environment as much as possible. Also you may be desensitized by properly prepared vaccination. Decreasing the intensity of these allergic reactions will decrease the intensity of the hypoglycemic reaction.

In addition to dietary treatment for hypoglycemia, it is desirable to use vitamin supplementation. The important B vitamins, vitamin C and mineral supplements may be needed in quantity. Laboratory techniques such as hair analyses for trace minerals and blood assays for zinc and copper will be helpful in deciding which minerals ought to be added to the program. The necessary B vitamins are B3, B6 and sometimes B1. Important minerals probably are chromium, zinc, manganese and magnesium.

Other adjuncts have been used during the initial stages of hypoglycemic treatment. These include a soluble calcium preparation called "Calphosan" given by intramuscular injection. Orthomolecular therapists have used an adrenal cortical extract, ACE, intravenously in a series of injections. Others seldom if ever inject these preparations. The idea of using ACE is to replace some of the hormones which a tired adrenal cortex is not preparing. Supplemental injections allow the gland to rest.

Those orthomolecular physicians who began their practice using megavitamin therapy have tended not to use ACE very much. Those who depended less on vitamin supplementation generally inject more ACE. It is possible that the use of megavitamins restores adrenal cortex function. This may explain why orthomolecular physicians who prescribe vitamin supplements do not use ACE injections as treatment nearly as often as the others.

Allergic hypoglycemics are aided by antihistamines and parasympathetic drugs such as bellargal.

Treatment of the hypoglycemic condition was divided by Ross into three stages. During the *first stage* of hypoglycemia care the patient may feel worse with symptoms. He experiences an increased craving for sweets and starchy foods, a craving similar to the withdrawal phase after eliminating any addictive drug. A non-addicted hypoglycemic may have less severe symptoms. Depression does appear, though, and only faith in the doctor's diagnostic skill and therapeutic wisdom sustains the patient. Occasionally depression becomes so severe that it requires antidepressant medication and, occasionally, admission to the hospital.

During the *second stage,* patients suffer from recurrent episodes of their typical hypoglycemic symptoms interposed with episodes of well-being. Each relapse brings back depression, but the enjoyable good periods come more and more frequently and last longer. Patients soon learn that dietary indiscretions precipitate the resurgence of symptoms. This is a valuable lesson, for it brings into play an evolutionary device which has allowed animals to learn which foods they can eat safely and which should be avoided. Humans being animals—though priding themselves on being the highest order thereof—will have an evolutionary instinct come into play.

Naturalists have shown that when an animal becomes ill within a few hours after eating a particular food, it will no longer have an interest in that food. Rats fed poisoned bait which does not succeed in killing them will avoid that bait again. A coyote fed rabbit meat containing sublethal amounts of lithium salts will become violently nauseated and vomit. Then it shuns that rabbit meat altogether. In one case a coyote shown a *live* lamb turned away and vomited because previously it had been made ill by lamb meat containing lithium. This is the way predators could be conditioned not to kill livestock. People, too, will find a certain food repulsive if it has made them sick and they are aware of the cause-and-effect relationship.

It is too bad that the sweet taste added to processed foods fool us into not tying hypoglycemia to symptoms of illness. Nature gives us no mechanism with which to deal with good-tasting foods that make us sick even after eating them for many years. People won't be persuaded that the deliciousness of junk pastries, pies, candies and cold cereals is bad for them when the result of their consumption doesn't show up for a long time. Food habits are extraordinarily difficult to change. We have to resort to reason to demonstrate the relationship between junk consumption and disease at a general level first, and at a personal level later. That is what we are attempting with this book—demonstration at least at the general level.

Personal demonstration is possible after you abstain from eating junk for a time. As long as you eat poorly every day, you will be ill in a low-grade way and not notice any immediate effect. After being off junk for several weeks, eating the stuff again will cause a resurgence of typical hypoglycemic symptoms. This shows the case-and-effect relationship clearly and is an especially valuable lesson for children.

If your child resents being put on the no-junk diet and resists your direction, it may seem sadistic, but here is a method for making your point clear: Persuade your son or daughter to eat *only* junk for one full day a week, usually Saturday. Let the child eat all that is desired of cold cereal coated with sugar, ice cream, chocolate bars, doughnuts with icing and so on. Feed junk food for breakfast, lunch and dinner. Most of the time the youngster will become ill and will quickly associate sweets with sickness. Now and then a retest will be required to prove the cause-and-effect relationship. If a *lot* of refined carbohydrate is consumed in one particular period, the lesson will be made clear.

Two periods during the year are critically dangerous to hypoglycemic people. After the Christmas and Easter holidays, there is a marked lowering of patients' blood sugar from the tremendous upsurge in eating candy and cookies. A fair number of people revisit their orthomolecular physicians then. They *had* been well, tried junk over the holidays, became ill again, and will, under the physician's direction, return to the usual junk-free diet, and once more recover.

A period that is dangerous for children is the summer hiatus from school. It becomes difficult to control a child's intake of junk, and parents usually give up until school begins again. Relatives, especially grandparents who don't understand the casual relationship, often play a pernicious part by feeding sweets to grandchildren surreptitiously. It is extremely difficult to counter the pervasive, almost ubiquitous drive in our society for junk food. Well-meaning but ignorant friends and associates continually urge patients to eat sweets. However, many determined hypoglycemics, once they are well, become full of missionary zeal and convert friends, relatives and neighbors to the junk-free way of life.

The *third stage* of hypoglycemia care is one of steady recovery from the condition. It occurs because by now you or a responsible family member has mastered the dietary measures required. Confidence with your manner of eating progresses steadily. Over time, a relapse can occur, and then you should immediately investigate for allergies which could have developed. When these are found and eliminated you will have recovered from hypoglycemia completely.

8

ORTHOMOLECULAR NUTRITION—PART II
Protein, Fat and Carbohydrate

THE EFFECT OF AN ARTIFACT-RICH DIET ON HEALTH

A dictum of orthomolecular nutrition is that most unprocessed foods contain a blend of all the nutrients. When digested in the gastrointestinal tract the nutrients are released more or less simultaneously. They become available for absorption into the blood. Distribution takes place among the various tissues, and the cells then have access to these nutrients for energy and growth.

There is a wide variation in the nutrient composition of foods. The range extends from foods very rich in protein such as meat, fish, poultry and seeds to those quite low in protein like apples and salad. Fats and carbohydrates vary in a similar way in their content within foods. This natural variation has been widely extended by processors who remove the food artifacts in their pure form. Pure protein, pure fat, pure starch or a variety of sugars are extracted and made available. These pure forms are *artifacts*—something created by human work, a modification from nature, produced artificially.

Textured protein sold as a meat substitute, ice cream and commercial pastry—a blend of pure fat, carbohydrate and sugar—are some of the readily available food artifacts.

A diet rich in such artifacts presents a complete imbalance, with no natural controls on the amount consumed of the nutrients—it is easy to consume too much or too little of any of the vital substances, to say nothing of the other nutritional losses, referred to earlier, caused by processing. You would be much less susceptible to an imbalance of nutrients if eating unprocessed foods.

PROTEIN

Protein-rich foods have been classified as high quality and low quality, depending upon the quantity and variety of essential amino acids present. Amino acids of a certain type are called *essential* because they cannot be made by the body and must be provided by food. The remaining amino acids are, of course, also essential for body metabolism, but they can be made by the body through conversion from other amino acids. As the body discontinues to make certain amino acids during the course of human evolution, as in the case of ascorbic acid, perhaps an increasing number of amino acids will become *essential*. It would be pleasant to think that the extra energy gained by omitting one of the metabolic functions may provide human beings with improved intelligence, more creativity or a greater ability to solve pressing problems.

A high-protein diet has advantages for many people, especially for those who have had relative hypoglycemia for many years. The glucose from protein is released slowly and does not overstimulate the production of insulin. Many find that a breakfast rich in protein prevents the occurrence of worries or tension, irritability, fatigue and sleepiness during the day. It provides for a moderate elevation of blood glucose, which is sustained.

Generally it is easiest to obtain high-quality protein from animals and fish, but it can be obtained also from vegetarian sources. A vegetarian must be highly knowledgeable about food values. Indeed, an uninformed vegetarian is more apt to find himself in nutritional difficulty than an uninformed meat eater. Some vegetarians turn naturally away from meat because they feel better subsisting on nonanimal foods. They may not be aware that possibly they are allergic to only one or two animal protein foods and really should avoid just these. Frequently they do not know that feeling healthier by avoidance is simply an allergy problem. Thus they avoid everything pertaining to animal foods. These are personal reactions, no different in principle than the effects of eliminating wheat or corn or some other cause of allergy.

An explanation is needed here about how to test yourself if you believe you are allergic to an animal protein or some other foodstuff. Anyone can determine whether an allergy is present by depriving himself of the particular food suspected for two weeks. Then reintroduce this item into your diet. If you feel well after doing without the food, and worse after you've reintroduced it, this would throw strong suspicion on that food as our particular allergen. Do the test again. If the same thing happens a few times, you have proved the food culprit as a cause of your discomfort.

A diet high in protein-rich foods to which an individual is not allergic cannot be harmful and may well be very helpful. You should aim for an optimum quantity. The guidelines available are crude and rough-figured. They are averages that are too high for a large number of the population and too low for an even larger section. Each person has to determine his own optimum amount. Then aim for something just above the optimum when eating only whole unprocessed foods. It is safer to eat more protein than less.

CAN YOU EAT TOO MUCH PROTEIN?

You certainly can eat too much protein if you include artifacts as sources. Natural food is unlikely to present a problem, simply because it contains other essential components, and its sheer bulk, eaten in quantity, makes it difficult to take in too much. But with the recent availability of almost pure protein, as present in textured protein meat substitutes, it will be possible to consume an overabundance. Too much protein intake throws an unnecessary burden on the body. This is undesirable and dangerous, for it will displace other essential foods and produce an imbalance.

In most cases, the high cost of protein will prevent an overabundant intake. Some people for personal reasons may consume protein artifacts to excess. These would not be foods naturally rich in the substance but foods made from protein artifacts such as gelatin desserts. This artifact fails as a good food in that it does not contain an adequate balance of the ten essential amino acids.

We interject a warning: dairy products, natural high-protein food, can cause allergy, especially since they are readily available and are used as high-protein snacks. A large number of my patients have reacted badly to increased consumption of dairy products. As a result, my policy now is to insist on a diet free of junk but without any emphasis on a high-protein diet. I no longer place special emphasis on the hypoglycemic diet. My views of the efficacy of this diet have been changing since I have found a fair number of people who, when following the hypoglycemic diet, develop allergies to the proteins it calls for. My new advice is not to increase the intake of protein or to call for frequent feeding, but simply to take *all* the refined foods away. This allows each person more individuality in the preparation of food, which they appreciate. Those are some of the reasons you won't see a specific hypoglycemic diet in this book.

My advice also is to be careful about foods which are liked or disliked excessively. Liking a food, you may eat too much of it. Disliking a food may be based on a long forgotten bad reaction to it. Yes, the dislike will linger on but the reason for it may not be remembered.

Even so, patients do train themselves to eat foods they dislike if they are advised to eat them. Having disliked milk, but told by me or some other doctor to eat milk products, patients will begin to consume milk in large quantities and so become worse. This may so intensify an allergy that small quantities, which in the past caused no difficulty, now cause severe reactions. Foods overly liked, on the other hand, may have an allergic-based addiction connected with them, which provides the basis for the excessive passion.

HAZARDS OF EATING TOO LITTLE PROTEIN

All the structural material of your body is built out of protein. Every reaction—nervous, circulatory, digestive, muscular, cerebral—is dependent in one way or another on protein or on the amino acids of protein. For this reason, too little protein present in the body is extremely serious. When its intake is deficient, all those reactions mentioned will slow down or stop altogether. Consequently, protein deficiency is much more pathological when protein requirements are high. For instance, children require high protein to build their bodies and surgical patients need high protein to repair wounds.

Once a structure or tissue has been developed by the body, it does not mean that it no longer needs protein. A human organ is not like an electric motor or other manmade object. Although a motor will operate until it wears out or breaks down, it is not continually rebuilt as it functions. Living tissue is rebuilt. It remains in a constant state of repair. Amino acids, the building blocks of all tissues, are constantly exchanged for new amino acids in the blood. If there is too little amino acid in blood, it will leach protein out of a tissue and may not leave enough to maintain that tissue in a healthy state.

Not every tissue suffers equal leaching. Vital organs hold onto their amino acids more tenaciously. Our major protein storehouse in the body is muscle. Muscles will lose protein first, become wasted, lose power, grow thin, and provide the emaciated appearance observed in a starved person. During starvation, when the caloric content of the diet is too low, protein will be taken to create energy too. That is the ultimate leaching process at work. It is what happens when the incorrect fad fasting is undertaken for weight loss.

An underabundance of protein will affect an infant. Infants grow rapidly and therefore require relatively more protein than in slower growth phases. If an infant is deprived of high quality protein, it will be permanently impaired. The brain may be affected, causing less intelligence, less adaptiveness and other developmental troubles. The baby may grow small in stature and body weight, a natural defense mechanism instituted by the survival instinct to spare protein for the brain to develop properly. The law of evolution dictates that the brain must be preserved at the expense of height, breadth, muscular strength and other body developments.

Adults need protein for repair and metabolic reactions. If high-quality protein is missing, the adult body will suffer from a lack of building blocks. For example, if a bricklayer requires three different types of brick, he will not be inconvenienced if he has too much of each kind. However, one kind of brick being missing may stop his work. In the same way, the cells of the body are not harmed by an excess of quality amino acid molecules floating in the cell fluid. The cell can take in what it requires of each amino acid and leave what it does not need. Lack of quality protein is serious, a state that the functioning body will not long endure without showing deficiency symptoms.

The only time a very great excess of amino acid could be harmful to the cell would be from the presence of a large number of molecules that might displace other essential molecules. The cell could be inconvenienced in the same way a person may be inconvenienced by the jostling of friends. A cell surrounded by a fluid medium containing inadequate quantities of amino acids would be much more seriously affected. Then it would have to shut down many reactions. It could not construct protein and might surrender its own limited supply of amino acids to other tissues in the body.

Your palate is an effective mechanism for determining your optimum needs. The appetite-regulating mechanism in the brain (called the *appestat* by the late Norman Jolliffe, M.D., Director of the New York City Department of Health's Bureau of Nutrition from 1949 to 1961) and the taste buds combine to tell your palate what you need and want, provided it is not perverted by a nutrient alteration or deficiency in food. High-protein foods are generally more palatable, and most people will consume enough if they are available. Yet, you can fool your palate with corrupters—sugar and salt—and most people use them to excess.

FATS AND FATTY ACIDS

The arctic explorer Stefansson lived for several years on the typical Eskimo diet and remained well. Stefansson found that the amount of meat he ate was unimportant as long as he ate enough fat, in the form of blubber, with it. On several occasions during a famine when game or fish was scarce or quite lean, he became weak and ill. But within a few days of eating blubber, Stefansson was well again. This illustrates the importance of fat in the Eskimo diet for maintenance in the cold North environment. In fact, Eskimos remain healthy as long as they follow their own diet uncontaminated by processed foods furnished by "civilization."

Fats, or lipids, are foodstuffs that contain no nitrogen. The length of their molecular chains determines whether they will be solid or liquid at room temperature. The degree of chain saturation with molecules also determines this. Short chain molecules form liquid fats, as do highly unsaturated long chain molecules. The hardest fats are long-chain, fully saturated ones. Fat molecules may contain less hydrogen and have double bonds. When hydrogen is added, these double bonds are destroyed and the fat becomes a saturated fatty acid. It holds more hydrogen but is not capable of absorbing any more hydrogen than it has up to that point. Liquid fats are thus made more solid by the addition of hydrogen. This can alter the fat's melting point and is called *hydrogenation*.

Fatty acids combine with a three-carbon molecule to form *tri-glycerides*. A fatty acid may have a right or left twist at one or more of its double bonds. Our body enzymes are so specific that an enzyme can react with a molecule that has a lefthanded twist and not react with one having a righthanded twist. The biological value of a fatty acid is determined by the length of its chain, the number of double bonds and the type of twist at these double bonds.

Certain long-chain fatty acids such as arachidonic acid are said to be *essential fatty acids*. They can't be made in the body. Other fatty acids, especially the short-chain ones, can be made easily in the body from carbohydrates or proteins. Some fatty substances, such as lecithins, are present along with the particular fats in which the nervous tissue is rich.

Fats build structures in the sheaths of nerves; they participate in most body reactions; they store energy. Each fat gram contains nine calories of energy compared to four calories for protein and four for carbohydrate. When calorie consumption exceeds calories used, the extra ones are stored in fat storage sites. An obese person demonstrates where those storage sites usually are located on the human frame.

When intake is less than utilization, the storage fat is slowly drawn upon by the rest of the body. This is a marvelous device for providing ourselves with a constant source of energy. Our primitive ancestors ate at infrequent intervals and probably fasted involuntarily for many days. If carbohydrate rather than fat were the means for storing our energy (as it is for plants such as the potato) our storage sites would be nine-fourths, or 225 percent, as bulky as they are now. We would be at least as wide as we are tall, and obesity would be a more severe problem than it is already. Obesity nowadays is more often caused by overconsumption of processed carbohydrates than by too much intake of protein and fat.

ESSENTIAL FATTY ACIDS

A very important nutrient—essential fatty acids (EFAs)—began to disappear from our diet about 75 years ago. Only 20 percent of our needs are available in the average diet today. Drs. D. Rudin and C. Felix call it the *nutritional missing link*. They have presented convincing evidence that this is one of the main factors producing many of the illnesses we have to contend with today.

There are two types of EFAs: omega-3 and omega-6. Both series are converted to various prostaglandins and must be in balance. *Fats and Oils* by Udo Erasmus is one of the best simple books that describe the chemistry and biochemistry of EFAs.

Omega-3 fatty acids are highly reactive. They are needed for growth, prevention of drying and flaking skin, integrity of cell membranes and many metabolic roles. These fatty acids are found in seafood and in cold climate plants. When compared with the omega-6 series, omega-3s are chemically more reactive, have lower melting points—they're more liquid at room temperature—and are more resistant to freezing (because they come from plants).

Omega-6 EFAs play an equally important role in maintaining health. The most important intermediate clinically is gamma linolenic acid (GLA). It is made in the body by adding one double (unsaturated) bond to linoleic acid. It is found mainly in plant seeds, notably in evening primrose, borage and black currant. One of the best sources of omega-6 fatty acids is linseed oil made from flax seed. Once very popular and widely consumed, linseed oil is now mostly available in health food stores. It is also very rich in omega-3 oils—up to 60 percent. Common vegetable oils have a lot of the omega-6 fatty acids but are deficient in the omega-3 type.

EFAs are converted into prostaglandins which help regulate the entire body. That conversion requires a large number of cofactors such as vitamins and minerals. Rudin and Felix list about 25 important reactions in the body that depend upon having the right amount and kind of prostaglandins. When there is a deficiency of EFAs, digestion is compromised and healing is retarded. For instance, the authors suggest that pellagra is due to the deficiency of prostaglandins and that this may occur for two reasons: there is a deficiency of (1) cofactors such as vitamin B3 (the best-known cause of pellagra) and (2) EFAs, so that even in the presence of these cofactors not enough prostaglandins can be made. They call the first type of pellagra *cofactor pellagra* (vitamins B3, B6 and tryptophan) and the second type *substrate pellagra*. The two pellagras are responsible for many chronic illnesses, both physical and mental, such as the schizophrenias.

Dr. David F. Horrobin has outlined the role of gamma linolenic acid in the biochemistry of the body and its clinical uses. He has been one of the foremost investigators who have brought EFAs to medical attention. As with all EFAs, GLA has two main functions: (1) to provide flexibility to cell membranes and control behavior of membrane-bound proteins and (2) to control a large number of rapid reactions in the body. Though there is no deficiency of linoleic acid in the diet, there may be a problem in the body making enough GLA. GLA may be needed clinically because:

1. Not enough is made or there is not enough substrate from which to make it.
2. There may be too rapid consumption of the imtermediates, for example, when there is a deficiency of antioxidants, excessive inflammation or rapid cell growth.
3. A particular body needs increased amounts of very important prostaglandins.

Horrobin lists the following conditions which had been helped by GLA: alcoholism, atopic eczema, breast pain and prostatic hypertrophy, cancer, cardiovascular disease, diabetic neuropathy, endometriosis, gastrointestinal disorders, liver disease, post-viral fatigue syndrome, premenstrual syndrome, renal disease, rheumatoid arthritis and other forms of inflammation, schizophrenia, Sjogrens syndrome and dry eyes associated with contact lenses, systemic sclerosis and viral infection. It is clear the GLA is not a specific treatment for anything, but that it has an enormous importance in the general health of the body. It helps repair biochemical problems which have helped create these pathological diseases. Six important nutrients are needed for normal EFAs formation: ascorbic acid, biotin, calcium, magnesium, pyridoxine and zinc. Vitamin B3 is also needed for conversion of GLA to prostaglandins. Copper inhibits metabolism, as can vitamin A. Horrobin writes, "It is important to emphasize that EFA's are essential nutrients which are being consumed every day and which must be supplied every day. As in any nutritional deficiency state, such as scurvy of pellagra, the required nutrient must be supplied regularly if the disease is to be kept at bay. In almost all the situations in which GLA treatment is being considered, there is an underlying condition which is not eliminated by the GLA but which can be kept under control, just like scurvy with vitamin C, if the GLA is constantly supplied."

The simplest way of getting GLA is by taking evening primrose oil and other GLA-rich oils. The dose range varies from under 1 gram per day to 10 grams for very serious conditions. The following program is recommended by Rudin and Felix:

1. Select the best oil. (All oils should be tested before you use them.) Ideally this is linseed oil, which tends to become rancid and develop a very bad flavor unless stored cold. Other oils are soybean, walnut and wheat germ. A 100-pound person can start with 1 tablespoon of linseed oil daily and a 200-pound person with 3 to 4. It is important not to take more than is needed as the extra oil can cause some side effects.
2. Adjust the amounts. Using one's health as a measure, examine such things as skin texture and feeling of well being. The amount of supplementary oil should be the smallest amount to maintain good health.
3. Balance the two series by using both linseed oil and some of the other oils. One needs more of omega-3 during the winter and less during hot weather. Fish oils are very good and also evening primrose oil which contains omega-6 fatty acids. (Dr. Horrobin is one of the main scientists to discover important clinical uses for evening primrose oil.)
4. Take supplemental cofactors (the vitamins and minerals described in this book). Fiber is also very important.

Obtaining the correct oils is not that simple. Finnegan discusses some of the problems in the preparation of commercial oils and fats in *The Facts About Fats*. If we are to use these essential nutrients with skill and safety, it is important that we understand their chemistry, what they do and some of the conditions for which there is clear evidence of their usefulness. It is especially important to know how these oils are made because they are very unstable—they have double bonds which are avid for oxygen. This is why linseed oil is used for a paint base. For the same reason, once the oils have been extracted, they do not store well. During deterioration or oxidation, the oils change so they have no value or may even be harmful.

Manufacturers have tried to avoid some of these changes by using what is called a "cold" pressing process that supposedly avoids using heat which increases oxidation and deterioration. But even when the oil is cold pressed, a lot of heat is generated in the process unless the oil is pressed so slowly that the heat has a chance to dissipate. (High quality oils must be produced by pressing at temperatures under 118°F.) Often this means that cold pressed oils are little better than heat treated oils. Finnegan contends that many companies are using the wrong processing methods and, by calling them cold pressed, are fooling the public into thinking they are not heat treated. Concludes Finnegan, "They need to be produced by light and oxygen excluding methods, bottled in containers that prevent the further exposure to light causing rancidity, and where possible they should be produced from third party certified organically grown seed." Fortunately, a few manufacturers produce products that have deteriorated very little and are stored under nitrogen until the bottle is opened.

CAN WE TAKE IN TOO MUCH FAT?

It definitely is possible to eat too much fat, inasmuch as fat artifacts are so readily available in the form of butter, cream cheese, oil, margarine and other items. With sugar mixed into the fat in the form of ice cream and rich pastries, the danger of excessive fat intake becomes all too apparent. Then the sweet taste of sugar perverts your palate. You can experience a hypoglycemic rebound by its consumption. Fat mixed with sugar is one of the combinations of artifacts which cause cerebral reactions. Furthermore, excessive desire for sweets encourages excessive consumption of fat—a vicious cycle, and the obvious reason for some people to be ice-cream addicts.

A good example of fat and sugar artifacts in combination is the cruller or doughnut. It is made from fat, white flour, sucrose, and frequently is surrounded by a variety of confectionery sugars or glazings. Crullers represent the pinnacle of poor eating, the ultimate in processed food poisoning.

You would find it difficult to overconsume pure fat artifacts by themselves. Fat quickly satiates your appetite, and the sensation of having eaten—fullness—stays much longer. Fatty foods are bulkier and require more time to be eaten as well.

Too much fat ingestion finally causes obesity. In addition, for some people, overabundant fat intake increases cholesterol and triglyceride blood levels. This is much less apt to occur if there is an adequate ingestion of plant fiber and lecithin along with the fat.

Lecithin increases the capacity of the bile salts to remove cholesterol. Nicotinic acid speeds cholesterol oxidation to its degradation
products also. In general, it is quite difficult to overconsume foods
rich in fat unless you make a studious effort to do so.

The attitude of the public has changed over the last few years,
and fat consumption has gone down. There has been a significant
drift from saturated to unsaturated fat artifacts as well. This anti-
fat attitude has been motivated by the widely publicized information that fats, by elevating blood lipid and cholesterol, are
principal causative factors in heart disease, mainly coronary
thrombosis. Adequate scientific data does not support this fats-
and-heart-trouble relationship altogether, but since the notion
is widely accepted, an examination of the reality of the belief
is needed.

The assumption that the fat portion of our food is responsible
for elevated blood fats has been challenged, and is contradicted
by a large amount of experimental evidence. There are two basic
hypotheses behind the anti-fat publicity:

1. That fat in our food causes elevated blood fats.
2. That elevated blood fats cause coronary thrombosis.

DOES FOOD FAT CAUSE HEART DISEASE?

Food fat by itself does not bring on heart disease. Populations
around the world eat very high-fat diets and do not have abnormal
levels of heart disease. In addition, there has been a steady increase
in coronary thrombosis in North America even though over the
past 35 years dietary fat consumption has decreased by about one-
third. At the same time, the amount of polyunsaturated fats in the
diet has increased substantially, while total calories have decreased
from 3,570 to 3,180 per day.

There is no general relationship between fat in our food and an
elevation of blood fats. There is no general relationship between
cholesterol and fat content of the diet and heart disease. Many
people continually eat large quantities of fat with no increase in
heart disease. The Somalis and the Samburus are examples. These
people are sheep and goat herders and eat mostly milk, blood and

meat. Their diet is about two-thirds saturated animal fat. According to the cholesterol hypothesis, they should have high incidence of heart disease; but they do not.

A variety of nutrient deficiencies can interfere with fat metabolism. An elevation of blood fat levels may result from any one or any combination of deficiencies. For instance, faulty fat metabolism resulting in an elevation of blood lipids can be caused by a deficiency of ascorbic acid, pyridoxine, lecithin and perhaps of other factors whose role is still uncertain. Doses of nicotinic acid greater than one gram taken three times a day lower cholesterol and triglyceride levels; a deficiency would increase them. Blood fats are also elevated by a deficiency of fiber. A diet rich in sucrose must eventually cause a deficiency of most nutrients and is associated with a deficiency of fiber.

Any person seeking advice on how to reorder his or her life to decrease the possibility of heart disease would be told to exercise, stop smoking, relax more and reduce fat intake. Accordingly, exercising restores muscle tone, uses up calories and improves your sense of well being. Smoking certainly is an abomination that causes a wide variety of diseases both physical and mental. The smoke not only affects the smoking addict but also anyone nearby forced to inhale the toxic organic chemicals and minerals. As for relaxing—well, everyone needs to relax at appropriate times to take stress from the heart and mind. Fat intake should be moderate because excessive fat consumption will lead to obesity, especially when combined fat is added to excessive sugar consumption. By itself though, fat consumption will *not* elevate blood cholesterol and triglyceride levels and is *not* a direct cause of heart disease.

Because of their isolation and history, the entire population of St. Helena, the island in the South Atlantic Ocean, 1200 miles west of Africa, already follows the four anti-heart-disease precepts. Their landscape is hilly and, as cars are not permitted on the island, the people get a lot of exercise. By tradition very few smoke. They lead relaxed lives for the most part. The population normally consumes a diet not excessive in fat. Yet they suffer from the same pandemic of heart disease as do other Western countries. Why? It may be that the St. Helena populace illustrates the destructive quality of sugar. Since 1900 their consumption of sugar has increased to the English level of about 120 pounds per year. Thus, in spite of practicing the four recommended ways of preventing coronary disease, this island group of people by overconsuming sugar has the modern high level of heart disease.

PREVENTIVE NUTRITION AGAINST HEART DISEASE

The *ideal diet* for preventing heart disease will be totally junk-free. It will contain optimum quantities of all the nutrients but will be particularly rich in niacin (vitamin B-3), pyridoxine (vitamin B-6), ascorbic acid (vitamin C) and vitamin E. It will contain optimum quantities of chromium, zinc and selenium and be rich enough in vegetable fiber to prevent any manifestation of the saccharine disease. Combined with this optimum diet will be a program of exercise, freedom from smoking and a stress balance struck between tension and relaxation. The optimum diet will induce relaxation since the individual is following a healthy lifestyle.

When his preventive nutrition program against heart disease is followed, normal cholesterol will be available from food. The body will need to make less cholesterol on its own behalf. Extra energy for such body synthesizing will be applied for other reactions. Ordinarily, the optimum cholesterol amount provided from food is equal to the quantity normally produced in your body. If you deprive yourself of eggs merely to lower cholesterol, your liver will simply make more cholesterol for body metabolism. Eggs also contain lecithin, which assists in balancing cholesterol intake. I suspect that disease syndromes due to inadequate cholesterol ingestion will soon be described in the literature as a consequence of the increased demand on the body to make more of its own. The low cholesterol artifacts have not been tested for long-term toxicity.

To assure optimum preventive nutrition against heart disease you will have to arrive at the appropriate diet on your own by trial and error. Depend on your taste and avoid highly refined adulterated foods that have industrial sugars added. Keep your weight at its ideal poundage for your body type by adhering to a trustworthy height, weight and body-build chart.

PROBLEMS ASSOCIATED WITH LOW-FAT DIETS

Few people voluntarily or spontaneously follow low-fat diets. However, as a large number are trying to reduce weight or avoid coronary occlusion, their diets may, as a result, contain a high proportion of unsaturated fats. There are several problems associated with such an unsaturated fat diet.

Low-fat diets are unpalatable for most people. There must be a certain enjoyment in eating which is hard to achieve with near-total avoidance of fats. Also, consuming little fat will leave a person feeling unsatiated, and the satisfaction of eating will last for a much shorter time. Some low-fat eaters remain hungry all day long, and this situation can generate a continuous low-grade irritability. Even worse, these people will often greatly increase their consumption of carbohydrates of the refined variety to get enough calories to maintain normal weight. The lack of a feeling of satiety plus the increased irritability make it difficult to remain on the low-fat or unsaturated fat diet. Within the framework of modern clinical nutrition, a low-fat diet is theoretically unsound and generally ineffective.

Furthermore, the increased difficulty in absorbing fat-soluble vitamins becomes apparent with a low-fat diet. Fat-soluble vitamins are ordinarily provided by fatty foods. Also the body has a minimum requirement for cholesterol. It uses the substance to build body structure, for certain reactions and as a material from which it makes hormones and the precursor of vitamin D-3. The diet low in fat that does not provide such cholesterol intake increases the body's need to manufacture the substance itself, with consequent risk of symptoms due to its deficiency.

THE CHEMISTRY OF CARBOHYDRATES

There is a common belief that all carbohydrates are the same. Also it is thought that all sugars are the same, since carbohydrates eventually break down into simple sugars such as glucose and fructose. What is overlooked in these incorrect assumptions is the importance of food bulk, the presence of other essential nutrients, the rate of sugar release in the digestive tract, and the absorption rate into the blood. Artifacts such as refined table sugar (sucrose) are not absorbed and metabolized as are the complex carbohydrates.

Carbohydrates consist of complex long-chain carbohydrates and short-chain carbohydrates. The latter are sugars. Each carbohydrate has a large number of molecules with five or six carbon atoms attached in the chain. Glucose, fructose and galactose are monosaccharides, a sugar of individual molecules which are attached to each other in a chemical bond. Glucose, the sugar usually given in 100-gram amounts before the common sugar tolerance test is done, is the main sugar in the blood and body tissues. It is an essential body sugar but is not essential as a pure substance in our food. All the cells, the brain cells more than the rest, depend upon glucose. The body makes it by splitting complex sugars and carbohydrates into their basic units, mostly sugar.

Conversion of carbohydrates into basic sugar units begins in the mouth when saliva is chewed into our food. Saliva contains enzymes which split (hydrolyze) carbohydrates into simpler sugars. Conversion continues in the stomach until the process is inhibited by the acidity of the stomach contents. It begins again in the small intestine, especially after the pancreatic juices are mixed with it.

Glucose is the energy sugar. The food industry advertises a false impression that sucrose, common table sugar made from beets or sugar cane, is a good source of energy. Such advertising is completely misleading. The truth is that a number of physical diseases, depressions, anxiety states, alcoholism and other addictions are the end product of quantity ingestion of sucrose. Table sugar and other refined carbohydrates bring on the saccharine diseases.

Paradoxically, glucose, needed by the body, but provided in pure form, could be dangerous also. Only slow release of glucose from food in conjunction with the release of other nutrients is safe; but pure glucose, an artifact devoid of other nutrients, is nearly as harmful as sucrose. Some violent reactions may be experienced among patients taking pure sugar for a glucose tolerance test. Symptoms are severe such as nausea, vomiting, headache and other unpleasant reactions.

Present in fruit is another monosaccharide, fructose. Fructose is somewhat less toxic than glucose or sucrose. It tastes sweeter weight for weight and less will be used for the same sweetness satiation. It does not stimulate the pancreas to release insulin. However, consumed in large quantities, fructose can be as bad as the other pure sugars because of the lack of a normal quota of nutrients. Fructose, like glucose, is a useful source of energy when released in the body from food such as fresh fruit. No physiological need exists for free fructose from any external sources.

Present chiefly as one of the components of milk sugar (lactose), galactose is less sweet than the others. It is also a monosaccharide.

Sugars which have two monosaccharides linked to each other are called disaccharides. Two common disaccharides are comprised of sucrose made with glucose and fructose, and lactose made with glucose and galactose. These are all hooked together. They are more complex sugars and must be split into monosaccharides before they are absorbed into the blood. Not splitting, they remain in the bowels as calories for bacteria to grow on. The body has enzymes to hydrolyze these double sugars.

To find out how much sucrose, the most common sugar, is consumed by any nation's individual citizen, merely divide the country's total sugar tonnage consumed by its total population. Tonnage will include sugar used in confectionery, soft drinks, breakfast foods, bakery products, canned soups and crystalline form. On the average, every man, woman and child in the English-speaking countries of the West consumes 125 pounds per person per year; of course, some consume much more and some much less.

Consumed sucrose is rapidly hydrolyzed, absorbed, shunted into the liver and converted into triglycerides. Triglycerides are then released into the blood and stored as fat deposits. When released into the blood too quickly without other nutrients present, sucrose is a highly toxic substance. Therefore, while sucrose in natural food is not toxic, the commercial or household form is.

Pure sucrose should be barred from human use and converted into alcohol as fuel for automobiles. Feed the leftover protein of sugar beets and sugar cane to livestock for its vitamin and mineral content. Sucrose is not fit for human consumption, since it creates ill health by its poisonous infiltration into the heart and mind of its user. At the very least the Surgeon General should print on sugar packages: "Use of this product may be hazardous to your health."

Beekeepers even contaminate honey with sucrose. In the spring, when insufficient pollen remains for foraging bees, they are fed sucrose syrup. This sugar poison is then deposited in the honey. Someone allergic to beet or cane sugar would be just as reactive to this contaminated honey as to sugar in the pure state. For this reason, late summer and fall honey is preferable, since less sucrose is fed to bees during those times of the year. Even with some contamination, honey is a worthwhile replacement for sugar because its fructose content is sweeter and less is needed. Used in the same quantity as sucrose, honey would be just as toxic.

Polysaccharides are complex saccharides in very long chains of glucose molecules. Among them are shorter-chained carbohydrates such as glycogen and long-chained fibrous foods such as bran. They taste bland, are not easily dissolved in water and have structural properties not found in simple sugars. They are much less toxic. Because of bulk, polysaccharides are eaten more slowly, hydrolyze slowly in the digestive system and enter slowly into the blood as glucose.

Natural, unrefined or unprocessed carbohydrates are surrounded and mixed with protein, fat, vitamins and minerals. Naturally occurring carbohydrates are good foods, contrary to processed carbohydrates such as starch. Starch is toxic but not quite as bad as the mono- and disaccharides. The degree of toxicity for a carbohydrate depends upon the degree of refinement. For example, whole wheat is non-toxic unless you are allergic to it. But during processing the wheat is cracked, ground and the central portion, the endosperm, gets sifted out. The outer coats of bran and germ and the coats next to them are taken away for other uses. When the whole kernel is used the flour is called a "100 percent extraction flour." If the middle or inner endosperm is used, it is called a "60 or 70 percent extraction." Thus the higher percentage extraction, the more germ and bran is present and the more nutritious the wheat flour. It is logical that if the wheat kernel's main function is to grow a new plant, the essential nutrients will be as close to the germ as possible.

DANGERS OF CONSUMING TOO MUCH CARBOHYDRATE

Excessive consumption of *unprocessed* foods almost exclusively carbohydrate in content such as rice, wheat and potatoes will cause obesity and produce a metabolic imbalance. Intake of too much carbohydrate will be associated with an inadequate ingestion of protein and fat. Dangers of excess intake are similar to dangers with taking too much of any food that is deficient in various essential nutrients. But unprocessed carbohydrates aren't likely to cause too much trouble, simply because of their bulk. It is difficult to over-consume too much of an unrefined carbohydrate at one time.

Processed carbohydrates present an altogether different situation.

These include all the food products rich in added sugar or prepared in a way that has dissipated a large proportion of other essential nutrients. Processed carbohydrates consist of such foods as polished rice, white flour and a variety of substances made from them. They can almost be branded as legalized poisons. The best use white flour can be put to is as paste for hanging wallpaper.

Excessive consumption of refined or processed carbohydrates is the major cause of a broad group of neuroses and a great number of physical illnesses. Until recently, these mental and physical sicknesses were looked upon as unrelated diseases with no known cause, but we know today that they arise from malnutrition. Amazing as it may seem to the person who has never had education in nutrition, eating an excess of processed carbohydrates is tantamount to condemning oneself to malnutrition.

The human body has not evolved over the centuries on a diet consisting of any of the simple sugars. Sucrose was not a staple in our diet until the last one hundred years. Our metabolism is ill-prepared to accept sucrose, and consuming it has severely undesirable effects. It is an empty food that supplies naked calories. It displaces true foods rich in essentials so that we create an artificial build-up in demand by the body for increases in ingestion of vitamins and minerals. Sucrose and other refined carbohydrates are a major cause of diabetes mellitus and hypoglycemia. The conclusion of Cheraskin and Ringsdorf is that "the ideal daily refined carbohydrate intake may actually be zero."

Refined sugar is particularly insidious since it produces addiction as severe as any drug addiction. The only difference between heroin addiction and sugar addiction is that sugar doesn't need injection, is readily consumable because of its availability and isn't considered a social evil. However, the strength of sugar addiction is just as strong as heroin addiction. One of my patients, a seven-year-old boy, exemplifies sugar addiction. He would sneak into the kitchen at three A.M. to steal handfuls of white crystalline sugar. Many adolescents grab for sweets even though they notice their behavior is normal when they avoid sugar and pathological when they consume it. Another of my patients drank three forty-ounce bottles of sweetened soft drink daily just to keep herself going. Otherwise, acute onset of hypoglycemia would drop her into depression and despair if even thirty minutes passed without a drink of sugar water.

Sugar addiction provides typical addiction withdrawal symptoms as severe as those accompanying withdrawal from drugs. During the withdrawal any food could activate symptoms. Too quick a withdrawal will see the patient develop severe depression or anxiety. I treated sugar addiction withdrawal with electroconvulsive therapy (ECT) years ago. Now my treatment includes assessment of the degree of addiction and if it is great, I taper off the patient from sugar slowly.

Sir Frederick Banting, who discovered insulin, noted while traveling through Panama that cane cutters consumed large amounts of carbohydrate by chewing sugar cane but contracted few cases of diabetes. Conversely, their Spanish employers, eating as much pure sucrose as their workers ate cane, had a very high rate of diabetes. The native workers got their sugar slowly and with vitamins and minerals included. The pure sugar that their employers ate was stripped of all its nutrients, and they consumed only naked calories. Also the cane cutters did not eat large quantities of other refined carbohydrates as did the employers.

Campbell has concluded that eating refined sugar is addictive, but eating the native sugar cane is not. He developed three sucrose rules which explain the relationship of sugar to humans. (1) The *rule of twenty years* says that an individual can resist the ravages of sugar consumption for twenty years, then diabetes appears. (2) The *rule of 70 pounds* suggests that a nation may consume 70 pounds of sugar per person per year before showing major physiological breakdown among its population. (3) The *rule of 20 percent* points out that in any population the whole caloric intake is less than 2400 calories, except where diabetes is common. The sucrose intake *with* the presence of diabetes will be more than 20 percent of the total calories. A nation's population that consumes less than 35 pounds of total sugar per person per year would be a lot healthier than one consuming notably more.

Yudkin states that sucrose consumption is one of the leading causes of atherosclerosis and coronary heart disease. It also markedly increases dental caries and periodontal disease, relates to dyspepsia and causes seborrheic dermatitis. Surprisingly, no experiments have been carried out to give laboratory animals huge quantities of sucrose to test its carcinogenic potential as was done with sucaryl and saccharin. Again let us reiterate that we agree with Yudkin that sugar should be banned from the market. This may take enforcement of the Delaney Act. The Delaney Clause against cancer-causing foods is a part of the basic FDA statute passed in 1958.

9

ORTHOMOLECULAR NUTRITION—PART III
Vitamin Supplementation

THE BATTLE FOR VITAMINS

When Casimir Funk coined the word *vitamine* he paved the way for the new science of vitamins in nutrition. But many battles remained to be waged for acceptance of vitamins as legitimate and necessary additions to the modern diet—and they still are going on. The most classical was Goldberger's war to establish that pellagra was a disease of malnutrition, caused by a deficiency of the amino acid tryptophan and vitamin B3 (nicotinic acid).

Dr. Goldberger's discovery was announced in Washington, D.C., on November 11, 1915: "What is believed to be a dietary cure for pellagra has been found in the results of experiments by the Public Health Service—the cause of the disease as well as the remedy, it was officially announced at the Treasury Department today. Assistant Secretary Newton, who has charge of the Public Health Service, spoke of the discovery as one of the greatest achievements of modern science in recent years. . . . It was established that persons whose diets lacked a normal proportion of protein seemed particularly subject to the disease while those whose food contained enough protein seldom were afflicted."

However, one year later, November 19, 1916, *The New York Times* carried a summary of a report from Drs. Thompson and McFadden, who had investigated pellagra carefully. They concluded there was no connection between nutrition and pellagra, which was, they said, an infectious disease caused by the sting of the stable fly. This monstrous conclusion was finally disputed after Goldberger injected himself with preparations of excrement from pellagrins, mucous from their nasal passages and scaly drippings from their skin and did not develop pellagra.

The interest and excitement over vitamins was tremendous between 1925 and 1940. One after another was isolated, named and identified. There was a race to be first to identify each new vitamin, with perhaps a Nobel Prize for the winner. This vitamin deficiency era reached its peak in 1942 when pellagra was nearly wiped out by the enrichment of flour with vitamin B3 in its nicotinamide form.

Interest in vitamins and nutrition faded from medical schools after that. They became the exclusive province of nutritionists and dietitians, and nearly every physician assumed there were no more avitaminoses to be treated. Popular writers and lay journalists took over the field of nutrition. The era of myths set in, such as the "one vitamin-one disease" concept. The false concept said that lack of a vitamin accounts for a specific disease, and that if the disease isn't present, there is no deficiency and hence no need for extra vitamins. This myth still prevails among some orthodox physicians. Ignored entirely is the fact that the deficiency diseases such as beriberi, pellagra and scurvy are the end result of months or years of severe deficiency and represent the premorbid condition. The false concept ignores entirely the many symptoms suffered during the developmental phase and concentrates on signs of deficiency that strike just before the patient is going to die.

Another silly myth is that the minimal daily requirement (MDR) applies to every individual. The MDR ignores a fact, too—that people are remarkably dissimilar biochemically, physically and psychologically. They don't look alike, nor do they have the same fingerprints; and they *do* have different requirements for various nutrients. Even if 90 percent of any population required only the MDR of vitamins, it would leave huge numbers of people needing 10, 100 or 1000 times as much. The minimal daily requirement, if it has any value at all, might do little more for many than prevent the classical deficiency diseases from appearing.

THEORETICAL BASIS FOR MEGAVITAMINS

About forty-five nutrients are required in optimum quantities. If you tried to take each nutrient in pure form and prepare a diet for each of them, it would be impossible to do. The complexity of the problem would tax the best computer. We are still fairly ignorant of the scientific bases of clinical nutrition. A few synthetic diets are available, true, but no one could trust himself to live on such a diet for any substantial time; some deficiency would surely show itself.

Fortunately, we do not need to plan our diets this way. We have adapted to the environment over millions of years to live on foods derived from plants and animals whose composition is not too different from our own bodies. Such food can readily be broken down into essential nutrients. Nature already has made the computations needed. All we have to do is revert to the whole unprocessed food consumption that we have already adapted to through evolution. Eliminate junk! Give preference to high-quality foods having diverse quantities of fat, protein, carbohydrate and fiber.

Of course, most of us in Western civilization do not consume an unprocessed diet; many *do* eat junk. Not only is it difficult to persuade people to eat what is good for them, but the medical profession plays a damaging role in delaying the applications of vitamin therapy developed by its colleagues. The medical use of vitamins has had to change slowly from prevention and treatment of deficiencies to a newer use of much larger quantities to treat conditions which are not clearly related to vitamin deficiencies. Certain foods can prevent and cure major diseases. This has been known for hundreds of years, but this knowledge has been narrow in distribution and seldom is applied on any substantial scale.

Any person runs the risk of getting either too much or too little of any essential nutrient. Generally too little of any nutrient is much worse, since it cannot be synthesized in the body. If too much is present, the cells extract what they require and leave the rest in the blood from which it is readily removed for future use by cells or as waste for elimination. Huge quantities of vitamins taken in could be dangerous only in the same way that drinking too much water is dangerous. You get rid of what you don't need. For that reason, many physicians dissuade people from using vitamins by pointing to the economic loss of enriching the sewage with them. This argument has no place in science. Don't confuse clinical utility with economics.

The practice of orthomolecular nutrition recognizes that each person requires optimum quantities of each nutrient. How can you determine the individual quantities you need? So far, orthomolecular medicine is able to recommend only one way—trial and error— self-experimentation. We make this recommendation with the understanding that the majority of any population will benefit by the supplementation of one or more of the essential nutrients and that very few individuals are in complete tune with their daily nutrient requirements.

Dr. Roger Williams and his coworkers emphasize that vitamins work together as a team or orchestra. One plays in unison with the other. For example, pellagra is cured, not by vitamin B3 alone, but by vitamin B3 *plus* all the other vitamins we require. In pellagra, B3 is *relatively* the most deficient, that's all. There is no great drama involved. The same applies to scurvy and vitamin C. That is because organisms rarely live in an environment which is optimal for them. Suppose turtle eggs lived in an optimal medium. They soon would cover the whole surface of the earth because so many of them are fertilized and laid. Fortunately these optimal conditions will never exist for any species, as we mentioned in an earlier chapter, and life adapts to survive in suboptimal environments. Our own body cells will live with less than optimal nutrition and function at a lower level of efficiency. There is a wide variation of need for each nutrient. Levels adequate for one person will be inadequate for another. In planning nutritional treatment for any individual these relationships must be considered.

MEGADOSE VITAMINS

Because of the need to emphasize that doses recommended were much larger than what was prescribed by the medico-nutritional establishment, the term *megadose* has come into common use. It is not a good term, however, because *mega* meaning *great, large* and *powerful* frightens people and becomes a focus of attack. A better term for vitamins recommended in optimum doses would be *optidose*. Nobody is against optimum health that optimum-dose vitamins would stimulate. The shrill attack against using larger than average doses could be muffled this way. We will continue to refer to megadoses in this book and in orthomolecular medicine, but they should be thought of as optidoses.

Traditional psychiatrists already have accepted megalithium therapy. My colleagues in mainstream psychiatry are not disturbed whatever at using large quantities of lithium therapy, simply because no one has thought of calling it megalithium therapy. This is so even though the difference in the quantities used as compared to the daily intake in a normal diet, which is only 2 mg. per day, is just as striking for lithium as it is for the vitamins.

In time, every vitamin will probably be found to be useful in megadoses for certain conditions. The number of combinations of vitamins possibly suitable for administration in megadoses is vast. The individuality of the body's needs and responses makes it unlikely that one pill will ever be devised to do the whole job.

Along with prescription of the no-junk diet, megadosage of vitamins is one of the main components of orthomolecular medicine and orthomolecular psychiatry. Not all vitamins are given in megadoses. When the nutrition is optimum, it is necessary to supplement with only a few. It is impossible to say that one vitamin is more important than another; they work together. Returning to our metaphor of vitamins working in unison as in an orchestra, at times one set of instruments is featured while the rest of the orchestra stays in the background; the same occurs with vitamins.

An imbalance is present when a vitamin is lacking. This is much more common than an imbalance resulting from an excess of any vitamin, which is rare indeed. Water-soluble vitamins are readily excreted if more is present than is required. To ensure an optimum combination, the simplest way is to use slightly more than required for best results. With some vitamins, several grams per day may be required, while others need considerably less than one gram per day as supplementation. Danger of overdose imbalance is rare when the usual orthomolecular doses are used.

Most clinicians intuitively know of the enormous variation in their patients' response to medication. The study of pharmacology and therapeutics teaches this. One patient may develop diarrhea on 250 mg. of ascorbic acid per day while another can consume 40 grams per day with no difficulty. Individuality determines the need for individual care. One patient may not be able to take 25 mg. of a tranquilizer because of a reaction of excessive drowsiness, and others might remain unaffected by 1000 mg. of the same tranquilizer.

Even identical twins are not alike because of unequal division of the fertilized egg. It is inconceivable that each egg would receive an identical allotment of cytoplasm and cytoplasmic particles. A minor variation in any one of the thousands of enzymes present could produce a major variation in the biochemistry of the body.

It is therefore inconceivable also that every person would require the same daily intake of nutrients, or that any average minimal daily requirement would be suitable for everyone. If the figure were set too low, too many who abide by it would suffer from a deficiency; if too high, less harm would be done, but too many foods would be considered inadequate. It will forever be impossible to generalize the nutrient needs of everyone. Set your own optimum intake from the scientific guide we furnish here.

THE ORIGINS OF VITAMIN SUPPLEMENTATION

In the introduction of the *Annals* of the New York Academy of Sciences, Machlin divides the use of foods and more recently vitamins into five periods, some of which overlap:

1. From about 1500 B.C. to 1900: foods were empirically used to heal certain diseases.
2. Between 1880 and 1900: deficiency diseases were produced in animals and the vitamin hypothesis was developed.
3. From 1900 to 1980: vitamins were discovered, isolated, their structure determined and their synthesis established.
4. From about 1930 to the present and continuing into the future: biochemical functions were studied, dietary requirements were introduced and commercial production became prominent.
5. Beginning in 1955: health effects of vitamins have been recognized beyond prevention of deficiency disease and through the use of vitamins therapeutically.

The middle three periods represent the use of vitamins-in-prevention era and also make up the vitamin deficiency paradigm. It was built upon the following principles: (1) Vitamins are needed only to prevent vitamin deficiency diseases. (2) They are needed in small amounts. This made sense, since they were catalysts of reactions in the body, and catalysts are known to be needed only in small amounts as they are used over and over. (3) Any dose above these small preventive doses is undesirable, wasteful, bad medical practice and, to some, even criminal. These principles are still adhered to very vigorously by dietitians, nutritionists and physicians.

At the same time, some physicians have lost their medical licenses because of substantiated charges that they were using large doses of vitamins. Some hospitals still do not permit the use of intravenous ascorbic acid.

While the preventive vitamins paradigm was being established, information was accruing that the paradigm was incorrect, but that information was ignored or ruthlessly suppressed. In the middle 1930s just after it was recognized that niacin cured pellagra, the early pellagralogists found—I am certain to their great surprise—that the small doses of vitamin B3 which prevented pellagra and which cured early (acute) pellagra did not help patients who had chronic pellagra. They required 600 mg. per day, a huge quantity, compared with the tiny dose of less than 20 mg. needed to prevent pellagra. This proved that the optimum dose even to prevent pellagra from recurring ranged from 20 to 600 mg. daily. Chronic pellagra changed the body's chemistry (human and dogs) so that the small doses effective as a preventive were no longer adequate and much larger amounts were needed. The person with chronic pellagra had developed a dependency on vitamin B3. (A *deficiency* is present when the diet is so bad that even the small preventive doses are not provided. A *dependency* is present when the body's needs are so great that even the best diet cannot provide the right amount.)

The preventive vitamin paradigm has been very harmful to nutritional research. It inhibited investigations of the therapeutic use of vitamins for at least 30 years. It still has medical school departments of nutrition in its sway, and this is the information they pass on to their students. The preventive vitamin paradigm is correct only for the very few classical deficiency diseases and is totally incorrect for the rest of medicine.

Machlin credits our paper showing that niacin lowered people's cholesterol levels as starting the fifth period in 1955. He writes that though he chose that paper "somewhat arbitrarily," the "well accepted response of the vitamin . . . is a clear health effect beyond preventing the deficiency disease pellagra." He further describes the fifth period as the "recognition of health effects beyond prevention of deficiency diseases—new biochemical functions" when vitamins began to be used therapeutically. The second major boost to the concept of using vitamins therapeutically came with our paper showing that vitamin B3 was therapeutic for schizophrenics. But in sharp contrast to the general acceptance today of the role of vitamins in medicine, psychiatry still has not accepted it and remains where it was 45 years ago.

The latest therapeutic vitamin paradigm is based on the following observations:

1. We are all different and have different nutrient requirements.
2. Optimum amounts are needed, which range from smaller doses necessary to prevent deficiency disease to much larger doses to treat vitamin-dependent conditions like elevated cholesterol levels and too low levels of high-density lipoprotein cholesterol.
3. The following variables determine the optimum need: age, sex, physical stress including pregnancy, psychological stress, lactation, diseases (whether acute or chronic) and use of xenobiotic drugs. Thus there can never be any useful Optimal Daily Dose (ODD) schedule for everyone. There must be Optimal Recommended Doses (ORD) that are specific for each condition and for each disease. Thus for pregnancy there would be a pregnancy ORD, for early cancer a cancer ORD and so on.
4. Vitamins can be taken safely for a lifetime.

The therapeutic vitamin paradigm opens up the use of vitamins for optimum health to everyone. In sharp contrast with drugs which are very toxic and must be carefully controlled by trained professionals, vitamins are so safe they can be experimented with by any person, secure in the knowledge that they are as safe as any of the over-the-counter medications readily available today. People can become their own therapists. Experimentation will not do them any harm, provided they take a little time to examine the vitamin literature, including books such as this one. With drugs, too little is much safer than too much, but with vitamins a little more is much safer than too little if one wishes to obtain optimum health. If one takes more than is needed, there is no harm because the extra amount is not stored and is readily eliminated. There are a very few exceptions. Thus one can try to find the optimum by taking increasing doses until that is reached. And if that dose is exceeded, the body can readily deal with it. If too little is taken, the desired therapeutic effect will not be obtained. However, the difference between optimum and less effective doses can be narrow. I have seen schizophrenic patients who did not respond to 3 grams per day of niacin, but when this was doubled, they began to improve very quickly. The same principle does not apply to minerals and may not apply to amino acids, even though they also have a wide tolerance range.

The year 1992 was a watershed year and marks the great turn-around in medical interest in the use of vitamins for therapy. Now doses much larger than what had been accustomed to were being prescribed. It was inevitable but rewarding to see it finally come about. [In the mid-1980s *The New York Times* commissioned a freelance reporter to attend a meeting of the Huxley Institute of Biosocial Research (HIBR) in New York where A.H. was then president. Though A.H. initially refused to speak with him, the writer assured A.H. that he had never had an article rejected by the *Times*. With that assurance A.H. spent about 6 hours outlining HIBR's work and answering all his questions. The report never appeared.] The lay press, which had for years been toeing the medical profession's party line about nutrients and the RDAs, suddenly began to publish reports about the remarkable new therapeutic properties of vitamins. Since they feel free, at last, to publish this information, it is clear they are no longer afraid of the medical profession and that the profession has become interested enough not to object as vigorously as they might have earlier.

One of the first articles appeared in the March 10, 1992, *New York Times* headlined "Vitamins Win Support as Potent Agents of Health" by Natalie Angier. Though the *Times* had not been as enthusiastic at anytime in the near past, the article was still ambivalent. Here are a few of their subsequent reports:

—May 8, 1992, "Vitamin C Linked to Heart Benefit" by Jane E. Brody, who wrote: "It may also help prevent an early death from other diseases."

—Jan. 19, 1993, "U.S. Opens the Door Just a Crack to Alternative Forms of Medicine" by Natalie Angier.

—May 20, 1993, "Vitamin E Greatly Reduces Risk of Heart Diseases, Studies Suggest. Best Results Found in Those Taking Large Doses" by Jane E. Brody.

Time magazine was next with a cover story on April 6, 1992, "The Real Power of Vitamins," subtitled "New Research Shows They May Help Fight Cancer, Heart Disease and the Ravages of Aging." The Food and Drug Administration (FDA) as usual was not to be taken in by these claims (it has been cracking down on nutrient health claims for years). Dr. Walter Willett of the Harvard School of Health said, "At this time I say don't take megadoses, but I'm not ruling out that in two or three years we might change our mind." This was a great concession from the institution which 30 years earlier had killed interest in vitamin E by attacking the Shute brothers' claims that vitamin E was very therapeutic for heart disease—something everyone now recognizes. The *Time* report concluded: "But stay tuned. Vitamins promise to continue to unfold as one of the great and hopeful health stories of our day."

The Medical Post reported April 23, 1992, that vitamin C may lower heart disease risk. *Newsweek* finally joined ranks on May 8, 1992, with their story "Live Longer with Vitamin C" and again on June 7, 1993, with "Vitamin Revolution: The Good News: Nutrients from Food or Supplements May Help Us Prevent Heart Disease, Cancer and Other Chronic Ailments." There was even a good report in *The Readers Digest,* based on the *Time* report. (These stories are vaguely reminiscent of the kind of reports which appeared in the old *Prevention* magazine, *New Age Journal* and other health food-oriented magazines.) *The Harvard Health Letter, Johns Hopkins Medical Letter* and the *Diet-Heart Newsletter* have reported similar stories. Finally, the National Institutes of Health has created a new Office of Alternative Medicine to explore various alternative practices. I hope the study of vitamins is included in their mandate, unless they now consider megavitamin therapy to be mainstream medicine— which is where it ought to be.

The medical profession was alerted in 1993 by *The New England Journal of Medicine* that more Americans in 1990 consulted alternative practitioners than all U.S. primary care physicians—425 million visits compared with 388 million. The social demographic group which consulted these alternative practitioners for chronic conditions were nonblack, ages 25 to 49, who had relatively more education and higher incomes. Twelve percent of this group (51 million visits) sought megavitamin therapy. The authors advised the profession to ascertain their patients' use of alternative therapies. (I do not think this will be much help since most patients who have consulted me are not willing to discuss it with their practitioners because of the negative reactions they have had in the past.) The article concluded: "Medical schools should include information about unconventional therapies and the clinical social sciences (anthropology and sociology) in their curriculums. The newly established National Institutes of Health Office for the Study of Unconventional Medical Practices should help promote scholarly research and education in this area."

It would also help if *The New England Journal of Medicine* would relax its censorship of reports dealing with megavitamin therapy. Several years ago they absolutely refused to publish a rebuttal by Linus Pauling of an article on cancer and vitamin C that was faulty, badly done and little deserving of the publicity it generated. Nevertheless, vitamin therapy (megavitamins) is well on the way to sweeping the field.

VITAMIN A

Vitamin A is known as the anti-infective or anti-ophthalmic vitamin. It helps to maintain normal growth and bone development, protective sheathing around nerve fibers and healthy skin, hair and nails. It is quite important for retention of normal vision, since it is used up in the process of seeing. The reason vitamin A is called anti-infective is that it maintains healthy mucous in the respiratory system and thus fights off infection and allergic symptoms.

For many years Reich has treated patients with asthma with a combination of vitamin A, vitamin D3 and bone meal to supply calcium. Reich's doses of A range from 28,000 to 75,000 I.U. per day, while doses of D range from 5000 to 14,000 I.U. daily. On a very large series of 5000 cases, Reich's results have been favorable. Similarly, my use of these megadoses for asthma and other allergies has netted good results. This is a simple and safe therapy that, as with megadoses of other vitamins, has met strange resistance on the part of medical traditionalists.

THIAMINE—VITAMIN B1

Thiamine is the anti-polyneuritis or anti-beriberi vitamin. Water soluble, it is used as an adjunct in the treatment of certain depressions and is specific for Wernicke-Korsakoff disease. The megadose (optidose) level ranges up to 3000 mg. per day, but this is rare. The usual megadose range for an average person is from 100 to 3000 mg., most often nearer the lower level.

Thiamine is useful against alcoholism. Cade reported that alcoholics admitted to his hospital are routinely given intravenous multivitamins containing at least 200 mg. thiamine. They may require this twice a day. In spite of a great increase in the number of alcoholic admissions to the hospital, there has been steady improvement until the death rate has fallen to zero. In 1945-50, before thiamine treatment was used, eighty-six patients died of alcoholism complications. In 1956-60, eight people died, but no deaths have occurred from 1966 to now. Cade concluded "that because the mode of death was identical with that in beriberi, because thiamine deficiency has been demonstrated in a significant proportion of sick alcoholics, because deaths no longer occur when they are given thiamine, and because there have been no other discernible significant changes in treatment which are likely to have been responsible, thiamine is the therapeutic agent which is literally lifesaving in a significant proportion of patients." Thus thiamine—vitamin B1—has been clearly shown to have saved lives among alcoholics.

Thiamine is also the main component of a multivitamin program for treating multiple sclerosis (MS) and myasthenia gravis. Dr. F. R. Klenner has been using about 2 grams of vitamin B1 a day orally in divided doses with additional parenteral administration (by injection) as needed. The clinician reported progress for one parenteral patient in a series of cases. Dale Humphreys, a forty-eight-year-old music teacher, had his first MS attack January 1973 following influenza. He improved partially with use of ACTH (a protein hormone of the anterior lobe of the pituitary gland that stimulates the adrenal cortex). A second attack one year later practically confined him to bed or a chair and ACTH no longer helped. Dr. Klenner first met Mr. Humphreys in August 1974 and placed him on a comprehensive megavitamin program. Pain began to ease soon after and by August 1975, the patient was nearly normal. By year's end, his physician and his neurologist found he was normal. Dale Humphreys continues to engage in all his usual physical activities. Klenner believes this approach should be used for other neurological diseases.

RIBOFLAVIN—VITAMIN B2

Riboflavin is a maintenance factor for mucous membranes of the respiratory system and is essential for healthy eye tissue and skin tissue. The largest tablet of this vitamin available is 100 mg., which has not lent itself to megadose levels. The most common multivitamin tablet dose is only 5 mg., a reflection of the current attitude toward riboflavin. Vitamin B2 is important in the respiratory enzymes and probably has some value for some people in megadoses. My experience has been that there is no toxicity apparent even with 250 mg. per day dosage.

Vitamin B2 turns the urine bright fluorescent yellow, a property that makes it a good marker to add to tablets to determine if they are absorbed. Bright yellow urine indicates the tablet has disintegrated and its contents taken in by the body. Two properties of riboflavin in doses of 250 mg. per day is evident: it decreases the craving for sugar and it greatly improves vision, especially in elderly people.

NICOTINIC ACID (NIACIN)—VITAMIN B3

Vitamin B3 was the third B vitamin to be identified. In the mid-1930s researchers recognized that nicotinic acid was a vitamin. This simple chemical had been known for more than fifty years, but no one had suspected its role in nutrition. There are two chemicals with vitamin B3 properties, nicotinic acid and nicotinamide. Both are converted into coenzyme one or nicotinamide adenine dinucleotide (NAD). This is the active anti-pellagra enzyme. Nicotinic acid is often referred to as niacin, and nicotinamide as niacinamide.

Both niacin and niacinamide are similar members of the B-complex, but niacinamide is more generally used in treatment since the burning, flushing and itching of the skin that frequently accompanies nicotinic acid does not occur. In nature, nicotinic acid and nicotinamide are not free, as they are in enriched flour or in tablets, but are usually bound in the mono- or dinucleotide form. Sometimes they are so tightly bound that they are not hydrolyzed by the intestinal enzymes, and are therefore not utilized by the body. The vitamin B3 in corn is so bound, but can be released by cooking the corn with limestone (calcium). The nicotinic acid (or nicotin-amide) is therefore digested slowly and absorbed slowly with no substantial elevations in blood levels. Nicotinic acid in natural sources does not produce any vasodilation, but when taken in doses of 1 gram three times per day, it causes a sudden and marked elevation of blood level, producing physiological changes, which is followed by the excretion of large quantities. The use of vitamin B3 tablets is thus wasteful, even if essential.

I have run preliminary tests on a slow-release nicotinic acid capsule. It contains other factors, such as inositol, and releases its ingredients over an eight-hour period. In this way it more closely reproduces the absorption of the vitamin from food. Companies are now developing slow-release preparations or esters such as inositol niacinate which are almost free of the flush side effect, but are still effective in lowering cholesterol and increasing HDL. The slow-release capsule has the following properties compared to pure nicotinic acid in ordinary tablets: it has very weak vasodilator properties and seldom produces any gastric intestinal discomfort. One-quarter gram capsules taken four times per day were more effective in lowering cholesterol and triglyceride levels than 1 gram of standard nicotinic acid taken three times per day. This suggests that the optimum dose range for schizophrenics may well be reduced from 2 to 30 grams per day of standard nicotinic acid to 1 to 10 grams of slow-release nicotinic acid per day.

Nicotinic acid has broad-spectrum hypolipidemic properties which have caused it to be examined for its effect in reducing coronary disease.

In comparison to the other compounds used to lower cholesterol, niacin was like the tortoise just past the starting gate compared to the hares already in full flight all around the globe. By 1986 it had been established that niacin lowered triglycerides (LDL-TG), very low-density hipoprotein cholesterol (VLDL) and low-density lipo-protein cholesterol (LDL). The degree to which it lowered these cholesterol fractions depended upon the initial level. If the initial levels were normal, there was no effect. If they were high, the decrease was proportional to the initial level; with high levels the percentage decrease was greater. Hoffer and Callbeck had observed nearly 40 years ago that niacin also elevated total cholesterol if it was below 150 mg. percent. This may be due to its effect in elevating high-density lipoprotein cholesterol (HDL). Recent data suggest that lowering the low-density cholesterol fractions is not as important as it is to elevate HDL. Researchers have found that as little as 200 mg. of niacin daily elevated HDL. At this low level side effects are minimal.

However, for 30 years following our report there was a slow accumulation of papers in the medical literature confirming our findings and expanding on them, but very few physicians in the practice of medicine heard about it. There can be no patent on the use of niacin, and therefore it was never promoted by any major drug companies. Rather, physicians were swayed by the massive advertising in journals placed by companies that were promoting their own inferior products for lowering cholesterol.

In fact, vitamin B3 is the only compound so far tested over the long term which has produced a real decrease in cardiovascular disease. Major interest developed in the use of niacin for decreasing cholesterol only after the results of the National Coronary Drug Study were published. Between 1966 and 1975, five drugs used to lower cholesterol levels were compared to a placebo in 8,341 men, ages 30 to 64, who had suffered a myocardial infarction at least three months before entering the study. Both niacin and clofibrate decreased cholesterol levels to the same degree, but only niacin decreased the death rate significantly from all causes. Nine years later, mortality had decreased 11 percent and longevity had increased by two years in those taking it, with about 6,000 men alive at the end of the study. Niacin apparently decreased the number of nonfatal infarcts as well as reduced cholesterol. It is interesting to note that the results of the study do not support the view that there is a high correlation between blood cholesterol and cardiovascular disease.

Since this report, niacin is considered one of the foremost compounds for dealing with elevated cholesterol levels. We do not subscribe to the hypothesis that niacin was effective only because it lowered cholesterol levels. If this were a well-established relationship, we would have expected clofibrate to have the same beneficial effect. We think that niacin acts because it is a vitamin, not a xenobiotic drug, and that it improves the overall health of anyone taking it. We are now in the rapidly expanding phase of niacin use for lowering cholesterol worldwide. It is one of the safest and most effective compounds, with only minimal side effects.

The tortoise has won and one of the hares, clofibrate, is gradually losing its popularity of nearly 25 years. The newer statin drugs that act differently have been introduced with great fanfare, but it is difficult for a drug that can cost over $100 monthly to compete with a vitamin which has a proven beneficial long-term effect and costs about $10 per month. Perhaps that is why sales of Mevacor, Merck & Co.'s product for lowering cholesterol, have slumped.

We suspect that niacin may also work because it is the best known antagonist to adrenochrome. Adrenochrome is made in the heart muscle by oxidation of adrenaline. It is the reason why adrenaline is toxic to heart tissue. Adrenochrome is converted into adrenolutin which can be measured in the blood. It would have been valuable had the designers of the National Coronary Drug Study included niacinamide as one of the compounds tested. We suspect it would have yielded results similar to that found for niacin.

Recent findings have shown that vitamin B3 has many anticancer properties. This was discussed at an international conference entitled "Niacin, Nutrition, ADP-Ribosylation and Cancer" held in Texas in 1987. Conference organizers Drs. Jacobson and Jacobson hypothesized that niacin prevents cancer based on studying two groups of human cells with carcinogens. The group given adequate niacin developed tumors at a rate only 10 percent of the rate in the group deficient in niacin. Dr. J. Jacobson is quoted as saying, "We know that diet is a major risk factor, that diet has both beneficial and detrimental components. What we cannot assess at this point is the optimal amount of niacin in the diet. . . . The fact that we don't have pellagra does not mean we are getting enough niacin to confer resistance to cancer." In a recent report Jacobson and Jacobson compared the amount of NAD with the amount of the mononucleotide (NADP) in the red blood cells. Normal subjects who lived on a diet very low in vitamin B3 had 70 percent less NAD in their cells, with very little decrease in NADP. The ratio of NAD/NADP decreased from 1.8 to 0.5. They suggest that a ratio of less than 1 indicates that the subject is at increased risk for becoming vitamin B3 deficient and therefore of increased risk of getting cancer.

Vitamin B3 may also increase the therapeutic efficacy of anticancer treatment. According to one study, mice were injected with mammary adenocarcinoma cells and then given niacinamide, 0.2 gram/kg body weight, thirty minutes before they were given radiation. This is equivalent to 12 grams per day of niacinamide for an average human adult. Although the vitamin had no effect on tumor volume in these animals, the tumor volume decreased 86 percent after irradiation in niacinamide-treated mice and remained 79 percent lower at four weeks. Mitotic activity remained low in niacinamide-treated animals after irradiation but returned to preirradiation levels in nontreated mice. Researchers therefore suggest that niacinamide may have a role in the treatment of malignant tumors. In a number of other studies conducted in mice, niacinamide also increased the toxicity of irradiation against tumors because it enhanced blood flow to the tumor and also enhanced the effect of chemotherapy. Further evidence that vitamin B3 is involved in cancer comes from a Japanese report showing a direct relationship between the activity of nicotinamide methyl transferase and the presence of cancer in animals.

It should be noted that after World War II Dr. Gerson treated a series of cancer patients with special diets and with some nutrients including niacin 50 mg. 8 to 10 times per day, dicalcium phosphate with vitamin D, vitamins A and D and liver injections. He found that all the cancer patients benefited in that they became healthier and in many cases the tumors regressed. In a subsequent report, Gerson elaborated on his diet. He emphasized a high-potassium-over-sodium diet, ascorbic acid, niacin, brewers yeast and lugols iodine. I would consider the use of these nutrients in combination very original and enterprising. In fact. Dr. Gerson was the first physician to emphasize the use of multivitamins and some multiminerals.

However, one factor hampering work in this and other areas is its status as a member of a group of compounds called "orphan drugs." These are not patented, and no person or company has a financial interest in developing them, since the potential rewards are not commensurate with the costs of development. Orphan drugs have to gain public acceptance on their own merits. Upon taking them, your judgment as to whether or not you feel better or have benefited in any way will determine whether you want to use them. This has happened with ascorbic acid. Linus Pauling's immense prestige in publicizing vitamin C alerted the public, and the continued large-scale use of the vitamin has been due to general public satisfaction with it. We hope that the same thing will happen to nicotinic acid. Its hypolipidemic effect may become a factor in its popular use, if for no other reason.

But all vitamins used in megadoses are orphan drugs. As time moves on and more people are exposed to orthomolecular nutrition, megadoses of vitamins will become more commonplace. People will recognize their value as protectors against pollution and stress.

Then the orphan vitamin products will replace drugs. It is inevitable that physicians will one day come to prefer a nutrient over a nonnutrient for therapy. The body has mechanisms for dealing with nutrients, but must evolve new ones for dealing with foreign chemicals.

Nicotinamide is the form of vitamin B3 that does not produce a flush, is alkaline and induces no acidity in the stomach. However, it can be taken in a dosage that produces a central nausea and vomiting. If one goes above the optimum dose it will produce nausea. David Hawkins, M.D., uses this characteristic as a means of measuring the value of dosage. The dose is increased until nausea ensues, then decreased by 1 gram. The dose range for nicotinamide is 2-6 grams per day.

Vitamin B3 is a co-enzyme in fat metabolism and helps to control blood fat levels. It is important for the treatment of mental illness because of its effects on complex chemical interactions that affect the working of the nervous system. It has also been described as the anti-rheumatic vitamin; and the nicotinic acid flush is comforting to those who suffer from the symptoms of arthritis. This was described by Kaufman, but unfortunately, he published his final report about the same time cortisone was being promoted for arthritis and the information was buried.

I estimate that the use of large doses of vitamin B3 is now at the middle of the accelerating phase as more and more information is disseminated in the medical and popular literature. Interest has also spread to the other vitamins, particularly such antioxidants as vitamins C, E and beta-carotene, and to the antioxidant minerals such as selenium. Other diseases being examined where therapeutic doses of vitamins can be used are AIDS, cancer, cardiovascular disease, mental disease and senility. Within about ten years, the maturation phase will be reached, and even medical schools will be teaching students all about the therapeutic use of vitamins—about orthomolecular medicine.

NICOTINIC ACID TREATMENT FOR SCHIZOPHRENIA

Schizophrenic patients who have been ill one year or less, or whose relapse has been one year or less in duration, fall into what I classify as *Phase I*. This group includes those who may have been ill several times but have been able to recover. They are cooperative patients, able to follow treatment at home or are cared for by a family. I start these people on vitamin B3, three grams per day. Patients who are under age twenty-one, all women, and those men who, for cosmetic reasons would prefer not to flush in public, are prescribed nicotinamide. Children are intolerant of the flush and there is no point forcing them to experience this unless the nicotinamide does not work. The amount given should be below the nauseant dose level.

If my patients are forewarned, the nicotinic acid flush causes them very little difficulty. When it comes, however, it can be surprising. An orthomolecular physician in Detroit forgot to warn his patient, and after the fellow took his first gram he developed the flush. Becoming concerned, he phoned the nearest poison control center at a hospital. The intern on duty, hearing what he had taken and how much, exclaimed, "Oh, my God, you have taken a lethal dose. Call an ambulance immediately!" By the time the badly frightened patient arrived at the hospital the flush was nearly gone.

The flush eases with each dose until in most cases it vanishes or remains a minor problem only. If the dose is too low, the flush remains fairly intense. It is necessary to give enough to empty the histamine storage sites to a level at which there is no time to replenish them by the time the next dose is taken. It may require 6 to 8 grams per day for some people. You can minimize the flush by a variety of procedures:

1. Take 120 mg. of aspirin each day for two days before starting on the nicotinic acid (Kunin).
2. Take the vitamin after meals with a cold drink. Anything that reduces the rate of absorption into the blood will decrease the flush.
3. Use nicotinic acid combined with inositol. This is available as a single product, *Lenodil*, in Canada. It was available as *Hexanicotol* in the United States, but FDA policy prevented its development.
4. Use the pelletized slow-release preparations—effective at lower dosages.

A few patients have low thresholds for nicotinamide and nicotinic acid. Nausea may set in with either. They will require smaller doses of both to achieve an adequate vitamin B3 intake. There is a wide range between patients for the optimum dose, and alteration of dosage may be needed as treatment continues. One of my chronic female patients who is schizophrenic required 30 grams per day for a year. On 24 grams her symptoms came back. For the past seven years, however, a gradually reduced dosage to 3 grams has been adequate.

For cerebral allergy patients, nicotinic acids helps to control symptoms by depleting the histamine and heparin levels. If the foods to which the patient is allergic are removed, the need for nicotinic acid will drop to about 3 grams per day or perhaps disappear entirely.

Viral infections are critical for schizophrenics and may cause a relapse, which comes on as the infection begins to recede. Therefore, ascorbic acid is advantageous in the dosage of 3 grams per day for decreasing the frequency of infections and colds. It is best to use the crystalline powder form of vitamin C dissolved in water or juice. If it is too acidic, neutralize the supplement with small quantities of baking soda.

There may be indications for using thiamine, riboflavin, pantothenic acid, folic acid, pyridoxine and cobalamin along with niacin for some schizophrenic patients. Tranquilizers, antidepressants and all other drugs used in psychiatry will also be useful if indicated. Usual doses are prescribed. Patients will remain on the vitamin supplementation program for several months or years, depending upon their response. Various medications will have their dosage altered up or down until an optimum program is achieved. When the patient is considered well, he is advised to continue with his supplementation for up to five years. That is the best orthomolecular nutrition practice for schizophrenia. If by that time withdrawal of medication is followed with relapse, the individual may have to continue vitamin supplementation for life.

Failures among Phase I patients, or chronic cases who have been ill for many years in or out of the hospital, fall into my classification of *Phase II*. Phase II schizophrenics often are unable to cooperate. They are prescribed the same chemotherapy as Phase I and additionally receive a series of electroconvulsive therapy (ECT). This may be given in hospital or out-patient. These schizophrenics usually require larger doses of vitamins, along with mineral medication to increase zinc intake or to reduce copper levels (with penicillamine). After the ECT, chemotherapy is continued as before. A very small proportion of my patients, under 5 percent, require ECT.

Phase I patients are seldom cases of cerebral allergies, but Phase II schizophrenics have cerebral allergies in up to 50 percent of cases. Nonallergenics are treated as described; cerebral allergenics require a specialized approach.

PYRIDOXINE—VITAMIN B6

Pyridoxine, another one of the water-soluble B complex vitamins, has a coenzyme involved in an enormous number of reactions. Most of them affect the metabolism of amino acids. The conversion of tryptophan into NAD is dependent upon pyridoxine, and it has importance in red blood cell formation and on central nervous system hormones. Fats, carbohydrates and all proteins metabolize more effectively by means of pyridoxine. In its absence, typical pellagra is produced. It has been used for treating certain forms of learning and behavioral disorders in children, as Rimland reported.

Along with vitamin B3, Cott and others have found it useful in the treatment of hyperkinetic children. Pfeiffer et al. has shown that kryptopyrrole (formerly known as the mauve factor) binds pyridoxine. Patients with large quantities of kryptopyrrole will, therefore, exhibit a pyridoxine-deficient state. Pfeiffer has described this syndrome. Hoffer and Osmond described it clinically, but concluded that vitamin B3 was the important therapy. Pfeiffer's work suggests that pyridoxine may be even more important. Patients with kryptopyrroluria, according to Pfeiffer, should be treated with megadoses of pyridozine combined with zinc. The usual megadose level is 250 to 3000 mg. per day of vitamin B6 with the mode near the lower level. In a very few cases pyridoxine increases excitability in children.

There are several good indications for using pyridoxine, both for psychiatric patients and for patients with physical disease. Vitamin B6 should be taken by the following psychiatric patients:

1. Schizophrenics, many children with learning and behavioral disorders, children with infantile autism and any patients excreting large amounts of KP. (The urine test for KP is relatively simple and any modern laboratory can learn to do it with little difficulty.)

2. Cases of infantile autism. Dr. Bernard Rimland was a coworker

in the first double blind prospective controlled experiment which showed that pyridoxine was therapeutic in these cases. Dr. Rimland stated, "There are now 17 published studies—all positive—showing that high dosages of vitamin B6 and magnesium are a safe and often helpful treatment for autism. Thousands of parents are using B6 and magnesium to help their children. Almost 50 percent show worthwhile improvement and the vitamins are immeasurably safer than any drug."

Vitamin B6 should be taken for the following physical ailments:

1. Carpal tunnel syndrome. Dr. John Marion Ellis and Dr. Karl Folkers concluded that vitamin B6 50 to 200 mg. daily for 12 weeks cured the less affected hand in patients selected for surgery on the more crippled hand and halted atrophy of the thenar muscle. They suggested it is a cofactor for normal cortisone activity in tendons and synovium. They also reported one case where riboflavin alone was very effective in treating carpal tunnel syndrome, but when both vitamin B2 and B6 were given together, the results were even better. They concluded that this syndrome was the result of a double vitamin deficiency.

2. Too much KP in the urine. The double deficiency of vitamin B6 and zinc produce symptoms in the skin, including stretch marks on the body and white spots in the finger nails. When the two nutrients are provided, they clear, proving they are not calcium spots. Another indicator is premenstrual syndrome; women with it respond well to these two nutrients.

3. Protection against arteriosclerosis, heart disease and strokes. Vitamin B6 is one of the nutrients essential in the conversion of homocysteine to the nontoxic cystathionine. (This is discussed in a section on Folic Acid later in this chapter.) Dr. J.M. Ellis, who has been using pyridoxine for a long time to treat carpal tunnel syndrome with great success, observed that few of his patients had heart attacks. Hattersley provides a comprehensive outline of the relation between pyridoxine and the development of atherosclerosis. His interest was aroused when he heard about the pioneer work being done by internist Dr. Moses M. Suzman in Johannesburg, South Africa. Suzman theorized that atherosclerosis was a vitamin deficiency disease and suspected

multiple vitamin and mineral deficiencies, primarily vitamin B6. He published an abstract of his work using pyridoxine 200 mg., folic acid 5 mg. and vitamin E 100 to 600 I.U., all daily. He also used other nutrients in smaller amounts. Of 62 typical heart patients followed for an average of 52 months there were four reinfarcts (two were fatal). However, Dr. Suzman was not able to publish the main body of his data in medical journals because they found his ideas too novel. The peer review system of vetting papers to be published in medical journals effectively suppresses any idea the "peers" do not like. In fact, the reviewers are not "peers," since they are not informed about the treatment nor have they been taught anything about it as medical students.

For people who are well or nearly well and who wish to ensure they have enough B6, I recommend 50 to 100 mg. daily. For specific indications I recommend between 100 and 500 mg. daily. Larger doses have been used, but they are seldom needed. It may be necessary for children to also use magnesium to prevent pyridoxine from activating hyperactive behavior. This observation, first reported by Adelle Davis in one of her books, has been confirmed by many.

There are very few side effects of taking vitamin B6. The ones that do occur are minor and transient. Much has been made of the few patients collected from several medical schools who took between 2000 and 6000 mg. per day and developed peripheral neuropathy, which cleared after a year. The paper describing these results was quite inadequate because it did not report whether the patients were taking any other nutrients and what type of diet they were on. But based on this report the idea became current that vitamin B6 was toxic. Marks wrote, "It has been claimed that high doses of pyridoxine can lead to liver damage, interference with the normal functions of riboflavin and a dependency state. With the possible exception of the dependency states these suggestions are not substantiated by scientific data. The dependency states were very transient."

COBALAMIN—VITAMIN B12

Cobalamin is used to maintain the health of all body cells by production of nucleic acid. It maintains nerve tissue sheaths, helps in blood formation and the production of genetic material DNA and RNA and affects protein and fat cells. Studies of vitamin B12 in megadoses have been infrequent. Newbold suggested that some schizophrenics have low blood levels of the vitamin and improve when it is given to them. Many elderly patients also are low in B12 supplementation. Since it works together with folic acid, both should be used as cosupplements. The megadose level of cobalamin would range from 1 to 5 mg. per day by injection. Dosage for oral vitamin B12 is not known.

Vitamin B12 is absorbed from the intestine except in patients with pernicious anemia who cannot do so. Supplementation is usually given by injection, but recent evidence shows that giving tablets or sublingual lozenges is as effective. Up to 100 mg. per day have been given with no side effects. This vitamin has been used by many physicians for many years for their patients with chronic fatigue even though their blood levels are normal. There is no doubt that these patients have benefited. The clinical skill of these doctors was better than if one depended only on laboratory testing. Vitamin B12 has been used in megadoses by nearly every doctor, who was probably not aware that he or she was practicing orthomolecular medicine. Injecting 1000 mg. per day provides 1000 times the recommended daily dose.

ASCORBIC ACID—VITAMIN C

Ascorbic acid is the vitamin most commonly used as a supplement in the United States only. Of the 20 percent of the population taking vitamin supplements, over half take 1 gram or more of vitamin C daily. A major increase in consumption of vitamin C followed Dr. Linus Pauling's book, *Vitamin C and the Common Cold*. Long known to prevent scurvy with doses of under 50 mg. daily, it aids in iron absorption, help to manufacture adrenal cortical hormones, polysaccharide and collagen. It forms bones, teeth, cartilage and keeps up capillary permeability. Also vitamin C prevents oxidation of nutrients within the body, promotes growth and wound healing and forms white blood cells which fight infection, detoxify drugs and environmental poisons in the system. This important vitamin fights off emotional and environmental stress and protects the circulatory system from fat deposits.

Vitamin C is the safest nutrient known, and in the recommended dose from 1 to over 10 grams per day, it is remarkably free of side effects and toxicity. In fact, it has no toxicity since it does not kill anyone. To reduce the frequency and morbidity of colds, you should use at least 3 grams (3000 mg.) per day, although it has been estimated than an average of 8 grams per day is required to prevent colds in 95 percent of the population. The optimum dose varies enormously depending upon the individual and his or her age and state of health. To determine that dosage, you need to increase your daily intake until your bowels begin to move too quickly, causing gas and an increased number of bowel movements (this side effect makes it a very useful laxative). Once this level is reached, the dose is decreased and retained at the lower sublaxative level. It can be taken by mouth or injection. Up to 200 grams have been given daily by intravenous injection.

Every person suffers from a deficiency of ascorbic acid, or has a form of subclinical scurvy, because the human body does not make it. So the addition of vitamin C improves almost every function of the body. It has been recommended for a large number of diseases, including cancer and infections, especially viruses. Pauling's interest in this vitamin had stimulated major research investigations, especially in the treatment and prevention of the common cold and cancer. In fact, Cameron and Pauling's book *Cancer and Vitamin C* marked the beginning of the vitamin C cancer era. The idea has been resisted by the cancer establishment, but in spite of this, it is being used on an ever-larger scale as part of the treatment of cancer.

Pauling and Hoffer reported the results of their study on 134 patients (this was not a double blind prospective study). Almost the entire group were terminal patients who had already been treated with surgery, chemotherapy and radiation to one degree or another. The 101 patients who followed a vitamin C regimen, plus other antioxidants and B vitamins, had a much longer survival time— there were nine 10-year survivals, including one case of cancer of the head and the pancreas, several sarcomas and others—than the group of 33 who did not follow the program. The smaller group's short life span is a measure of how sick the entire group was. A recent survey of a second, much larger sample yielded the same difference in recovery rates.

With scurvy the blood vessels no longer retain their integrity and fluid leaks from them into the skin and the tissues. Rath and Pauling have shown that the body increases its production of lipoprotein cholesterol(a) in an attempt to overcome some of the symptoms of scurvy. The lipoprotein(a) [Lp(a)] does what the presence of vitamin C would do: plugs small leaks which develop and decreases the leakage of fluid from the vessels. But if too much Lp(a) is made—this could be a too-successful attempt to prevent fluid loss—the extra Lp(a) is deposited in the vessel wall and initiates arteriosclerosis, which builds up over a lifetime. This is one of the main factors, but not the only one, which is responsible for cardiovascular disease, including strokes and coronary disease. Elaborating on the work he completed with Dr. Linus Pauling, Dr. M. Rath noted that animals which make their own vitamin C make only small amounts of Lp(a), while animals that cannot make the vitamin make substantial amounts of Lp(a). There are probably other mechanisms which have developed over the past 20 million years to try to overcome the problems generated by the lack of ascorbic acid.

Vitamin C is needed by everyone. And the amount increases very rapidly in the presence of any pathology or stress. It has been found that the more serious the condition, the more vitamin C is needed. A good indicator of this is the ratio of ascorbic acid in its original reduced state to the amount of oxidized vitamin C (dehydroascorbic acid). Normally less than 5 percent of the total vitamin C in the body is in the oxidized state so that the ratio is better or higher than 20 to 1. However, when the individual is close to death, almost all the vitamin C is in the oxidized state and the ratio is very small. For other diseases the amount of oxidized vitamin C decreases. In people who are very sick and begin to recover, the amount of oxidized vitamin goes down quickly. It is apparent the vitamin C must be in the reduced state since only then can it function as an antioxidant. The best way to ensure that the ratio is very low is to take ample quantities of the vitamin.

VITAMIN E—THE TOCOPHERALS

Alpha tocopherol has been recommended as a preventive and treatment for cardiovascular disease, as a protective agent against free radicals in the body and as an antisenility factor. The last supposition is based on the hypothesis that free radicals (from oxygen, radiation, etc.) accelerate aging. Years ago, when I (A.H.) did not know what to expect, I added vitamin E, 800 I.U. per day to my multivitamin program. About one year later my hair, which had been graying, had regained most of its original dark color except the hair on my chest, which remains gray and white.

Vitamin E promotes normal growth and aids the functioning of muscle, blood and nerve cells. It helps in the absorption of unsaturated fats, fights off stress and acts as a detoxifying agent. Nair et al. reported on treatment of porphyrinuria with vitamin E for four patients. In all four cases the typical biochemical changes were present, but they were corrected. The orthomolecular doses for vitamin E range from 800 I.U. to 3000 I.U. per day. A normal dose range is 200-800 I.U. daily.

Vitamin E was discovered in 1922 and was first isolated from wheat germ in 1936. The fat-soluble vitamin is absorbed into the walls of the intestine, where it is combined with other fats into chylomicrons and distributed throughout the body. It is almost all carried in the low- and high-density lipoproteins. Its major role is as a scavenger of free radicals, which are highly reactive fractions of molecules. If allowed to remain, free radicals will damage cell membranes and amino acids rich in sulfur.

Vitamin E is nature's best antioxidant for protecting cell surfaces. One vitamin E molecule is used over and over and can protect against 1000 free radical molecules. It must have other uses as well. It has only recently become popular. For long it was laughed at as a vitamin in search of a disease. Now it is known to prevent many diseases: it regulates platelet aggregability, prevents peripheral vascular disease and modulates the immune system.

Vitamin E supplementation enhances the immune response. A 1992 issue of *Nutrition Reviews* reported that a controlled experiment with older people given 800 I.U. improved their immune function. This report suggested that decreased immunity in the elderly might be due to a deficiency of vitamin E. Vitamin E deficiency, in a classical sense, does not occur in adults but is found mainly in premature infants. There it causes increased hemolysis of red blood cells and a decreased red blood half life.

After vitamin B3, vitamin E was the second vitamin used in large doses. Dr. Evan Shute, who did early research on the effects of vitamin E with his brother Wilfred on more than 30,000 patients, describes six properties of vitamin E: (1) It is an antioxidant and improves the ability of tissue to use oxygen. (2) It prevents the formation of emboli from clots and extension of the clots. (3) It is a vasodilator for the capillaries. (4) It improves damaged capillary fragility. (5) It resolves some scars. (6) It may improve muscle power in athletes and in animals. Not surprisingly, it has been found to be therapeutic for managing thrombosis (he referred to 57 published reports), gangrene, indolent ulcers, thromboangiitis obliterans (13 papers), thermal burns, radiation burns, cardiac disease, congenital heart disease, acute and chronic rheumatic fever, hypertensive heart disease and coronary heart disease.

Dr. Marks discussed the following indications in his more recent review: (1) cardiovascular disease; (2) premenstrual syndrome: (3) tissue ischemia, which is common in myocardial infarction, stroke and renal failure (vitamin E reduces ischemia and is very important in dealing with these conditions); (4) cancer prevention (studies show an inverse relationship between vitamin E status and the development or risk of dying from cancer); (5) protection against environmental pollutants (it suppressed increased lipid peroxidation in cigarette smokers); and (6) enhanced immune function.

Drs. Wilfred and Evan Shute recommend doses from 400 to 8000 I.U. daily. The usual dosage range was 800 to 1600 I.U., but they report that they had given 8000 I.U. (about 8 grams) without any toxicity. I usually use between 400 and 1200 I.U, daily, but for Crohn's disease I have been giving 4000 I.U.

I have not yet seen any side effects from vitamin E administration at suggested doses. Dr. Marks reports that adults can safely be given 100 to 800 I.U. but excludes adults with alteration of vitamin K status or metabolism. Ingestion of 1200 I.U. has increased the coagulation defect produced by vitamin K deficiency or by warfarin treatment. Drs. Shute advise starting with small doses for patients who have rheumatic heart disease and very slowly working up the dose. The reason is that if too much is given at the beginning, the increased strength of the heart beat may create some difficulty. The same applies to heart failure from hypertension. The initial dose should be small and gradually increased so that the final dose can safely reach 800 to 1200 I.U.

The history of vitamin E, its massive rejection for about 40 years and its increasing acceptance today is very interesting and contains many lessons for physicians and medical schools. The only reason it was so thoroughly rejected is that physicians knew hardly anything about vitamins. It is clear that vitamin E will play an ever-increasing role in the prevention and treatment of disease. It is now widely recognized as an antioxidant vitamin intimately involved in the biochemistry and physiology of the body and with a host of diseases. The Shute brothers were deprived of the recognition they deserved, though at the end of their lives they had some recognition from orthomolecular physicians. They were the first doctors who had to face the unreasonable and unrelenting opposition of the medical establishment for their espousal of megadoses of a vitamin. That opposition was totally unscientific.

However, the lay vitamin literature was well acquainted with vitamin E and its usefulness. There was ample literature from which to learn. Thus in 1972 Dr. E. Di Cyan, a friend of mine, wrote his excellent book *Vitamin E and Aging*. This book even today is very up-to-date and foreshadowed many current interests in the medical profession, which at the time were totally ignored and laughed at.

A FEW CLINICAL HEALTH STUDIES OF VITAMIN E

The November 19, 1992, *New York Newsday* carried a report that vitamin E had decreased the risk of heart disease between one-third and one-half. Two studies were conducted at the Harvard School of Public Health. In one study of 87,245 women, Dr. M. Stampfer et al. found that during an eight-year followup, women who had taken at least 100 I.U. of vitamin E daily for two years had a 46 percent lower risk of having a heart attack. The second study on men by Dr. E. Rimm et al., based upon 51,529 subjects, showed a 37 percent lower risk. They found that there was not enough vitamin E in food to reach these daily levels. Considering that 40 percent of all deaths are caused by heart disease, with 2,000 people a day, or about 750,000 people per year, dying from it, it's impossible to calculate how many lives would have been saved if the Harvard group had taken their responsibility seriously and examined vitamin E claims in 1950 instead of waiting until 1992. That is the real cost of medical cynicism.

Two recent reports show that vitamin E helps heart patients get well from bypass surgery and angioplasties. Dr. D.S. Sgoutas, Department of Pathology and Laboratory of Medicine at Emory University, found that 35.5 percent of the angioplasty patients taking vitamin E suffered from restenosis, while 47.5 percent of the control placebo group did. Dr. T. Yau at the University of Toronto reported that presurgical supplementation of vitamin E helped the heart pump during the high-risk five-hour postoperative period. Controls did not do as well.

Vitamin E may be working its way into psychiatry following reports that it had a slight effect in decreasing the symptoms of tardive dyskinesia in patients. This aroused some to consider its role there as an antioxidant and its possible effect in decreasing the oxidation of catechol amines to their oxidized derivatives (these are compounds like adrenochrome). This is an interesting hypothesis and corroborates our views published in the mid-1950s. However, the Parkinson Study Group reported in *The New England Journal of Medicine* in 1993 that vitamin E 2000 I.U. daily, given to patients for an average of 14 months, had no significant effect on the disease.

The June 1992 *American Journal of Epidemiology* reported that people who took vitamin E regularly for at least six months had half the expected risk of oral cancer. This is based upon 1,100 patients with oral cancer and 1,300 normal controls. The amount of vitamin in multivitamins was not enough, and they had to take pure vitamin E supplements, at least 100 I.U. per day. Several other similar studies are underway.

FOLIC ACID

Folic acid is another safe water-soluble vitamin. It has been used in doses up to 15 mg. daily. There was a report that this dose caused gastrointestinal disturbances, but this was not seen in another study with the same dose. Most patients do not need more than 5 mg. Recently it has been proven that women will give birth to babies with spina bifida and similar neural tube defects (NTD) much less frequently if they take supplemental folic acid 1 mg. In fact, Dr. Smithells in 1981 showed that giving pregnant women extra folic acid decreased the incidence of NTDs. The immediate reaction to the original findings was one of strong disbelief and hostility, and the establishment refused to advise women to take folic acid until the requisite number of double blind experiments were done. At last they were satisfied 11 years later, culminating with a 1989 report in *The Journal of the American Medical Association*. Folic acid provided protection for most causes of the defect.

Even in women with a family history, the frequency of babies with the defects was more than five times greater—18 per 1000 against 3.5 per 1000—in women who did not take the vitamin in the first six weeks of pregnancy. How many babies could have been saved by such a simple solution? I (A.H.) cannot recall in the past 40 years a single female patient of mine on vitamins giving birth to any child with a congenital defect. I have been able to advise them all that they not only would not harm their developing baby by taking vitamins but that their chances of giving birth to a defective child would be greatly diminished. I was frequently questioned about this by my patients who had been told by their doctors that they must stop all their vitamins while pregnant. They looked upon vitamins as toxic drugs. I am still asked the same question for the same reason today.

However, governments can learn and respond. It is now official that pregnant women should take folic acid in order to prevent spina bifida and other birth defects. The U.S. Public Health Service has issued the following advisory: "In order to reduce the frequency of NTD's (neural-tube defects) and their resulting disability, the United States Public Health Service recommends that: All woman of childbearing age capable of becoming pregnant should consume 0.4 mg. of folic acid per day for the purpose of reducing their risk of having a pregnancy affected with spina bifida or other NTDs." This amount will not be provided by most diets and requires supplementation. The U.S. Public Health Service is considering fortifying bread and other foods with folic acid, though it should be noted that some of it will be destroyed by heat.

Folic acid is also one of the nutrients involved in the prevention of arteriosclerosis. That is such a complicated phenomenon it is not surprising a large number of factors are involved, including ascorbic acid, nicotinic acid, pyridoxine and choline. J. Challem in *The Nutrition Reporter* reviewed the recent literature and concluded that the common factor is homocysteine, which is quickly changed in the body to cystathionine. Folic acid is one of the vitamins needed for the rapid conversion of homocysteine to the nontoxic cystathionine. High levels of homocysteine are now recognized as a risk factor in heart disease. Dr. M. Stampfer analyzed blood from 14,916 male physicians, all of whom had not had a heart attack. Five years later, 271 had suffered heart attacks. Of these, 31 had extremely high blood levels of homocysteine. Several other studies have found the same relationship. For example, a study at Oregon Health Sciences Center showed that 40 percent of patients who had strokes had high homocysteine levels. It is elevated in only 5 percent of the normal population.

Folic acid has been found to decrease the odds of getting lung cancer, and it has also been shown to reverse changes found in the cervix as measured by the Pap smear. Butterworth and his colleagues found that patients with low folate levels were more likely to develop cervical dysplasia. I use it for these conditions.

Another indication I have found is for elderly patients who develop a hand tremor which makes it difficult for them to write. Giving them folic acid 5 to 10 mg. daily will often remove this problem in a week or so. There is a remote danger that giving folic acid will mask pernicious anemia, the vitamin B12 deficiency, but the level of vitamin B in the blood will show whether this is a problem.

A deficiency of folic acid is clearly related to psychopathology. When Young and Ghadirian reviewed the medical literature, they found that folic acid deficiency was high in patients with depression, senility and schizophrenia and in epileptic patients on Dilantin. Medical patients with folic acid deficiency suffered more from psychiatric symptoms. Giving folic acid to these patients produced substantial improvement. They concluded that "all patients in certain diagnostic categories should receive vitamins." However, they recommended only very small doses. In sharp contrast Dr. L. Kotkas used larger doses with success and without any evidence of toxicity. Dr. Paul Godfrey, Institute of Psychiatry, London, reported that folic acid speeded recovery from depression in patients where one-third were folate deficient. The overall outcome was impressive. Abou-Saleh and Coppen also found that folic acid deficiency is common in psychiatric patients. Patients given 10 mg. daily responded in two to three months; but it took five months for gastrointestinal and neurological symptoms to improve on 10 mg. weekly.

A recent study showed that half the American population does not get enough folic acid. Stampfer recommended that 1 to 5 mg. of folic acid be taken daily. Because there is an inverse correlation between homocysteine and the intake of vitamins, this is enough to decrease elevated homocysteine levels in blood. It is clear that orthomolecular therapists will have to give much more attention to this important vitamin.

THE NONTOXICITY OF VITAMINS

Many sweeping generalizations have been made about the dangers of hypervitaminosis. Before any statement can be made about toxicity, one should specify the exact vitamin, the toxic dose and the duration of treatment. Otherwise, when examined in the light of their nonspecificity, these statements become meaningless.

Indeed, every chemical, when used in quantities larger than can be disposed of by the body, is toxic. Patients can even suffer from water intoxication. One of my obese schizophrenic patients lost 60 pounds of water in a couple of weeks after he was prevented from spending all day at the water fountain drinking. To discuss intelligently the toxicity of a vitamin, you must have two particular values: the optimum effective dose and the toxic dose of LD 50. This *LD 50* is the dose which, given over a specified period of time, will kill half the subjects. For example, if 100 mg. of saccharine fed to thirty rats kills fifteen of them from cancer, the LD 50 is 100.

The toxic dose divided by the therapeutic dose is the *therapeutic index*. If the therapeutic index is low, the compound is toxic; if it is high, it is nontoxic. If 1 gram per day is the optimum dose, and 2 grams per day is the LD 50, the therapeutic index is 2—the optimum dose is only half the amount which would be lethal to 50 percent of those to whom it is administered. Obviously such a drug or supplement would be hazardous to use. Another way to consider the therapeutic index is as the ratio between the amount of a drug which will kill and the amount required to be effective. Using our example above, if 100 mg. of saccharine kills half the rats (this is a hypothetical example, *not* a comment on the Food and Drug Administration's use of experimental evidence to ban saccharine), but only .02 mg. is required to produce the desired sweetness effect, the therapeutic index is 500, indicating a relatively safe drug.

Insulin may fall into the class of dangerous drugs. It has a low therapeutic index, and users know that insulin has to be used with great caution. Nicotinic acid had a high therapeutic index of 70. This is arrived at in the following manner: the optimum dose of nicotinic acid may be 3 to 30 grams per day for a person. If we use the average of 15 grams per day, we can determine the therapeutic index by first looking at animals. For animals the LD 50 is about 5 grams per kg. For a 70 kg. man this would be 350 grams per day, giving a therapeutic index of 23. But if we substitute the much more common dose of 3 grams per day per person taken instead of 15 grams per day, the therapeutic index becomes 70, indicating a safe product.

Vitamins have more favorable therapeutic indices than chemicals like tranquilizers and antidepressants. Additionally, the sheer bulk of a substance like a vitamin will make it relatively safe. It is difficult to consume large quantities because of this bulk. If three small tablets of an antidepressant is the recommended daily dose, it is a simple matter to commit suicide by swallowing 200 of the tablets. It is doubtful, however, that anyone could swallow 100 grams of any vitamin in tablet form without vomiting. Once, one of my patients, in a fit of anger, swallowed 100 tablets (50 grams) of nicotinic acid. The only result was a very sore abdomen. There is no record of any suicide with vitamins as the medium of death.

AN "AVERAGE" ANTI-STRESS VITAMIN FORMULA

People have often asked me for a single formula of minerals and vitamins that they could turn to without going to the bother of self-experimentation. Orthomolecular physicians have avoided suggesting such formulas. An anti-stress formula, it must be remembered, has to be individualized; there is no general prescription for every person, and there is no "average" megadose vitamin and mineral supplementation program.

Yet the clamor goes on. People *want* an "average" anti-stress vitamin formula. So, while urging that you keep in mind that individuals vary greatly in their needs, I have chosen to reveal what I take every day as a means of countering the various pressures of modern life and in order to live the full measure of years allotted *homo sapiens.*

Basically, one should start with good nutrition, which takes into account individual needs, and only after that has been shown not to be effective, does one turn to the use of megadoses of vitamins and mineral supplements. Certainly eat a sugar-free diet under any circumstances. Here is the anti-stress formula I take daily.

Supplement	Dosage
Thiamine, vitamin B1	100 mg.-300 mg.
Niacin, vitamin B3	3000 mg.-6000 mg. (people with cholesterol problems should take the nicotinic acid form)
Pantothenic acid	100 mg.-300 mg.
Ascorbic acid, vitamin C	3000 mg.-6000 mg.
Tocopherol, vitamin E	200 I.U.-800 I.U.
Vitamin A Vitamin D }	together in 3-9 cod liver oil capsules
Mineral calcium Mineral magnesium }	together in 3-6 tablets of dolomite
Zinc gluconate	30 mg.-60 mg.
Chromium	from brewery yeast
Iron	if anemic only, and on doctor's prescription
Avoid copper	

VITAMIN AND MINERAL GUIDE

VITAMIN A

Also known as the anti-infective or anti-ophthalmic vitamin. Usually measured in U.S.P. units.

Natural sources: Colored fruits and vegetables, dairy products, eggs, margarine, fish liver oils, liver.

Functions: Builds resistance to infections, especially of the respiratory tract. Helps maintain a healthy condition of the outer layers of many tissues and organs. Promotes growth and vitality. Permits formation of visual purple in the eye, counteracting night-blindness and weak eye-sight. Promotes healthy skin. Essential for pregnancy and lactation.

Deficiency: May result in night blindness, increased susceptibility to infections, dry and scaly skin, lack of appetite and vigor, defective teeth and gums, retarded growth.

VITAMIN B1

Thiamine, thiamine chloride. Also known as the anti-neuritic or anti-beriberi vitamin. Generally expressed in milligrams (mg.), occasionally in units. 333 units of B1 equal only 1 mg.

Natural sources: Dried yeast, rice husks, whole wheat, oatmeal, peanuts, pork, most vegetables, milk.

Functions: Promotes growth, aids digestion, essential for normal functioning of nerve tissues, muscles and heart, necessary for proper metabolism of carbohydrates and fats.

Deficiency: May lead to loss of appetite, weakness and lassitude, nervous irritability, insomnia, loss of weight, vague aches and pains, mental depression and constipation. In children, a deficiency may cause impaired growth.

VITAMIN B2

Riboflavin or vitamin G. Measured in milligrams (mg.).

Natural sources: Liver, kidney, milk, yeast, cheese and most B1 sources.

Functions: Improves growth, essential for healthy eyes, skin and mouth, promotes general health.

Deficiency: May result in itching and burning of the eyes, cracking of the corners of the lips, inflammation of the mouth, bloodshot eye, purplish tongue.

VITAMIN B3

Nicotinic acid (niacin)
Niacinamide (nicotinamide)

The functions and deficiency symptoms of these members of the B-complex are similar. Niacinamide is more generally used since it minimizes the burning, flushing and itching of the skin that frequently occurs with nicotinic acid.

Natural sources: Liver, lean meat, whole wheat products, yeast, green vegetables, beans.

Functions: Important for the proper functioning of nervous system. Prevents pellagra. Promotes growth. Maintains normal function of the gastrointestinal tract. Necessary for metabolism of sugar. Maintains normal skin conditions.

Deficiency: May result in pellagra, whose symptoms include inflammation of the skin, tongue; also gastrointestinal disturbance, nervous system dysfunction, headaches, fatigue, mental depression, vague aches and pains, irritability, loss of appetite, neuritis, loss of weight, insomnia, general weakness.

VITAMIN B6

Pyridoxine. Measured in milligrams (mg.). If it is designated in micrograms (mcg.) remember that it requires 1000 micrograms to equal 1 milligram (mg.).

Natural sources: Meat, fish, wheat germ, egg yoke, cantaloupe, cabbage, milk, brewer's yeast.

Functions: Aids in food assimilation and in protein and fat metabolism, prevents various nervous and skin disorders, prevents nausea.

Deficiency: May result in nervousness, insomnia, skin eruptions, loss of muscular control.

VITAMIN B12

Commonly known as the "red vitamin" cobalomin. Since it is so effective in small dosages, it is the only common vitamin generally expressed in micrograms (mcg.). Vitamin B12 is available in 1 mg. to 100 mcg. doses in sublingual tablets. With the exception of patients with pernicious anemia, the oral form is as good as the injectable form.

Natural sources: Liver, beef, pork, eggs, milk, cheese.

Functions: Helps in the formation and regeneration of red blood cells, thus helping to prevent anemia; promotes growth and increased appetite in children; a general tonic for adults.

Deficiency: May lead to nutritional and pernicious anemias, poor appetite and growth failure in children, tiredness.

VITAMIN C

Ascorbic acid, cevitamic acid. Expressed in milligrams (mg.), occasionally in units. 1 mg. equals 20 units.

Natural sources: Citrus fruits, berries, greens, cabbages, peppers. (Easily destroyed by cooking.)

Functions: Necessary for healthy teeth, gums and bones; strengthens all connective tissue, promotes wound healing, helps promote capillary integrity and prevention of permeability; a very important factor in maintaining sound health and vigor.

Deficiency: May lead to soft gums, tooth decay, loss of appetite, muscular weakness, skin hemorrhages, capillary weakness, anemia.

VITAMIN D

Viosterol; ergosterol, "sunshine vitamin.'" Measured in U.S.P. units.

Natural sources: Fish-liver oils, fat, eggs, milk, butter, sunshine.

Functions: Regulates the use of calcium and phosphorus in the body and is therefore necessary for the proper formation of teeth and bones. Very important in infancy and childhood.

Deficiency: May lead to rickets, tooth decay, retarded growth, lack of vigor, muscular weakness.

VITAMIN E

Tocopherol. Available in several different forms. Formerly measured by weight (mg.), now generally designated according to its biological activity in International Units (I.U.).

Natural sources: Wheat germ oil, whole wheat, green leaves, vegetable oils, meat, eggs, whole grain cereals, margarine.

Functions: Exact function in humans is not yet known. Medical articles have been published on its value in helping to prevent sterility; in the treatment of threatened abortion; in muscular dystrophy; in the prevention of calcium deposits in blood vessel walls. Has been used favorably by some doctors in treatment of heart conditions. Much further research needs to be completed before a clear picture of this vitamin will be obtained.

Deficiency: May lead to increased fragility of red blood cells. In experimental animals deficiencies led to loss of reproductive powers and muscular disorders.

VITAMIN F

Unsaturated fatty acids, linoleic acid and linolenic acids.

Natural sources: Vegetable oils such as soybean, peanut, safflower, cottonseed, corn and linseed.

Functions: A growth-promoting factor; necessary for healthy skin, hair and glands. Promotes the availability of calcium to the cells. Now considered to be important in lowering blood cholesterol and in combating heart disease.

Deficiency: May lead to skin disorders such as eczema.

VITAMIN K

Menadione.

Natural sources: Alfalfa and other green plants, soybean oil, egg yolks.

Functions: Essential for the production of prothrombin (a substance which aids the blood in clotting); important to liver function.

Deficiency: Hemorrhages resulting from prolonged blood-clotting time.

VITAMIN P

Citrus bioflavonoids, bioflavonoid complex, hesperidin.

Natural sources: Peels and pulp of citrus fruit, especially lemon.

Functions: Strengthens walls of capillaries. Prevents vitamin C from being destroyed in body by oxidation. Beneficial in hypertension. Reported to help build resistance in infections and colds.

Deficiency: Capillary fragility. Appearance of purplish spots on skin.

CALCIUM PANTOTHENATE

Pantothenic acid. A member of the B-complex family.

Natural sources: Liver, kidney, yeast, wheat, bran, peas, crude molasses.

Functions: Not clearly defined as yet. Helps in the building of body cells and maintaining normal skin, growth and development of central nervous system. Required for synthesis of antibodies. Necessary for normal digestive processes. Originally believed to be a factor in restoring gray hair to original color. This function has not been substantiated.

Deficiency: May lead to skin abnormalities, retarded growth, painful and burning feet, dizzy spells, digestive disturbances.

FOLIC ACID

A member of the vitamin B-complex.

Natural sources: Deep green leafy vegetables, liver, kidney, yeast.

Functions: Essential to the formation of red blood cells through its action on the bone marrow. Aids in protein metabolism and contributes to normal growth.

Deficiency: Nutritional macrocytic anemia.

CHOLINE

A member of the vitamin B-complex family. One of the "lipotropic factors."

Natural sources: Egg yolks, brain, heart, green leafy vegetables and legumes, yeast, liver and wheat germ.

Functions: Regulates function of liver; necessary for normal fat metabolism. Minimizes excessive deposits of fat in liver.

Deficiency: May result in cirrhosis and fatty degeneration of liver, hardening of the arteries.

INOSITOL

Another member of the B-complex family.

Natural sources: Fruits, nuts, whole grains, milk, meat, yeast.

Functions: Similar to that of choline.

Deficiency: Similar to that of choline.

METHIONINE

Dl-methionine. One of the essential amino acids.

Natural sources: Meat, eggs, fish, milk, cheese.

Functions: Building new body tissue; helps to remove fat from liver.

Deficiency: May lead to fatty degeneration and cirrhosis of liver.

BIOTIN

One of the newest discoveries in the B-complex family.

Natural sources: Brewer's yeast. Present in minute quantities in every living cell.

Functions: Growth-promoting factor. Possibly related to metabolism of fats and in the conversion of certain aminoacids.

Deficiency: May lead to extreme exhaustion, drowsiness, muscle pains and loss of appetite; also a type of anemia complicated by a skin disease.

LYSINE

L-lysine monohydrochloride. One of the essential amino acids.

Natural sources: Meat, eggs, fish, milk, cheese.

Functions: Building new body tissue and also such vital substances as antibodies, hormones, enzymes and body cells.

Deficiency: Not definitely known as yet.

RUTIN

Natural sources: Buckwheat.

Functions: Similar to that of vitamin P.

Deficiency: Similar to that of vitamin P.

PABA

Para amino-benzoic acid. Belongs to the B-complex group.

Natural sources: Brewer's yeast.

Functions: A growth-promoting factor, possibly in conjunction with folic acid. In experimental tests on animals, this vitamin when omitted from foods, caused hair to turn white. When restored to the diet, the white hair turned black.

Deficiency: May cause extreme fatigue, eczema, anemia.

THE IMPORTANT MINERALS

CALCIUM: Builds and maintains bones and teeth; helps blood to clot; aids vitality and endurance; regulates heart rhythm.

COBALT: Stimulant to production of red blood cells; component of vitamin B12; necessary for normal growth and appetite.

COPPER: Necessary for absorption and utilization of iron and formation of red blood-cells.

FLUORINE: May decrease incidence of dental caries.

IODINE: Necessary for proper function of thyroid gland; essential for proper growth, energy and metabolism.

IRON: Required in manufacture of hemoglobin; helps carry oxygen in the blood.

MAGNESIUM: Necessary for calcium and vitamin C metabolism; essential for normal functioning of nervous and muscular system.

MANGANESE: Activates various enzymes and other minerals; related to proper utilization of vitamins B1 and E.

MOLYBDENUM: Associated with carbohydrate metabolism.

PHOSPHORUS: Needed for normal bone and tooth structure. Interrelated with action of calcium and vitamin D.

POTASSIUM: Necessary for normal muscle tone, nerves, heart action and enzyme reactions.

SULPHUR: Vital to good skin, hair and nails.

ZINC: Helps normal tissue function, protein and carbohydrate metabolism.

NOTE: The symptoms noted in these pages should occur only when the daily intake of the vitamins mentioned has been less than the minimum daily requirement over a prolonged period. These nonspecific symptoms do not alone prove a nutritional deficiency but may be caused by any of the great number of conditions or may have functional causes. If these symptoms persist, they may indicate a condition other than a vitamin or mineral deficiency.

10

ORTHOMOLECULAR NUTRITION—PART IV
Mineral Nutrients

THE SOURCE OF ALL LIFE

Most scientists assume that all life arose out of the sea, a solution rich in minerals that covers 70 percent of the earth. Life is considered to have originated from a mixture of organic and inorganic molecules which organized into chemicals and then interacted. It would be impossible for any living cell to avoid contact with minerals, or to exclude them from its interior—too much energy would be expended for such avoidance. Indeed, any chemist who must prepare pure water, a liquid totally free from metallic ions, can tell you the enormous energy cost required simply to eliminate minute quantities of these elements.

Thus no life could develop if minerals were excluded. They provide structural and functional support, and for each element there exists an optimum quantity that furnishes maximal support for a cell. Nature already furnishes these optimum quantities so that minimal amounts of energy are needed to either increase or decrease amounts inside a cell. Any quantity less than the optimum would eventually lead to a deficiency state, and cellular malfunction might express itself in some obvious manner. For instance, a mineral excess, if it could not be gotten rid of easily, would produce a toxic state.

As nutritional science developed, more elements were seen as being essential to the human organism. Elements needed in larger quantities, such as calcium, phosphorus, sodium, potassium and magnesium, were recognized relatively early. Other elements, required in such miniscule amounts that it was impossible to measure them accurately by the primitive methods used at the time, were recognized later; they are called *trace elements.*

Trace elements are divided into four categories: (1) those considered *absolutely* essential, such as iron, cobalt, iodine, molybdenum, copper, selenium, zinc, manganese, chromium and tin; (2) those considered *possibly* essential, such as nickel, fluorine, bromine, arsenic, vanadium, barium and strontium; (3) those considered *non-*essential such as aluminum, mercury, cadmium, silver, gold and lead; (4) those elements which in even very low concentrations are *toxic,* probably because they are difficult to eliminate, such as arsenic, lead, cadmium, mercury and bismuth. Possibly every element, including the toxic ones, is essential but in such minute quantities that it is impossible ever to test whether life can exist in their absence.

By forming weak or strongly adherent chemical bonds (such as metalloenzymes), trace elements are involved in nearly every physiological reaction. For example, they carry oxygen in the blood and grow nails and hair. Or an element such as calcium gives structural rigidity to bones and teeth. Often they are associated with the vitamins in enzymes and coenzymes.

Like the vitamins, minerals must act in concert. Any cell deficient in a single mineral nutrient will fail to perform at its best level. As a safety measure, it is generally best to have slightly more of these elements than is necessary, since a cell can exclude much of what it cannot use and the body can eliminate more. Minerals, however, do not allow for the same spread of safety as do the vitamins. Take as a rule of thumb that any mineral which can be excreted readily, such as zinc, may be considered relatively safe even in quantity. Those that are excreted slowly, such as mercury, should be considered toxic.

The optimum diet that we have described will provide all the essential elements in about the appropriate quantities. Natural foods in our optimum diet have incorporated elements from their surroundings during the period of growth and development. It is quite presumptuous of humans to think that they can tamper with nature, given our present state of nutritional information. Only unprocessed foods offer the proper quantities of mineral nutrients.

Mineral requirements vary with the age of a person and his/her special events such as childbirth and disease. Rapid growth of a child demands greater mineral quantities, especially of calcium and magnesium. In separate texts Williams and Pfeiffer listed the amount of mineral nutrients required by a human adult. We have divided the elements into three groups on the basis of these authorities' rough estimates.

Mineral nutrients in *group one* are those for which the daily requirement is 350 milligrams per day or more. These include

sodium	5 grams
potassium	4 grams
phosphorus	2 grams
calcium	1 gram
magnesium	0.35 gram (350 mg)

Mineral nutrients in *group two* are those for which the daily requirement is 2 to 15 milligrams per day. These include

iron	15 mg.
zinc	15 mg.
manganese	5 mg.
copper	2 mg.
chromium	2 mg.

Mineral nutrients in *group three* are those for which the daily requirement is less than 1 milligram per day. These include molybdenum, cobalt, selenium, lithium and iodine.

Natural foods are the best sources of minerals; and second to those are the foods which have not been damaged by modern food processing. Unlike the vitamins and amino acids, minerals are not destroyed by heat. Water-soluble minerals, however, are easily leached out by any process which exposes the food to solutions. Some minerals may be removed by substances which combine with them, called *chelating agents*. To understand chelated minerals, we will first define the terms involved in detail. For instance, *minerals*, as has been said, are elemental substances, many of which are essential to life, and are involved in many complicated biological activities in the human body. Then there are the amino acids, the building blocks of all protein. By the word *chelation* (pronounced *key-lay-shon* and taken from a Greek word meaning *claw*) we mean the process by which minerals are held, as if by a claw, by amino acids or other organic compounds. Some commercial minerals sold in health food stores have been clelated, that is, bonded in a "claw" with amino acids.

Chelation of a mineral with an amino acid is a natural step in the absorption and use of a mineral by the body. Minerals chelated with amino acids exist in nature. They combine naturally for absorption into our systems via the digestive tract. When non-amino-acid-chelated minerals such as sulfates or gluconates reach the intestine, they are there chelated for absorption, if amino acids are available for a chelate to form. Amino-acid-chelated minerals help side-step this part of the digestive process because they are already bonded with amino acids. They are a specific type of complex with a valence (combining capacity) of 2 able to be chelated. However, potassium, with a valence of 1, and phosphorus, with a valence of 3 or 5, can be chelated by complexes. To be chelated, potassium would need a valence of 2, which is similar to having two arms for the amino acid claw to grab. With three or five arms, phosphorus acts like a negative anion or carrier thus forming a complex or salt. Chelated minerals appear to be more quickly absorbed.

Some commercially prepared foods have lost rich mineral portions discarded because of the vagaries of food technology. Food processors, concerned more with appealing to the public's palate than with serving its nutritional needs, throw out the mineral cooking waters as waste.

Also, when plants are grown on soils which are deficient in various elements, they will have too little of these elements in their structure. Consumption of mineral-deficient foods will eventually lead to an insufficiency state, just as if we ate processed pulp. Certain natural foods in the form of plants may become toxic because they have accumulated too much of an element such as selenium. The concern about mercury in fish is a good example of contamination. Certain ocean waters have been rendered impure by contact with mercury, and the animals living there have absorbed the poison, making them unfit to eat.

The best guide to good mineral nutrition is to follow the same principle suggested in the previous discussion of vitamins and processed food: *if the item is manufactured, don't eat it.* Be cognizant, though, that some edibles supposedly uninjured by humans might still contain too much or too little of mineral nutrients, owing to the inevitable variability of soils, crops and growing conditions.

Besides books written by Williams and Pfeiffer, two other reference sources for information about minerals are Underwood and Newbold.

SODIUM AND POTASSIUM

Both sodium and potassium are intimately involved in the transfer of energy. Sodium tends to remain within the fluid surrounding the cells, while potassium is held within the cell. Energy is needed to maintain their proper ratios. In vegetables there is a higher ratio of potassium to sodium, but the reverse is true for animals. On the other hand, processed vegetables, especially the canned variety, are higher in sodium. Consumption of only processed food will cause you the risk of accumulating as much sodium as to possibly throw an unnecessary burden on the kidneys, which must excrete it. A physician's concern about kidney and heart disease, the ultimate organ victims of too much sodium, should make him wary of excess sodium in canned food.

However, H. L. Newbold, M.D., found his patients to be sodium *deficient*. One gram a day of sodium supplementation allowed them to improve. Patients with Addison's disease experience severe fatigue partly because of lack of sodium: they do not have enough sodium-retention hormone. Sunstroke will also cause severe sodium loss. Since it is easily gotten rid of, the ideal is to take more sodium than required. Sodium goes out with the sweat and urine. Indeed, sodium deficiency has become an increasing problem in recent years because of the introduction of diuretic drugs that are used for edema resulting from allergy and other causes.

Only if the kidneys are unable to excrete enough waste will there be an excess of potassium present in the body; mental confusion will then be the resulting symptom. More common is potassium deficiency with its accompanying muscular weakness, fatigue, constipation, as well as mental confusion. Junk food tends to be low in potassium. This includes anything overdosed with salt to make it more palatable. Because the manufacturing process removes so much of the natural flavor from food, copious quantities of salt and sugar are added, and become contaminants.

People taking diuretics run into trouble with potassium deficiency. They should take extra potassium in the form of foods naturally rich in the element such as oranges, bananas and freshly prepared vegetables.

PHOSPHORUS, CALCIUM AND MAGNESIUM

Since phosphorus combines with other substances in most foods, it is difficult to sustain a phosphorus deficiency. The element is used by the body for bones and teeth in combination with calcium. Eighty percent goes for this purpose, and the rest involves itself with energy-transfer reactions. Phosphorus bonds itself with nicotinic acid and calcium to carry on physiological processes.

Calcium is the firming structural agent of bone and teeth, and that is how the element is used 99 percent of the time. Only about 1 percent is free in the body fluids, but a constant calcium level is required in the extracellular fluid and blood. The large reservoir of the mineral maintained in the bones makes this possible. It is transferred from fluid to bone and back again as needed. Calcium ions help clot blood and stimulate the nerves. Surveys have shown that approximately 30 percent of our population is deficient in this element.

Yet the main food sources of calcium consist of common foods: milk, whole grain cereals and meat bones. Processed cereals have much of their calcium removed though, and people eating mainly highly processed edibles such as this can develop a calcium deficiency.

Low-protein diets and high-protein diets alter calcium metabolism and require supplementation. Calcium deficiency symptoms may come on with enforced bed rest from illness, an excellent reason to get a patient up and about as soon as possible.

Symptoms of calcium deficiency are muscular irritability; softening of the bones, especially serious in the aged; and rickets in children. Symptoms of too much calcium absorbed into the body consist of interference with blood coagulation, depressed nerve function and possibly kidney calculae (stones). Kidney stones will not occur unless there is a concomitant deficiency of pyridoxine (vitamin B6) and magnesium.

Calcium and magnesium supplements are needed if you are allergic and unable to consume dairy products. A satisfactory supplement is dolomite in tablets or powder. Dolomite contains roughly two parts of calcium for each part of magnesium. No danger of mineral imbalance will occur with this substance, since it tends to be insoluble, and the amount absorbed will depend upon the acid quantity in the stomach. To increase absorption, additional hydrochloric acid may be needed.

Like calcium, magnesium involves itself with many body reactions. Its deficiency is serious and causes depression, irritability, tremors, irregular heartbeat, sometimes muscle spasms and, rarely, convulsions. Magnesium deficiency is apt to appear in alcoholics and tends, with the associated deficiencies of thiamine and niacin, to cause delirium tremens. Cirrhosis of the liver and hardening of the arteries are other results of lack of magnesium. Highly processed foods are missing in the mineral, as they are in other essentials. Magnesium supplementation will be required for those who take a lot of thiamine.

Although rare, an excess of magnesium in the body can cause depression of the nervous system. In fact, the element was once used as an anesthetic.

ZINC

Among the most essential components of our diet, zinc has been shown to be deficient in a large proportion of the population. Its recommended daily dose is 15 mg., but from the changes produced in food by modern technology, we are in constant danger of not getting enough. Amazingly, the changeover from galvanized iron pipes to copper pipes in our plumbing has removed one of the valuable sources of zinc. Zinc salts in soil are readily leached away by rain and take a large amount each year from the food plants that otherwise would accumulate it. In some areas zinc is an important constituent of fertilizer used in otherwise imperfect soils.

Other factors decrease human zinc intake. For instance, preparation of food so purifies it that the fibrous fractions which are richest in zinc and other minerals are removed. Thus white flour contains only eight parts per million of zinc nutrient compared with thirty-five parts per million in the whole wheat. As mentioned before, water in which food is cooked may be thrown away as waste, and this action throws out zinc with the water. According to Carl C. Pfeiffer, Ph.D., M.D., in his book *Mental and Elemental Nutrients*, even usually adequate diets are liable to be not up to normal standard in zinc.

The richest zinc source is oysters, which contain up to ten times as much as any other good source. Also wheat germ and bran are relatively rich in zinc, but the phytic acid in the wheat product may bind some of it and prevent total utilization.

Zinc insufficiency has been shown to produce various physical changes. Among them are retardation of growth as a result of unpalatability of food; keratogenesis, a particularly severe skin lesion in rats and mice that resembles psoriasis in people; delayed wound healing; interrupted reproduction; diminished learning capacity; and general alteration in protein and carbohydrate metabolism.

Considered an essential component in the action of insulin, zinc appears to be abundant in the islets of Langerhans, and the prostate gland contains the highest concentration in the body. Furthermore, zinc seems related to sexual function, and impotent males so deficient in the element require many months to regain normal potency when given adequate amounts of it. Pfeiffer has presented evidence that growth in adolescent boys may be retarded in some by the meager zinc supply taken up by sex glands and organs. His observation may explain why adolescent boys often are of smaller stature than girls of the same age who don't have similar zinc requirements for sexual maturation. Only later do the boys increase their body zinc levels, when growth is once more resumed vigorously.

Human skin holds about 20 percent of all the body's zinc. Elasticity of this organ will be the result, and defective zinc content of skin makes stretch marks appear over hips, thighs, abdomen, breasts and the shoulders. Hair and nails won't grow well either, and zinc-defective fingernails and toenails will be brittle and show white opaque spots on them. The hair may lose some of its natural pigment. Some other skin lesions may develop as well. A girl relapsing into schizophrenia, whom I recently examined, had all these skin, hair and nail changes. She had discontinued her orthomolecular nutrition program and suffered the unfavorable effects.

Alert physicians and surgeons routinely administer zinc to convalescing patients after burns or other trauma. It is used before and after optional surgery too, since the rate of healing will be markedly improved.

Subnormality in zinc also disrupts the sense of taste and smell. Severe malnutrition may ensue as a result. Foods taste flat or become unpalatable, which effectively prevents their consumption, and zinc supplements will have to be taken to correct the problem.

Pyridoxine deficiency and zinc deficiency combined have been proven to be related to mental disease. Several mental problems, including schizophrenia and learning or behavioral disorders in children, are not single homogeneous conditions. Zinc deficiency is one of a number of metabolic faults affecting the function of the brain in each syndrome. It combines with pyridoxine deficiency due to the presence in the body of a substance known as *kryptopyrrole*. Over thirty years ago, kryptopyrrole was demonstrated for the first time to be present in the urine of schizophrenics by my research group. One of my biochemists, Donald Irvine, later identified its makeup. Pfeiffer and his colleagues at the Brain Bio Center confirmed the finding and then went further to demonstrate that the substance combined with both pyridoxine and zinc to produce a double deficiency.

Pfeiffer's researchers showed that a close relationship prevails between the amount of kryptopyrrole excreted into the urine and the depletion of zinc in the body. A careful clinical examination of patients who excreted a lot of the substance revealed that they displayed a typical schizophrenic syndrome but also had some clearcut differences.

In original research with Humphry Osmond, M.B., M.R.C.P., F.R.C. Psych., I had shown that the mental condition of patients not diagnosed as having schizophrenia who excreted large quantities of *mauve factor* (the original term for kryptopyrrole) resembled schizophrenia much more than the neuroses. This was especially apparent when careful examination using tests such as the HOD test were made and comparisons were undertaken with respect to treatment and outcome of treatment. (The HOD test is a written test which was developed by A. Hoffer and H. Osmond as a determinant of schizophrenia, now in general use in orthomolecular psychiatry; for a description, see Chapter 4.) Our findings were generally ignored until Pfeiffer and his colleagues began their studies. They called patients who excrete mauve factor *pyroluriacs*. This is a particularly significant term inasmuch as it draws attention to the essential nature of the disease. The pyroluriac patient tends to have his psychosis activated by stress. He shows neurological symptoms, is unable to remember his dreams and has the physical characteristics of zinc deficiency described, such as striae and white opaque marks in the nails. Urine examination for kryptopyrrole will confirm the diagnosis—first morning specimen range should be under 20 micrograms per 100 milliliters of urine. Treatment must include large quantities of zinc and pyridoxine. Then treatment response will be satisfactory.

The importance of this kryptopyrrole work should not be under-estimated. It is one of those findings where a well-defined relation-ship is shown between biochemical abnormality and psychiatric syndrome. When injected into animals, kryptopyrrole has also been shown to be toxic. It produces neurological, electroencephalograms and behavioral changes. These are the exact alterations reported by Pfeiffer in his observations of the pyroluriac group. Pyroluriac chil-dren may develop any of several learning and behavioral disorders, while adults develop a form of schizophrenia.

According to Pfeiffer, zinc deficiency will probably be found in the following conditions:

- During pregnancy.
- During the first year of life, when the infant has too much copper and requires more zinc to balance and eliminate the copper excess.
- During rapid growth.
- During puberty, especially in the adolescent male.
- During the teen years when considerable premenstrual tension is present in girls. This tension may be stimulated by birth-control medication, which elevates blood copper levels.
- During any severe stress. Note that chronic zinc deficiency and pyridoxine deficiency may predispose toward cancer. Wounds and burns require much zinc for healing, and hyper-tensives tend to be low in zinc and too high in copper.
- Elderly people may develop confusion that is misdiagnosed as senility simply from defective intake of zinc.
- During excessive intake of copper. Even 2 mg. per day of copper will accumulate and eventually produce toxicity if zinc levels are low. Too many preparations including vitamins con-tain added copper. There is so much copper in our water that no copper should be added to our pills and tablets, but it is.
- During starvation, zinc will be lost. Then both cadmium intake and copper levels will be too high.
- During any serious illness. Chronic leukemia, for example, is associated with very low zinc levels. Note that there is no adverse effect by calcium on zinc absorption.

Remarkable safety has been observed with ingestion of zinc salts. In one study, sixteen geriatrics were given 220 mg. of zinc sulfate three times a day. Six patients did develop diarrhea. The plasma zinc increased in four weeks from a normal level of 100 micrograms per 100 ml. to 150 mcg. Beneficial changes took place in patients. I myself have been using zinc dosages at those levels for many years without any adverse side effects other than what one would see with any nonspecific intolerance to tablet medications. Pfeiffer reports that he has treated over 1700 patients with zinc with no serious side effects also. Simkin using 220 mg. three times each day found very positive effects in treating patients with rheumatoid arthritis. There were very few side effects.

IRON

Hemoglobin holds most of the body's iron. This complex red substance, derived from the combining of iron and protein, carries oxygen to the tissue cells throughout the bloodstream. Very little iron is present in muscle, but a small quantity is carried in the blood plasma bound to transferrin, a beta globulin substance. If free iron ions were floating in the plasma, the effect would be toxic. Consequently, it is noteworthy that iron deficiency will cause an insufficiency of hemoglobin with resultant anemia.

Dr. Paul Cutler found that iron overload was very common and caused depression, lethargy and disabling fatigue. He successfully treated seven patients with the chelating drug deferoxamine. It is given by injection 10 mg./kg. twice weekly until iron levels have returned to normal and symptoms are gone. High doses of iron are associated with an increased risk of heart disease since iron increases the formation of free radicals in the body. Antioxidants such as vitamin E and ascorbic acid inhibit excess oxidation reactions.

Pfeiffer believes that iron deficiency anemia is much less of a problem than commercial advertising would have us believe. In disguise, zinc and pyridoxine deficiencies can cause anemia, and that may be the condition attributed to lack of iron. He recommends, therefore, that serum iron levels should be taken for a more accurate diagnosis of iron deficiency anemia. It is more likely to occur where extensive blood loss takes place, as with excessive menstrual flow, a large loss over a short period or a small loss over a longer period. For this reason, women are more apt to suffer from anemia between puberty and the menopause. Iron deficiency anemia diagnosis must involve a search for the source of the blood loss.

Thomas Sydenham, an English physician, reported three hundred years ago that simple iron salts were helpful for some cases of chlorosis. Iron is found in the greatest concentration in lean meat, organ meats, dark green leafy vegetables and whole-grain cereals.

In contrast with zinc, of which it is difficult to accumulate an excess, oversaturation is relatively simple with iron. A variety of factors, when there is no chronic blood loss, will increase the iron absorption. If it continues for many years, too much iron absorption will lead to toxicity. This toxicity may appear in men after age forty; its symptoms will not be specific, and seem to be associated with various forms of malnutrition. In the old days, when iron cooking pots were used extensively, it was possible to obtain too much iron from the action of acidic foods in dissolving iron from the pots; this is no longer a danger because of the widespread use of aluminum, glass and stainless steel vessels.

An attempt by the Food and Drug Administration to increase the amount of iron present in food by enriching cereal grains aroused much controversy. Most white flour already contains additional iron, as well as thiamine, riboflavin and nicotinamide. The FDA's move was stalled by a vigorous counterattack of physicians and nutritionists who were concerned about the dangers of further buildup of iron levels in the body.

MANGANESE

The body contains 10 to 20 mg. of manganese, with the diet providing 2 to 9 mg. About 45 percent is absorbed from food, and 4 mg. is excreted daily. Manganese deficiency is associated with growth impairment, abnormalities in bone, diabetic-like carbohydrate changes, lack of coordination, tardive dyskinesia and convulsions.

As does the mineral zinc, manganese decreases the absorption of copper. Zinc and manganese work synergistically to reduce copper levels. Zinc alone increases copper excretion in schizophrenics threefold. However, giving zinc alone may induce a manganese deficiency. Adding manganese increases the excretion even more. The combination is a valuable treatment for schizophrenia. Like many of the other trace elements, manganese participates in a number of body reactions. It is required for the synthesis of acetylcholine, which is a neurotransmitter, and a deficiency may be causally connected with diabetes mellitus as diabetics seemingly have less manganese in their bodies. The nutritional importance of manganese is discussed by Dr. Freeland-Graves.

Tranquilizers create a major toxic reaction called tardive dyskinesia, which is a motor disorder that can be irreversible. The tranquilizers bind to manganese, are excreted carrying it with them and so cause a deficiency. About 25 percent of patients on tranquilizers a long time will get it. However, it does not occur when orthomolecular regimens are used. In fact, Dr. R. Kunin found it very helpful in removing tardive dyskinesia very quickly. I have seen the same response to manganese in the few patients who have come to me with this toxic reaction. Patients I have treated since 1955 do not get this dreadful condition. Manganese also plays a role in seizure disorders not related to drugs.

Doses up to 30 mg. are safe but are seldom needed. I usually use less than 50 mg. doses. If the drug companies would put 1 mg. of manganese into every tranquilizer table, tardive dyskinesia would disappear. I recommended this to one company, but nothing has been done about it. Good natural sources of manganese are tropical fruits and tea. Perhaps English schizophrenics who drink tea do not get tardive dyskinesia as often as American patients.

Rarely has manganese toxicity occurred, and then only from industrial accidents, not from food or tablets. Too little manganese is a more likely condition and for the usual reasons of depletion of the soil. The addition of lime to soil binds manganese in a way that greatly decreases the amount present in leafy material grown for food, and good processing also diminishes the content of this mineral. In cereals, manganese, as with most minerals, will be found in the bran and germ which is removed from white flour.

COPPER

Copper has been called the fourth heavy metal intoxicant by Dr. Pfeiffer. Its daily requirement in human nutrition is probably under 2 mg. per day, and this level is so small that it is hardly likely that any diet will contain less. A few infants, fed only a dairy milk diet, have been known to develop a true copper deficiency, but no other cases are known. Among all his patients tested, Pfeiffer found no one in whom blood copper levels were low. The small amount of copper required by the body is necessary for the synthesis of hemoglobin. In animals, lack of the element may occur when they graze on grass growing in copper-deficient soils. Living in the same area, though, people do not develop any such evidence of insufficiency.

Babies are born with high copper levels in their bodies. From five to fifteen years will pass before a person reaches lower and more normal adult levels.

An excessive ingestion of copper will present health problems. The widespread use of copper pipes in our plumbing systems brings about leaching of the mineral into our water supply. It's a good idea to avoid drinking the first water that comes from the tap. Let it run for perhaps five minutes in order to reduce the copper levels found in water that has lingered for a long time in copper pipes.

The belief that copper deficiency is a problem has become so well entrenched that many vitamin or mineral preparations contain added copper, which is only a contaminant. That is why in the "average" vitamin formula given in Chapter Nine, it is suggested that you avoid taking in any more copper.

Copper levels are increased in the blood by the use of estrogens, as in birth control medication. This is the probable cause of depression arising from this medication's ingestion.

For decades it has been suspected that high blood copper is associated with schizophrenia, and now much evidence to confirm this has been found. Adult psychotic patients have an excess of copper that has apparently produced a schizophrenic syndrome or depression; such an excess is also connected to learning and behavioral disorders in children. Carl Pfeiffer has expressed concern about copper as a cause of senility. He points out that copper supplementation is a definite possibility for senile causation.

Food overdosage with copper offers no danger, and the best sources for the mineral are grains and vegetables. Zinc and manganese decrease copper absorption and decrease copper blood levels. Therefore, zinc and manganese supplements are advantageous as copper diluents. To sum up, evidence exists that both iron and copper excesses are undesirable.

CHROMIUM

First recognized as an essential element in 1957, chromium has been shown to increase glucose tolerance in rats. The glucose tolerance factor (GTF) should be considered a new vitamin, suggests Dr. Pfeiffer. GTF is an essential co-factor in the activity of insulin and contains one atom of chromium, two molecules of nicotinic acid and several amino acids. Now commercially available as chromium picolinate, it has received intensive investigation as a treatment for diabetes mellitus and other carbohydrate diseases.

Whether chromium deficiency occurs is dependent upon the amount present in the drinking water, which is variable. However, insufficient chromium is a more common state than excess chromium, since the best sources are thrown away as food waste. As are other mineral nutrients, chromium is present in bran and germ of grains. Whole wheat contains about 1.7 micrograms of chromium per gram, while white flour made into bread contains only .14 microgram per gram. This mineral is also stripped away from white sugar in the refining process, even though the cane or beets tend to be high in its content. The best sources for chromium are the easily available brewer's yeast, sugar beet molasses, which is harder to get, and such meats as liver and beef.

Early investigations pointed to chromium as a toxic substance rather than an essential element. This probably was thought because so little was needed by the body. As with other elements active in such low quantities, the procedure would be to use too much at first and observe its toxicity, which is what happened. Chromium is *not* toxic, however, and it is impossible to get too much of it from any food source.

SELENIUM

In just over thirty-five years, selenium has changed from being considered highly toxic to being classed as one of the essential trace elements. It is in the group of minerals required in amounts of less than 1 mg. per day; about 200 mcg. per day is recommended. As with other highly potent elements, it is toxic in high dosages, but these are rarely derived from food sources, as our present diets are apt to contain foods not up to par in selenium. The mineral is very unevenly distributed in the soil, varying from concentrations producing toxicity in plants utilized by grazing animals to total absence. Populations living on selenium-rich soils have less cancer. Selenium-rich soils are found in the Great Plains and Rocky Mountain states. The Northeast, East and Northwest of the United States are very low in selenium as is southern British Columbia and Vancouver Island. Southern Vancouver Island, which also has more mercury, has a very high incidence of cancer. Animals on the island must be given selenium or they will not grow and thrive.

Selenium's uneven distribution does not preclude its having several important functions. First, it does protect animals against toxic levels of trace poisons such as cadmium and mercury. Selenium (1) promotes growth, (2) protects against mercury, cadmium, arsenic, silver and copper and (3) protects against cancer. Indications for supplementing with selenium include anticancer, anti-aging and as an antidote to heavy metal poisoning. Selenium also greatly increases the efficacy of vitamin E. Third, selenium is a possible inhibitor of cancer. It acts as an antioxidant and prevents chromosome breaks and it is known that when selenium intake has been low, the cancer rate has been high. In a recent study it was found that people had low selenium levels before they had their myocardial infarction. The therapeutic dose is between 200 and 600 mcg. daily. Patients have taken up to 2000 mcg., but I do not recommend it.

Selenium also has antidepressant properties, and many patients may prefer it to the major antidepressants. Benton and Cook found that subjects receiving 100 mcg. of selenium compared with a placebo had improved mood over a five-week period. I have been giving my depressed patients 200 mcg. twice each day when they do not want to take drugs, and the results have been good. Patients on diets low in selenium will probably respond the best.

The best food sources for selenium are brewer's yeast, garlic, liver and eggs. Foods from animal sources are richer in the element than are plant foods, and processing greatly decreases its content in food.

LITHIUM

Lithium is used for the treatment of manic-depressive psychosis in large doses (megadoses) ranging around 1000 mg. (1 gram) per day. Some time ago a suggestion was offered that lithium levels in water were related to depression: where lithium levels were higher there was less depression. The suggestion was never explored and presents a worthwhile topic for further biochemical research.

Other than as antipsychotic therapy, lithium has no known use in the body, and has been considered one of the neutral or innocuous elements, neither therapeutic nor harmful. An average diet contains about 2 milligrams per day. Its only possible general use as an essential trace element is for mood control. This proposition would be difficult to examine, however, as it would be hard to feed animals a lithium-free diet even if they could describe their moods to us, and it would certainly be impossible to maintain human subjects on diets free of lithium. It occurs naturally in many foods.

Megalithium or megamineral therapy has been readily accepted as orthodox psychiatric treatment, in contradistinction to the opposition confronting megavitamin therapy. Orthomolecular psychiatrists can't say or understand why there is this paradoxical reaction from orthodox psychiatrists. I have been using 300 mg. of lithium per day for a number of patients to improve energy levels, remove fatigue, eliminate depression and alter mood changes associated with multiple food allergies, and the results have been gratifying.

COBALT

Other than being an essential component of vitamin B12, cobalt appears to have no role in the body. There has been no evidence of human lack of cobalt, but it has occurred in cattle and sheep in Australia and New Zealand from poor soil. In 1966, an epidemic of cobalt toxicity took place in Canada when the mineral was added to beer to preserve its foamy head. A large number of heavy beer drinkers who had poor nutrition were poisoned.

MOLYBDENUM

Our diets are probably as defective in molybdenum as they are for reasons similar to those behind our chromium deficiency. Modern food technology removes the mineral nutrients. As a result most people will need orthomolecular nutritional supplementation in the form of unprocessed foods heavy in molybdenum. These include animal organs, shellfish, many vegetables (especially lima beans, lentils, green beans, potatoes and spinach), grains, fruits and sunflower seeds. The mineral may prevent dental caries and may protect against esophageal cancer.

There appears to be an inverse relationship between molybdenum and copper. This is affirmed by sheep grazing on pasture rich in molybdenum, which develop a copper deficiency and fail to produce pigment in their wool. By alternating between high-molybdenum and high-copper feeding, it is possible to produce wool banded black and white.

TOXIC MINERALS

Various toxic elements are known, and include lead, mercury, cadmium, bismuth and perhaps aluminum. Paradoxically, they may be required elements, but with such low dosages needed it's impossible to determine what the dosages are. There will be no shortage of these minerals, since contamination of our environment provides more than enough abundance. No individual will ever show a minus quantity.

DIAGNOSING METAL TOXICITY

The final diagnosis of metal toxicity is made by laboratory tests such as blood analysis, urine analysis and hair analysis. Hair analysis remains controversial, with most physicians ignorant of the technique and its value or strongly opposed to it. Since it is seldom done by regular laboratories, the increasing demand for this analysis is being met by private laboratories and is readily accessible today.

Dr. J. Campbell reviewed hair analysis as a diagnostic tool. Since 1983 there have been over 1,500 citations on hair analysis. It is measured using an atomic absorption spectrophotometer. The results are reproducible and reliable. They are very valuable for measuring the mineral status of the body using live tissue. The mineral status measured represents the status at the time the hair was still in the follicle. Thus it is possible to examine hair serially and determine what happened some months before.

Campbell summarized the important relationships between the values in hair and other measures. Copper levels in hair are correlated with copper levels in liver. High cadmium is related to hypertension, aluminum to Alzheimer's disease and lead levels to atmospheres rich in lead as near lead smelters. Low chromium and zinc were related to diabetes; high levels of calcium and magnesium indicated osteoporosis or decalcification. All low minerals indicated malabsorption. As an illustration of its usefulness, Weber et al. found that malnourished children had lower hair zinc while copper and iron levels were higher. Hair zinc levels were a good measure of nutritional status. Cromwell and coworkers found hair analysis useful in distinguishing between violent and nonviolent criminals. Vance and his group found that hair analysis showed several elements were involved, including mercury which was higher in the hair of Alzheimer's patients.

Campbell concluded that hair analysis was useful for screening: (1) populations at risk for toxic metal exposure; (2) people working in the mining and metallurgy industry; (3) children with learning and behavioral disorders; (4) people associated with violence and other antisocial behavior; (5) and diagnosing metabolic disorders before they became well entrenched.

LEAD AND MERCURY

Lead has contaminated our environment through its free use in gasoline, paint and the manufacture of common articles. *Mercury* has contaminated lake and river water where industrial waste chemicals have been dumped. It has gotten into fish flesh and thus poisoned people who ate it.

Mercury is a highly toxic liquid mineral that vaporizes very easily. It has been known for many years as a brain toxin that causes psychosis. The mad hatters of Europe were mercury-intoxicated hat makers. Very rarely has mercury been inhaled in excess from faulty purification of air, as is definitely the case with lead. However, in one month about 20 years ago I saw three men with the schizophrenic syndrome caused by prolonged inhalation of pure liquid mercury. Eliminating the mercury eliminated the psychotic condition. Marlowe and his colleagues have found higher levels of lead and mercury in the hair of emotionally disturbed children.

The major source of intoxication from mercury comes from our mouths—from the mercury amalgams dentists have introduced. The mercury is thereafter absorbed both from the vapor and from direct contact with tissue in the gums. However, this view is stoutly attacked by both the dental profession and the medical profession. The debate is as vigorous for mercury from our amalgams as it was for lead in gasoline and as it is for fluoride, but it has not yet entered the public arena as have the other two controversies.

Dr. Hal Huggins is one of the early and strongest critics of the use of mercury amalgams. He is now supported by many investigators. The sharpest scientific support comes from Dr. Murray J. Vimy, clinical professor in the Department of Medicine, University of Calgary, and Dr. D. Shwartzendruber, chair of the Biology Department, University of Colorado. Dr. Shwartzendruber presented evidence to the Washington State Dental Disciplinary Board which held hearings in 1991 on a proposed restriction regarding dentists making statements against the use of mercury amalgams. He noted that mercury amalgams contain over 50 percent mercury, 35 percent silver, 13 percent tin and lesser amounts of copper. Contrary to the view put forward by the dental profession, mercury is not harmless when present in the amalgam with other metals, since it gradually disappears from the amalgams and seeps into the rest of the body. It is released as a vapor that increases with chewing. The amount released accumulates daily. The mercury lodges in the tissues, is absorbed by the lungs and intestinal tract and accumulates in the brain and other organs. Methyl mercury is absorbed from the mouth and goes directly to the brain. Shwartzendruber added that it affected all tissues as a general toxin. There is no safe level except zero. He concluded that the World Health Organization had determined that amalgams were the prime source of human mercury exposure. In his view people generally looked upon mercury toxicity as close to asbestos and DDT, above lead paint and auto emissions and slightly below PCBs and uranium mining.

Dr. Murray Vimy also reported the results of his studies with sheep to the Washington State Dental Disciplinary Board Public Hearing. He placed mercury amalgams in sheep, and within 30 days substantial amounts of mercury were taken into their tissues. The same occurred with monkeys. He then referred to studies which showed that Alzheimer's patients have 5 to 8 times as much mercury in their brain than the normal population. The greatest amount was found in those parts of the brain where the Alzheimer's lesions were present. He concluded that (1) mercury is released from amalgams; (2) it is released continuously when we chew; (3) in animals it is taken into the tissues, particularly the liver, gastrointestinal tract and kidneys; (4) it can induce pathopathology in sheep; (5) removal of the mercury improves kidney function; (6) there is a link to Alzheimer's disease; and (7) there is a link with development of antibiotic-resistant bacteria. In the face of such testimony, the board eventually decided not to make their pernicious recommendation.

It has also been shown that mercury fillings also weaken the effectiveness of antibiotics against bacteria. Experiments carried out at three medical centers, including the University of Calgary, University of Georgia and Tufts University School of Medicine, on monkeys showed that these animals developed a resistance to mercury and to antibiotics. This means that for some patients the usual amount of antibiotics will be inadequate and they will have to be given much higher doses. For others the antibiotic will be ineffective at any dose. The implications are chilling. Some bacteria were resistant to six antibiotics. However, the dental association laughed at this possibility. Said one member, "I have amalgam fillings in my mouth and I'm not going to take them out."

Recently Siblerud found that a very significant deterioration of psychological health occurred in people with mercury amalgams. They were more depressed, had less peace of mind and had more problems in concentration. They had more than twice as many complaints, including sudden outbursts of anger, depression, irritability and anxiety. They craved sweets more, smoked more and drank more coffee and alcohol. A further study on subjects after the mercury was removed showed that 80 percent felt much better. They were less nervous, less depressed, felt more confident and their memory was better. Recently one of my female patients, who had been depressed for many years and had failed to get well after two years of psychiatric treatment, had all her amalgams removed. Within a few weeks she was free of depression.

Not everyone needs to have their amalgams removed, even though that would be ideal. But whenever a person has any physical or mental problem for which there appears to be no cause and which has remained untreatable, it is important to examine whether mercury amalgams might be a decisive factor. Dentists take special precautions not to expose themselves to mercury. Even their associations which strongly defend the use of mercury advise their members not to be exposed to it. They think it is all right to maintain continuous exposure in one's mouth but not in their offices. Even undertakers now have to be careful. With so many bodies being cremated containing mercury, there is a great danger that the mercury vapor will injure them while working.

Dentists should have mercury analysis of blood and urine and certain conductivity tests in the mouth, plus professional examination of their teeth. Everyone should insist that no new mercury amalgams be used so they will gradually be replaced with other material. When the demand for other, safer compositions becomes noticeable, manufacturers will surely meet the demand, and dentists will learn the necessary skills with which to work with these materials.

Heavy-metal intoxication will produce hyperactivity in children, the schizophrenic syndrome in adults and probably some cases of senility. Treatment requires removal of the metal by the use of chelating agents. *Chelates*, as described previously, are substances that combine with toxic minerals and allow their elimination in the urine. Ascorbic acid has chelating properties. The best course of action is to avoid contamination by these toxic metals. Unfortunately, the average person is not aware of the dangers of these common substances and has no idea of how to avoid them. Treatment of trace element toxicity lies in the province of orthomolecular medicine through use of orthomolecular nutrition.

NICKEL

Adult humans consume about 0.5 mg. per day of nickel. It may be essential, and a deficiency in the chick will produce several pathological changes. Nickel is present in higher concentration in ribonucleic acid (RNA) than in the surrounding material and may play a role in maintaining the configuration of the molecule. It is also thought to play a role in pigmentation in some animals. Vegetables contain more nickel than do animals. Tea and buckwheat seed are particularly rich in it, as are herring and oysters, but it is low in meat, eggs and milk. By itself, nickel is relatively nontoxic, but organic compounds such as nickel carbonyl are very toxic. They produce respiratory changes and are carcinogenic. Cigarette smoke contains nickel carbonyl, and the quantity found in fifteen cigarettes per day smoked for one year has been shown to be carcinogenic. High serum levels of nickel are found after myocardial infarction, strokes and severe burns while very low levels are found when cirrhosis of the liver is present. Diets which avoid junk foods have adequate amounts of nickel.

TIN

Tin may be another essential trace element in mammals; however, very little is present in newborn infants. It arrives in the body later on. It tends to accumulate with age, especially in the lungs. Because tin is absorbed very poorly, it is relatively nontoxic. The average consumption is about 2 mg. per day. Foods stored in tin cans absorb some tin, even when they are lacquered, but lacquering does reduce solution in the food. High levels of tin intake can cause anemia, but this is prevented by adequate amounts of iron.

FLUORINE

Fluorine is one of the most controversial elements, since it has not yet been shown to be an essential trace element, but it does increase the strength of teeth and bones. It is being used to treat osteoporosis. When present in water at about one part per million, fluorine tends to decrease caries of teeth. If too much is present, mottling of the teeth occurs, and this mottling is irreversible. It does not prevent gum disease caused by bad nutrition and the consumption of junk food, especially sweets. Dean Burk has gathered evidence that there is a positive relationship between the presence of added fluoride to drinking water and the increased incidence of cancer in those communities that add it. There is also evidence that levels of fluoride in drinking water are related to the development of thyroid disease; the higher the fluoride level, whether natural or fortified, the more thyroid problems are found in the community.

Generally, the authors do not favor the compulsory consumption of fluoride. People who wish to treat their teeth with fluoride have every right to have this done by using topical application of fluoride preparations to their teeth. But they must not be lulled into thinking this means they can continue to eat sweets to their hearts' content. Those who do not wish to ingest fluoride should not be forced to do so. Ideally, if communities determine by majority vote to obtain their fluorides in this way, there should be two sets of water supply giving each householder a choice.

BROMINE

Bromine is not an essential trace element, as far as we know; however, future experiments may demonstrate that it is. It can interchange with chloride in the body. Marine plants are naturally richer than land plants in bromine, and potassium bromate is added to some flours to hasten the maturation of flour. This is another example of adding something to our food for cosmetic reasons even though it has no nutritional value and might be deleterious.

ARSENIC

Arsenic compounds have been favorite poisons of industry and murderers for many years. With the introduction of hair analysis of arsenic, the murderer is much less apt to remain undetected. Arsenic compounds have been used for therapy in the past. For instance, Ehrlich's famous substance 606, "the magic bullet," was the first substance found to be toxic against spirochetes of syphilis. Apparently the pure mineral is not that toxic. In the mountains of central Europe natives used to eat 1 to 2 grams per day of the mineral arsenic because they believed it helped increase endurance at high elevations, and may still do so.

VANADIUM

Vanadium is essential for rats and chickens and perhaps for people too. It is rapidly used and then excreted as urine. It is present in high concentration in fats and vegetable oils. In such concentration, it lowers cholesterol levels. Vanadium is nontoxic, as it is poorly absorbed; about 2 mg. per day is present in the diet.

STRONTIUM

Strontium is not an essential trace element, unless it is required in such low quantities that it will be difficult to ever establish it as an essential dietary component. Because strontium tends to accumulate in bone, radioactive strontium, one of the products of atomic explosions, is particularly hazardous.

ALUMINUM

Increased quantities of aluminum are apt to be ingested nowadays, compared to past years, because it is used for making cooking utensils. Acid cooking fluid will increase the solution of aluminum. It is also present in baking powders and in antacid preparations. Excess aluminum hydroxide gels will reduce blood phosphate and have an adverse effect on bones. It has no use in the body. About 35 mg. per day of aluminum is normally consumed. Pfeiffer has suggested that excess aluminum may be a factor in the genesis of senility.

The evidence pointing to aluminum as one of the causes of Alzheimer's disease is powerful and becoming stronger. Prof. D.R. Crapper McLachlan, director of the Centre for Research in Neurondegenerative Disease at the University of Toronto, concluded that public health efforts to reduce exposure to aluminum would reduce the incidence of Alzheimer's disease. He reviewed four lines of evidence: (1) aluminum-impaired learning and memory performance in animals; (2) aluminum-induced neurochemical changes in the brain, where it interferes with over 65 different reactions in the body (even moderate increases of aluminum in the blood are toxic); (3) many epidemiological studies supporting the hypothesis; and (4) a study showing that if aluminum is removed using deferoxamine (a substance that binds aluminum and reduces the amount in the body), there is less deterioration compared with a control group.

Although aluminum is found in food and added to drinking water, many processed foods, toothpaste and a variety of cosmetics, Dr. McLachlan made the following suggestions: (1) exposure to aluminum should be minimized; (2) public action is necessary; (3) aluminum content should be listed on packages and in cosmetic products; (4) municipal processed water should be regulated so there is less than 50 mcg. per liter and eventually less than 10 mcg.; and (5) daily intake should be lowered to 3 mg. or less.

GOLD AND SILVER

Gold and silver are not required nutrients. They are probably toxic because of the strong oxidizing properties of their salts. Gold is used for some forms of arthritis when nothing else has worked, but it has to be employed with great care. Orthomolecular physicians prefer to use vitamin B3, which is probably more effective and nontoxic. Silver was used in the form of a drug, argyrol; it caused some undesirable reactions and is no longer used in medicine.

IODINE

Iodine deficiency was first suggested in 1830 as an environmental factor causing hypothyroidism. But like many discoveries in medicine, a number of decades were required before the idea was taken seriously. Iodine is a component of the thyroid hormone thyroxin. When there is too little iodine, there is a deficiency of thyroxin. This results in pathological changes in the thyroid gland and in the rest of the body. When this occurs early in life, physical and mental growth is stunted, producing cretinism and feeblemindedness. About 100 to 200 micrograms of iodine per day are required. Foods grown on soils deficient in iodine will contain so little of the element that people living on produce from these soils will develop iodine deficiencies. Large areas of the earth are said to be goitrogenic because of this.

The best food sources for iodine are water, especially in regions where there is enough, in the soil and from seafood. To be on the safe side, only iodized salt should be used. Those who wish to increase their iodine intake without increasing their salt intake may do so by taking more seafood and by adding products from the sea like kelp in their diets. Increasing iodine intake in this way may even decrease the tendency for developing cancer of the breast. It so happens that the glandular tissue of the breast bears some similarity to the glandular tissue of the thyroid gland.

TREATMENT OF MINERAL TOXICITY

The source of the toxic mineral must first be determined and withdrawn. Then an orthomolecular diet should be instituted. Removing additives decreases the toxic burden on the body, and adding fiber increases the excretion of toxic minerals. Then chelating compounds should be used. The safest is ascorbic acid, which should be given in optimum doses. The three other chelating compounds which bind minerals and remove them are penicillamine for copper, desferoxamine for aluminum and iron and EDTA for iron and other compounds. (When chelating compounds are given by vein in a series of treatments, it is called chelation therapy.) Finally, one should use natural antidotes such as selenium against mercury and cadmium, zinc and manganese against copper and zinc against cadmium. Psychotic reactions, whether schizophrenic-like or toxic, are best treated with optimum doses of vitamin B3 as well as whatever drugs they may need.

11

How to Find Out If Your Diet Is Normal

There are many people who are well and therefore do not need to modify their diet. They have found the diet to which they are best adapted. Any modification of their diet would likely make them worse if it were continued for a long time. However, if you have any doubts about your diet or your health, you need to find out for yourself it you have good health and see if it can be made better by changing the foods you consume. There are two aspects to this. The first is the short-term outlook: Are you well now? The second involves a long-term outlook. Since the mean age at death is now close to 75, most people will live many decades. In my view one's state of health ought to be so good that there is no deterioration toward the end of one's life.

PRESENT STATE OF HEALTH

Most people know when they are in good health. They are able to feel rested and relaxed after 6 to 8 hours of sleep, and they awaken in the morning feeling well and looking forward to the day. They enjoy the food they eat. At work or at home they have enough energy to do what they want and need to accomplish. They carry on throughout the day without becoming excessively sleepy or tired, nor do they become excessively tired in the evening. If such changes occur in the midmorning or midafternoon, they usually indicate that food allergies are present. During the day and later on at home they remain in good humor, free of depression unless there is something which would depress any other normal person, such as the loss of a job, death of a friend or family member or a major disappointment or loss. When they do feel sad, this clears in time as it does for normal people. They do not suffer prolonged, deep depression long after the event which precipitated it has passed. They enjoy their work or profession, or if it cannot be enjoyed, they tolerate it and find other activities to make up for what they are not getting from their work. They make decisions which are rational most of the time. They are able to deal with stress, and when they get sick, they recover in fewer days than most people who are not well. If this is your state of health, you are in my opinion in good health.

I use four main criteria for evaluating the state of health of my psychiatric patients: (1) Are they free of signs and symptoms? (2) Are they getting on reasonably well with their family? (3) Are they getting on reasonably well with the community? (4) Are they working either at home or on the job, and are they paying taxes? I define work as any activity a person does whether or not they are being paid to do it. Paying taxes indicates one is able to work and is one of the best measures of recovery. Very few schizophrenics on tranquilizers are able to work. If my patients fail to achieve even one of these four main points, I do not consider them well.

To evaluate your own health you should ask yourself the following questions:

1. Do you have enough energy to do what you want to do or are you suffering from fatigue? Are you tired too much of the time, especially when it's not appropriate to be tired?
2. Is your mood fairly stable, with swings into depression or cheerfulness appropriate to events around you? Would such swings be considered appropriate by other people in similar circumstances?
3. Do you feel well? Or do you have symptoms which indicate you are suffering from any disease? If this is the case, you should consult your doctor and clear up whatever disease you have. If you do not have any known condition, you should then determine whether you are suffering from one of the many forms of malnutrition, from a defect arising from poor diet, from a vitamin or mineral deficiency or from any one of the nutrient dependencies.

IF YOU ARE WELL

Not much needs to be done when you are well. Either you are already on a good diet to which you have adapted, or you have a marvelous constitution and biochemistry so that you can remain well even on a less-than-perfect diet. Your only concern is for the future. It would be wise to tighten up the diet by following the principles described in this book and to supplement this by taking the optimum amount of vitamin C and a good B-complex preparation one or more each day. Many people are surprised how much better they feel after following a program for several months. They had considered themselves normal, but when they felt so much better afterward, they realized they had not been well originally.

Many years ago a high school teacher came to see me with his identical twin schizophrenic brother. His brother had been ill for many years and was not able to work. I prescribed vitamin B3 and vitamin C for him and arranged to see him regularly to follow his progress. Several months later the normal brother asked me whether he could take the same vitamins. I assured him that he could. He had seen great improvement in his twin and wondered what the supplements might do for him. A few months later he confirmed that he felt much better on the vitamins.

I have seen the same realization in families where the mother and/ or wife became my patient. I advised her to follow a good diet, usually eliminating sugar, junk foods and very often milk, plus any other food she might be allergic to, and outlined which vitamins to take. Very often the husband, who was well, did not want to give up sweets and desserts, and my patient did not want to deprive him of these. After a few months my patient would often tell me the whole family had had the flu and she had remained well; in the past she would have developed the same infections that they had. Then, after many months of preparing two sets of meals, one for herself and one for the rest of the family, she would decide to place the whole family on her diet, primarily because she was now well. Then I would hear from her how her husband was more energetic, less irritable and more relaxed and the whole family was much healthier.

Every person, no matter how well they feel, can determine very easily how well they really are by placing themselves on a natural diet with or without supplements.

IF YOU ARE NOT WELL

The first step is to have a medical checkup by your doctor. Anything you and the doctor find must be corrected. After that you should follow a procedure of improving your diet and adding the correct supplements. It is desirable to do this with medical supervision, but you may find it very difficult to find a physician or nutritionist able to advise you, though this field is opening up very rapidly. If you cannot find a trained professional to advise you, the next best thing is to read everything you can about how to do so, in addition to this book. Then take the following four steps.

Step 1.   Eliminate all junk foods from your diet, especially all the free sugars and any food you suspect you might be allergic to. Add vitamin C 1 gram after each meal. Stay on this diet for at least one month. If by then you feel well, this is your diet. If you are not any better or have gained only a little, examine your diet again for other possible food allergies. Then eliminate them and carry on for another month. If you cannot find any other food allergies, go to step 2.

Step 2.   Add a good B-complex tablet or one of the stress tablets. I like the B-complex 50 or 100 preparations. You can take as many as you wish, but in most cases 1 to 3 tablets per day will be adequate. These all contain riboflavin, vitamin B2, which will color your urine yellow. This is a good test of whether or not the vitamins are being absorbed in the gastrointestinal tract. Stay on this program for several months. If you have not reached the state of wellbeing you want, then start to add other individual vitamins. The main objective of this book is to describe these nutrients and how to use them well enough so that you can use them safely. All these nutrients are compatible and can be taken together, usually with food. Nutrients are compatible with all medication and with each other.

Step 3.   For the rest of your life keep reviewing both your diet and the supplements you are taking because requirements change with age, sickness and degree of stress. There is only one way of knowing, and that is to be alert to the changes in your body and to the changes you must make in your diet. It is necessary to maintain a continual adjustment between your needs and the foods you eat.

Step 4.   If you are still not well, you probably have very serious problems and will have to consult specialists in the field of ortho-molecular medicine and psychiatry.

12

The Treatment of Cancer

WHY I STARTED TO ADVISE CANCER PATIENTS

It was my practice in 1960 to test the urine of patients for what we then called the *mauve factor*, now known to be kryptopyrrole (KP). We had found it in the majority of schizophrenic patients but in hardly any normal subjects. To my surprise, it was also found in many patients with cancer of the lung. In fact, one patient diagnosed with organic confusional psychosis arising from lung cancer metastases to the brain became mentally normal three days after starting niacin and vitamin C therapy. To my further surprise, this patient, who had been placed on terminal care, kept coming for over 30 months. One year after he started taking these two vitamins, his lung were entirely clear, and the head of the cancer clinic began to think he had never had cancer in the first place.

I then examined the urine of 34 cancer patients for KP. Only one had been given any vitamin therapy. Thirteen excreted KP, and their mean survival was 647 days after their urine was tested. The 21 without the factor lived 297 days.

My second patient, a 16-year-old girl with an osteogenic sarcoma (Ewings sarcoma), was scheduled for an amputation in a month. I started her on niacinamide and ascorbic acid 3 grams each daily. When her tumor regressed, surgery was canceled, and she has remained well since 1962.

Another patient's recovery convinced me that this treatment ought to be examined much more. In July 1979 a patient, age 59, was referred to me with a tumor of the head of the pancreas that was obstructing her bile duct. After surgery to unblock the duct, she was discharged from hospital and began to take ascorbic acid 10 grams daily. I increased this to 40 grams per day and added vitamin B3 and a few other nutrients. Six months later no tumor was visible on a scan, and her original bile duct had reopened. The owner of a bookstore, she has told everyone about her recovery through vitamins. Her friends who developed cancer got themselves referred to me, and each year the number of new patients has increased until now it has reached almost 1,500 new cases each year.

By the time I had treated about 45 patients, it had become evident that the patients who were able to follow an orthomolecular program lived a lot longer than did those who did not. I discussed my preliminary results with Dr. Linus Pauling, who urged me to follow up every patient I had treated. Our report was published in 1990.

SOURCES OF PATIENTS

If special diagnostic and therapeutic advice was required, a patient was referred by his or her family doctor or general practitioner, who remained in charge of the patient's treatment. This meant the patient had already been diagnosed, evaluated and treated for physical ailments. The majority of patients referred to me were psychiatric, including the usual run of depressions, schizophrenics, addicts, behavioral problems and children with learning and/or behavioral disorders.

At first almost all the patients had already been given surgery, irradiation and chemotherapy in various combinations. They came because they had failed to respond, relapsed or no further conventional treatment was indicated. A large number of the patients had already exhausted their physical and emotional resources, and by the time they came to see me they were no longer able to cope even with the minor demands that a nutritional program placed upon them. This was especially difficult for single patients; those with families or spouses fared much better with family support. Many of the patients were desperate and had planned to travel to clinics in Mexico or elsewhere to receive alternative treatment but put this off after seeing me. Some went even after that. They were thus highly motivated, an important factor.

Only in the past few years have I been seeing a larger number of early patients where it is possible to start them on a nutritional program at almost the same time they start conventional therapy. This is the ideal; someday, the whole armamentarium of treatment will be started simultaneously for every cancer patient.

THE TREATMENT PROGRAM

The treatment was almost the same for every type of patient and cancer, since it was aimed at improving their physical health and was not directed at the type of cancer. Of course, treatment was also individualized, since the response varies so much with different patients. Before advising them on the nutrients they were going to take, I discussed the type of nutritional program they should follow and had them observe the following general food rules:

1. Avoid, where possible, all prepared foods containing added sugar. It is possible with this rule to greatly reduce the amount of additives present in commercially prepared foods. It is prudent to avoid all additives as much as possible, especially since they are suspect as potential carcinogens.
2. Decrease intake of salt. This follows the reduction of all processed foods containing added sugar, since they also tend to be rich in salt.
3. Reduce fat consumption as much as possible. Generally, I ask patients to eliminate all dairy products, which is one of the easiest ways of cutting down fat intake.
4. Reduce, but not eliminate, intake of animal protein and increase intake of vegetable foods, raw as much as possible.

Because many patients are physically very ill and have lost a lot of weight, I also try to increase their food intake, using total food preparations such as Boost and Ensure, as needed.

VITAMINS

Ascorbic Acid

There was evidence in the medical literature that ascorbic acid used in optimum doses was therapeutic for cancer patients, but it was only after Linus Pauling became interested, examined the literature and published his book with Ewen Cameron, *Cancer and Vitamin C*, that there was more of a surge of interest in the scientific world than in the medical profession. After a review of the enormous medical literature, Stone also concluded that vitamin C was helpful in the treatment of cancer. Most of the studies used small doses, but Stone believed that much higher doses should be used, especially since vitamin C is one of the safest nutrients known. In one study, for instance, 4 grams daily was shown to improve health and increase tolerance to x-rays. Stone also pointed out that many of the symptoms of leukemia were symptoms of scurvy. White blood cells contain 20 to 30 times as much ascorbic acid as normal cells and sequester the body's supply, producing scurvy in other tissues. He suggested that sufficient vitamin C be given to saturate these cells and leave enough for the rest of the body.

Goth and Littmann found that cancer started in organs whose ascorbic acid levels were under 4.5 mg. per 100 mg. Benade, Howard and Burk at the National Cancer Institute found that ascorbate was highly toxic to Ehrlich's ascites carcinoma, but the institute ignored their work. More recently a number of other researchers provided more supporting data for the earlier Cameron and Pauling studies.

By the early 1990s there was much more interest in the connection between ascorbic acid and cancer. Physicians have begun to recognize that ascorbic acid is one of the most powerful natural antioxidants. Since free radical theories are sweeping the field, it now makes sense to consider all the natural antioxidants, of which vitamin C is one of the best known and most effective. Frei, England and Ames report that ascorbic acid is the most effective water-soluble antioxidant in human blood plasma and suggest that it is of major importance for protection against diseases and degenerative processes caused by oxidative stress. They even suggest that the

RDA should be increased from 60 to 150 mg. daily, thus pointing to the inadequacy of the present RDAs.

The subject of a conference held in London in 1989 and published as a supplement to the *American Journal of Nutrition* (vol. 53, January 1991) was "Antioxidant Vitamins and B-Carotene in Disease Prevention." The evidence showing the relationship between antioxidants such as vitamin C to cancer prevention and to other conditions was very powerful, leading Dr. W. A. Pryor, who summed up the meeting, to conclude: ". . . it may not be many years before the concept of the RDA is broadened, with one daily intake of a nutrient being recommended to prevent known vitamin deficiency diseases and a substantially higher value recommended to optimize the disease-preventing properties of these nutrients. Thus, there is reason for considerable hopefulness about our ability to reduce the incidence of the most life-limiting of the chronic diseases within the coming decades, with the consequent improvement in health, life span and well-being of our citizens."

Another meeting held in 1990 in Bethesda, Maryland, was cosponsored by the National Cancer Institute. One of the factors leading to this meeting was Dr. Linus Pauling's persistent demand that the institute seriously examine the claims that ascorbic acid was useful in the treatment of cancer. The main conclusions arising from this meeting supported the use of vitamin C for the treatment of cancer as follows:

1. Ascorbic acid protected plasma lipids against oxidative damage. It scavenged free radicals, destroying them before they reached the membranes where they could do so much damage.
2. Ascorbic acid decreased the toxicity against normal tissue of drugs used in chemotherapy and decreased the toxicity of radiation, but it did not protect the cancer.
3. Ascorbic acid had anticancer properties. It protected cells against transformation into cancer by methylcholanthrene.
4. An epidemiological survey of the field showed that in 33 out of 46 studies vitamin C was protective, decreasing cancer incidence and mortality.
5. Ascorbic acid had properties that make it an important part of any cancer treatment.

Ascorbic acid is required to make connective tissue so it can help contain or restrict the spread of cancer cells. It is also needed to make noradrenaline and activate hormones. But its major role is to act as an antioxidant minimizing damage caused by oxidative processes. (A later review by Pauling and Rath expands the properties of ascorbic acid into the area of cardiovascular and other diseases.)

Treatment: Usually I advise patients to take 12 grams of crystalline material per day in three divided doses rather than swallow 24 of the 500-mg. tablets. If they can tolerate this amount, they are advised to slowly increase the dose until it becomes almost like a laxative; it usually causes frequent bowel movements and gas when the sublaxative dose is exceeded. They then decrease the dose to a value below this level, with which they are comfortable. Most patients remain on at least 12 grams, but a few go much higher— up to 40 grams per day. After they are well for a few years, many of the patients slowly decrease the dose to a substantially lower level. A few patients are also given intravenous ascorbic acid by their physicians. A very small number of patients cannot tolerate even 50 mg. of ascorbic acid and cannot follow the program. There is a vitamin C preparation called ester-C which is more tolerable for these very sensitive patients.

Ascorbic Acid Decreases Toxicity of Irradiation and Chemotherapy: Ascorbic acid increases the killing effect (toxicity) of irradiation and chemotherapy at the same time that it decreases the toxicity in normal tissue (thereby increasing the therapeutic index). In one study 54 women with cancer of the cervix were treated with irradiation. Half of the group were pretreated for one week with a vitamin-mineral preparation containing vitamin C, and the other half were not. The treated group yielded the best response. Along with other researchers, Hanck concluded that ascorbic acid increased survival and decreased adverse effects of irradiation. In one study, 67 percent of the vitamin-treated group were free of symptoms after six months, compared with 45 percent of the control group. Almost all listed side effects of irradiation were less frequent in the vitamin-treated group. Ascorbic acid reduces one of the dangerous side effects of chemotherapy and radiation—their mutagenic potential.

Vitamin B3

Recent findings have shown that vitamin B3 does have anticancer properties. Niacin and niacinamide are essential in the chemical reaction that produces poly (ADP-ribose) polymerase, an enzyme that is activated when strands of deoxyribonucleic acid (DNA) are broken. Carcinogenic factors such as radiation and chemicals damage the DNA, and this enzyme repairs or counteracts the damage. This was discussed at a 1987 international conference in Texas entitled "Niacin, Nutrition, ADP-Ribosylation and Cancer."

Dr. M. Jacobson, one of the conference organizers, is quoted as saying, "We know that diet is a major risk factor, that diet has both beneficial and detrimental components. What we cannot assess at this point is the optimal amount of niacin in the diet.... The fact that we don't have pellagra does not mean we are getting enough niacin to confer resistance to cancer." (As noted previously, about 20 mg. per day of niacin will prevent pellagra in people who are not chronic pellagrins; the latter may require 25 times as much niacin to remain free of pellagra.)

Vitamin B3 may also increase the therapeutic efficacy of anticancer treatment. Niacinamide in mice increased the toxicity of irradiation against tumors. Kjellen et al. concluded that the combination of normobaric carbogen with nicotinamide could be an effective method of enhancing tumor radiosensitivity in clinical radiotherapy where hypoxia limits the outcome of treatment. It increases radiosensitivity of the tumor cells and enhances blood flow to the tumor. Additional evidence that vitamin B3 is therapeutic for cancer arises from the National Coronary Drug Study (see discussion of vitamin B3 in Chapter 9).

Vitamin B-Complex Preparations

It is very rare for patients as sick as those with cancer who have also undergone the stresses involved in conventional treatment to have an increased need for only one or two vitamins. Therefore I consider it good policy to reinforce them with vitamin B-complex preparations. The doses need not be very high. I use preparations which provide 50 or 100 mg. each of the first four vitamins in the series (thiamin, riboflavin, niacinamide and pyridoxine) and smaller quantities of the others. However, there is growing evidence that folic acid deficiency increases the risk of certain types of cancer. Butterworth et al. reported that low red blood cell folate levels enhanced the effect of other risk factors for cervical dysplasia, a predecessor of cervical cancer. I used folic acid 5 to 10 mg. per day for a few patients with lung cancer. Smaller amounts are present in the B-complex preparations.

Beta-Carotene

Many presentations at the 1989 conference in London discussed the anticancer properties of beta-carotene. For example, Dr. W.A. Pryor said, "At present, the strongest evidence for an anticarcinogen effect for the antioxidant nutrients appears to exist for beta-carotene." The doses used ranged from 25,000 to 100,000 I.U. The only side effect at the high doses is cosmetic—it gives a slight orange tinge to the skin.

Selenium

In his excellent review Foster found strong evidence between low selenium intake and higher incidence of cancer. In a 27-country survey of breast cancer mortality the same relationship was found, and other minerals were also involved. Cancer incidence is lower where soil calcium is very high but higher where soil mercury is high. However, some studies yield conflicting data, with little or no difference in blood selenium levels between breast cancer and controls. One study of 4,480 subjects of whom 111 developed cancer showed a significant but small decrease in selenium in the patients who developed cancer.

The effect of selenium has not been examined extensively. Selenium was administered in one study of 18 patients with precancerous lesions in the oral cavity. There was a complete remission in two patients; five showed partial remission, six minor improvements, and there was no response in five. When selenium was stopped, growth resumed in 7 out of 18 cases. In a double blind experiment to test selenium's safety on 40 healthy miners, researchers concluded that using selenium was safe and effective to humans with low selenium status. They found that selenium protected lymphocytes against DNA damage induced by ultraviolet radiation and the carcinogen 3,4 benzopyrene.

Frequently recurring reports in the news media about the dangers inherent in excessive exposure to sunlight continually remind and frighten some people about the possibility of getting skin cancer. However, these reports do not discuss the connection between the nutritional health of the population and their susceptibility to cancer of the skin. Since ultraviolet radiation increases the formation of free radicals, it would not be surprising that increasing the availability of antioxidants would prevent some of the toxic reactions to ultraviolet radiation. It has been shown that selenium is such a preventive nutrient. Given to hairless pigmented mice orally or as a lotion, selenium protected them against damage from ultraviolet irradiation. Burke confirmed these findings when she reported that both oral and topical selenium supplementation decreased the incidence and chronic damage from ultraviolet irradiation without being toxic. Mice treated with it had delayed onset and markedly lesser incidence of skin cancer.

Selenium is a good antioxidant. It is synergistic with vitamin E, the body's best-known fat-soluble antioxidant. I would therefore suggest that the three best-known natural antioxidants—ascorbic acid, vitamin E and selenium—be used to protect people against the toxic effect of excessive ultraviolet irradiation. The daily dose would be 200 mcg. selenium, 800 I.U. vitamin E and 3 or more grams of ascorbic acid. It should not take too much time to test these antioxidants in controlled studies. But because the danger from ultraviolet-induced skin cancer and melanoma is potentially so great, it would be prudent to take these simple nutrients as a precaution. They, of course, have other advantages as well.

Selenium also has antidepressant properties. Benton and Cook gave 50 subjects 100 mcg. of selenium daily. They found that the lower the level of selenium in the diet, the more frequent were reports of anxiety, depression and fatigue. Following five weeks of selenium therapy there was a significant decrease in the level of depression.

Zinc and Copper

Zinc deficiency was not recognized until 30 years ago, but since then an association has been found with a large number of conditions such as growth retardation, skin disorders, delayed healing, birth defects, taste and smell disorders, loss of appetite and immunological deficiency. Zinc deficiency induces immunodepression. Thymus-dependent acquired immunity is affected most severely. This is well known and is becoming increasingly important because of the widespread inadequate intake of zinc. Zinc plays a large number of roles in host defense responses: (1) It contributes to plasma defense integrity; (2) it aids functioning of binding sites; (3) it inhibits phagocytic functions in high concentration; (4) low body stores are associated with dysfunction of T cells; (5) nucleic acid and protein synthesis is dependent on zinc; and (6) it plays a key role in metalloenzyme functions.

With zinc deficiency, spleen and thymus decrease in weight, lymphocyte count is reduced, the response to antigens is decreased, immunoglobulin levels are decreased, T-cell helper function is interfered with, and susceptibility to infection is increased. It should not be surprising that zinc deficiency is related to cancer and treatment with zinc may be therapeutic.

The literature over the past five years appears to be in almost unanimous agreement that zinc plays a major role in cancer prevention. There is also powerful evidence that the ratio of blood copper over blood zinc is a good measure of the presence and severity of the cancer. Copper and iron are present in melanomas, but not in nevi. Zinc was not present in either. Using toenail clippings, researchers found that zinc levels were lower in 379 cancer cases compared with 514 control subjects. Subjects at greatest risk for oral cancer had low zinc levels. Their selenium levels were also low.

Alterations in copper/zinc values and their ratios have been shown to be related to cancer stages and could be used to diagnose and monitor treatment. There is an inverse relationship between copper and zinc. A deficiency of one will cause an increase in the other. The easiest way to bring copper levels down is to increase the intake of zinc. Fortunately, zinc is a very safe trace mineral and can be given in useful dosages for long periods of time with hardly any side effects.

With all this evidence of the importance of zinc, I decided to include adequate zinc in the supplemental program for cancer patients who came to me for nutritional advice. I used the following daily compounds: zinc sulfate 220 mg., zinc gluconate 50 mg. and zinc citrate 50 mg.

In summary, patients with cancer have elevated serum copper

levels, elevated ratios of copper/zinc and may have low zinc levels. The higher the ratios, the more malignant the disease is and the poorer the prognosis. It is likely that these indices will become generally used in helping with diagnosis, in following treatment and in estimating prognosis.

STUDYING THE EFFECTS OF ORTHOMOLECULAR THERAPY ON CANCER PATIENTS

The 1990 study conducted by Hoffer and Pauling is based on a series of 134 patients with cancer referred to me by their physicians between July 1978 and April 1988. Patients were treated for cancer by their physicians and/or the cancer clinic, and I treated them with orthomolecular therapy.

I started the 134 cancer patients on an orthomolecular treatment program of dietary advice and nutrient supplements. Dietary advice included eliminating all foods containing added sugar to eliminate most common additives as well as dairy foods to decrease fat intake. The major supplement was vitamin C in doses starting at 12 grams per day, with vitamin B3 at 1.5 grams and smaller amounts of the other vitamins, as well as selenium and zinc.

Gathering Data

Of the 134 patients, 33 chose not to follow the treatment regimen. They were still receiving standard treatment depending upon their condition, but for a number of reasons could not follow the nutrient program. These reasons included being too sick, too nauseated from chemotherapy, not believing there was any point in trying and discouragement by their doctors who had originally referred them or by members of their family. I also decided to exclude all the patients who were not able to remain on the vitamin program at least two months. This was an arbitrary cutoff point but one I considered valid. With all the patients I have given orthomolecular doses of nutrients over the past 40 years, it has been my experience that it takes at least two months and sometimes much longer before the program kicks in. There is no evidence that these controls were significantly different from the patients who did follow the program. For example, 85 percent of the control group received conventional therapy compared with 85 percent of the treated group.

The study was designed with four cohorts; the mean age of the four cohorts was 53.1, 52.8, 51.9 and 55.3 years. However, two cohorts were merged into one after analysis showed they were very similar. (1) The first cohort was the pseudo control group of 33, with all types of cancer, who did not follow the treatment protocol and who survived 5.7 months. (2) The second cohort of 40 patients with cancer of the breast, ovary, uterus, cervix and fallopian tubes had 22 survivors. Mean survival time was estimated to be 99 months (over 8 years). (3) The third cohort of 61 patients with the remaining cancers had 29 survivors. Mean estimated survival time was 67 months (over 5 ½ years).

This was not a prospective double blind comparison study, but it was possible to use the patients who did not follow the program as a valid concurrent control. We used the Hardin Jones biostatistical analyses of mortality for cohorts of cancer patients, which was developed by Pauling in 1989. This method addresses the problem of evaluating mean survival time for a cohort with few survivors at the termination of the study and for a cohort with many survivors at the termination of the study.

Psychotherapy

All the cancer patients were also treated with the type of psychotherapy that any physician ought to use. Their diagnosis was discussed in detail, treatment was explained and prognosis was described. The psychotherapy had to include enough information to increase the patient's hope that something could and would be done. One of the most important psychotherapeutic variables, hope is generated by discussing cases of patients with similar cancers and outlining how they have dealt with their tumor and results of treatment. Patients were advised to attend meetings of the Cancer Victors Society and Hope groups. Visualization was also discussed, but little time was required for this, since most of them had already heard of it and had started practicing it before they saw me. If faith, hope and a positive attitude do nothing more than increase compliance to treatment, they are beneficial.

Followup and Evaluation of Results

Every patient was contacted personally. If they were no longer alive, I spoke to members of their families, usually spouses, or to children. If no contact was possible, I spoke to the referring physician. I also obtained copies of the records from the Cancer Clinic. Some of the cancer patients were my patients for previous psychiatric problems and I had continued to follow them as needed. Some became psychiatric patients after they were advised about treatment for their cancer. In terms of evaluation I decided to use the hardest of all data—survival. If patients spoke to me, they met this criterion, but I was also able to determine how they were getting along.

Quality of LIfe

It is difficult to measure quality of life quantitatively, but it is relatively easy to find out whether patients and their families were more comfortable. A large proportion of my patients told me they were more contented, more functional and suffered less pain. Frequently they were able to decrease the amount of narcotic. Even when they lived for a short time after they saw me, they felt they had benefited, and often after their death, families would tell me how grateful they were that the patient had suffered so much less. I have not had a single complaint from my patients. This contrasts strongly with conventional therapy characterized by severe discomfort of many kinds, nausea, fatigue of long duration, loss of hair and so on. In fact, orthomolecular therapy tends to decrease the discomfort caused by conventional therapy. This is also difficult to quantify, but I believe my patients were telling the truth when they reported that they were better able to tolerate radiation and chemotherapy. Their surgeons were often surprised by their rapid recovery from surgery, and they were quickly discharged from hospital.

Conclusions

We concluded that 80 percent of the patients who followed the regimen in cohort 2 had a probable survival time 21 times that of the controls and for cohort 3 it was 13 times that of the controls, or all patients had a probable survival time 16 times that of the controls. The mean survival of patients from each group who died was about 10 months, or about twice as high as for those who did not follow the program. The mean survival of the controls—5.7 months—was about the same as that for ambulatory patients who had reached or were close to the terminal stage of cancer, with 85 percent having received potentially curative or palliative conventional therapy.

The differences in duration of life after I first saw all the patients were analyzed using two approaches: (1) The group of 101 in cohorts 2 and 3 was compared with the smaller group of 33 in cohort 1. (2) The same group of 101 was compared with 19 patients who never started on the program. The therapeutic results were significantly better for the orthomolecular-treated group using both methods of comparison. The survival rates for all 134 patients can be compared by oncologists with the results they get using a similar group of very sick treatment failures. The survival curves for the 134 and for the 101 on vitamins alone are much closer to each other than they are to the group of 19 who did not start the program.

In a report published on the study, we concluded, "The much longer mean survival time of 81 of the similar patients who followed the regimen, 92 months, must surely be attributed to this regimen." We also said, "On the basis of these results and of those reported by Cameron and his collaborators we strongly recommend that patients with cancer follow the regimen described in this paper, as an adjunct to appropriate conventional therapy. We also join Ewan Cameron (Cameron & Campbell, 1974) in recommending that physicians consider administering large amounts of sodium ascorbate by intravenous infusion to patients with advanced cancer. Cameron himself gave intravenous ascorbate, usually 10 g/d for about 10 days, as well as oral ascorbate continued indefinitely, to each of his patients, and other physicians have reported the successful use of intravenous ascorbate."

13

Case Studies in Orthomolecular Nutrition

RECOVERIES FROM DISEASES

Every orthomolecular physician can tell of dramatic recoveries in patients who had previously failed to respond to any other therapy. Each recovery is a sparkling jewel added to the treasure chest of precious memories. Recoveries from disease for patients are the doctor's immutable rewards beyond price.

A personal friend living in New England once sent me a Christmas card expressing gratitude. She reported that her adopted daughter had received a bachelor's degree in special education. Throughout her university training, the young woman had been on the dean's list. My friend's daughter is one of my jeweled memories. I first met her when she was a little girl, seven years old. She was brought to me for treatment advice because at the time she was suffering from several problems. She had a reading disorder, did not speak clearly, still wet her bed and was developing serious behavioral troubles. The little girl had been born in one of the state's mental hospitals, from which she was adopted. Her biological mother was a chronic schizophrenic and spent most of her time confined in institutions.

I advised the adoptive mother, my friend, to place her daughter on 3 grams of nicotinamide a day with treatment to continue until age eighteen. For the first two years progress was slow, but after that the little girl began to improve quickly and has been normal since. She discontinued taking the vitamin just two years ago. Undoubtedly this young woman, now trained as a special education teacher to help children such as she had been, would have had to obtain her education in special schools for the retarded if she had not taken this dramatic turn for the better.

Another case that well represents orthomolecular medicine in practice also offers a reward for me that can't be measured. About twenty years ago I was invited to see a sixteen-year-old girl confined to the hospital for the previous six months. She had been under the care of another psychiatrist, whose treatment consisted of tranquilizers to which she did not respond. She was typically schizophrenic: saw visions, heard voices, was paranoic, showed hostility toward her parents for no reason, had depression and spoke of suicide frequently. My treatment program included the full gamut of megavitamins and a sugar-fee diet, for a case that I had estimated would not be difficult. I held her in the hospital for a time with the idea that if she failed to respond to orthomolecular nutrition, I would then prescribe a series of shock treatments (ECT). Indeed, she did not improve, and it became necessary to give her seven electroconvulsive treatments.

To my disappointment, the teenager showed no change after the shock treatment either. I realized that I was dealing with a very complicated problem. However, for fear that she would become alienated from her family altogether through such a long hospitalization, I discharged her. She returned home with a heavy megavitamin program and a heavy quantity of tranquilizers required to keep her from committing suicide. Of course, she was fed a diet free of junk foods.

I observed no change in her during monthly visits for over a year. It made me terribly sad because I sensed that I had failed, and I visualized her future—in and out of mental hospitals, chronically tranquilized and subject to all the side effects that go with tranquilizers and anti-depressant drugs. The girl realized her dismal future also, for she was very bright when she was not tranquilized.

It was then that I decided to investigate the young woman's allergies, following lines of inquiry suggested by remarks of William Philpot, M.D., Marshall Mandell, M.D., and other orthomolecular physicians at various scientific meetings. My patient agreed to engage in a four-day fast. She said, in fact, that she would agree to anything to get well. I have to admit that I was skeptical that something so simple as not eating for four days would do anything to help the patient with whom I had tried and failed for such a long time.

To my surprise on the fourth day of her fast, my patient appeared absolutely normal, reverted to what her personality had been: cheerful, alert, happy, smiling, adjusted, friendly with her parents;

she heard no voices, saw no visions and was at ease with everyone. I began extensive tests for the young lady's food allergies. As soon as I gave her a glass of milk, the girl became completely psychotic within the hour; her schizophrenic symptoms returned as before.

Over the next several weeks we tested for other food allergies. I found a host of foods to which she responded adversely. It soon became clear that my patient had so many allergies that it was practically impossible for her to eat. At that time the family found it necessary to move to a distant city where their daughter accompanied them. Her symptoms returned and another psychiatrist attended to her. He hospitalized her and rediagnosed the girl as not being psychotic at all but as merely a "bad" person. She was confined to a special school with rigorous controls on her. Eventually she ran away and made her way back to my office almost a year after I had last tested her.

This time I instituted an addition to my orthomolecular nutrition program. I put into use a number of anti-allergy compounds which would decrease my patient's reactivity to the foods she was allergic to. Improvement was again dramatic and, happily, lasting. She returned to having a normal personality and was able also to eat practically everything that was not junk food—with two exceptions.

She knew she was violently allergic to milk. But one evening my patient ate a large quantity of peanut butter and again within the hour turned psychotic. She was rushed to the nearby hospital emergency room. By chance, the medical intern on night duty was a former patient of mine, a recovered schizophrenic, who called me right away. I told him not to let the hospital people do anything to her, just get her home as soon as possible. The intern wrote a strong recommendation that the young woman should be discharged. She was! Now she knows that she must avoid milk and peanuts. She has remained well since.

This girl's story illustrates that orthomolecular psychiatry is the practice of internal medicine against mental disease. The case required megadosed vitamins, an anti-allergy approach, anti-depressant drugs, ECT, a junk-free diet and other elements of an overall approach. The extent of her problem indicates that the orthomolecular physician should never give up on treatment. The secret of success in therapy is to keep trying. The patient will finally get well!

Any competent physician can accomplish therapeutic success with mental disease even with no special training in psychiatry. Naturally we will always need psychiatrists for that small number of patients who require so much time and skill that the average general physician or family practitioner cannot provide it. But I am absolutely convinced that when orthomolecular medicine becomes widely established, we will need a lot fewer psychiatrists than we have today.

The psychiatry of "talk therapy" is going the way of the dodo. And as people become educated to the incorrectness of the "one disease-one drug" approach currently the rage among medical doctors, they will demand a complex treatment program similar to our orthomolecular nutritional therapy. We use a whole variety of things to help our patients.

SUCCESS STORIES FOR VARIOUS ILLNESSES

Nothing shows what's possible with orthomolecular nutrition better than case studies. We've assembled cases of people with a variety of illnesses who should not have recovered, but who did very well on individualized treatment programs. These cases represent what can happen, not what will happen with every patient treated this way. They suggest that it is worthwhile to try this treatment because if one member of a class responds, others surely will also.

Amyotrophic Lateral Sclerosis

When P.M. (born 1923) came to A.H. in 1977, he complained that for the past two years he had experienced difficulty walking—he walked with a limp, he could not walk more than 20 minutes and he couldn't walk on his toes. He had always been nervous and tense. His thumb and forefinger on the left hand had become awkward, and he could not flex his left wrist. A neurologist had diagnosed him with upper-motor neuron disease, amyotrophic lateral sclerosis (ALS), which is known as a killing disease. He had started to take a few vitamins three weeks before and believed he had gained some strength, was less tired and the sense of pressure around his neck had decreased.

Initial Treatment: I started him on niacinamide 3 grams, thiamin 1.5 grams, pyridoxine 250 mg., ascorbic acid 3 grams, all daily, and thiamin by injection 100 mg. I.M. and liver extract 1ml. I.M. twice each week. This was based upon a program developed many years before by Dr. Fred Klenner of Reidsville, N.C.

Continuing Treatment: A year later P.M. told me he was walking better but that he was losing strength in his right wrist. He was not certain whether the vitamin program was doing any good. I suggested he discontinue the regimen as a test, and a month later he reported that he had resumed the vitamin program. He went off again six months later for six weeks, but this time he felt much worse and was finally convinced it was necessary for him to keep on the program. I increased his vitamin E to 800 I.U. twice each day because I had seen a patient with Huntington's Disease who did not become well until his vitamin E had been increased to 3200 I.U. (Animal studies have shown that vitamin E is helpful for some muscular dystrophies.) Two and a half years after first consulting me, he reported that his condition was stable, and he was able to walk without a limp for as long as he needed.

P.M. came back in 1988 and said that he was about the same but that he would like to try anything new that might be available. I advised him to take coenzyme Q10 30 mg. three times per day. (By then I was familiar with Dr. Karl Folker's work with this coenzyme and muscular dystrophies.) Two weeks later he called to report how excited he was by his dramatic improvement. Before he had been able to walk about one mile, but now he could walk any distance and had even been hiking in the mountains. He was not tired, and he had a lot more energy.

In October 1992, P.M. began to deteriorate when he was no longer able to get any liver extract and had to stop the injections. (He still searched for a source of liver because he was convinced his deterioration had come after he was not able to get anymore.) He was then on vitamin E 800 I.U., pyridoxine 200mg., dolomite 640 mg. twice, thiamin 500mg., Q10 60 mg., niacinamide 500 mg., ascorbic acid 4 grams, folic acid 5 mg., selenium 200 mcg. and zinc citrate 50 mg., all daily. By May 1993 he had deteriorated more, especially his right hand, which he could no longer close. I increased his Q10 to 180 mg. and his folic acid to 30 mg.

Only 50 percent of patients with ALS live 3 years after diagnosis, 20 percent live 5 years and 10 percent live 10 years. Rarely does anyone live more than 10 years. This patient had only a 5 percent chance of surviving 18 years, which is proof of the power of ortho-molecular nutrition.

Idiopathic Thrombocytopenic Purpura (ITP)

E.A., age 35 (born 1953), was referred to A.H. in April 1988. Her physician wrote, "She suffers from recurrent idiopathic thrombocy-topenic purpura [ITP]. She has had a splenectomy which did not help and is now maintained on Prednisone. She was on Prednisone for six months from June 1987 to January 1988, and when she came off of it, her platelets immediately dropped and she required plate-let transfusion. She is eager to consider alternative therapy and has requested to see you." ITP, probably one of the autoimmune dis-eases, is a common condition. About 60 percent of patients respond to corticosteroid treatment, but only 20 percent of the original group stay in remission. Splenectomy helps about 80 percent. Other treatments are used, but even with the most efficient combination of treatments, only a partial response is seen, and the side effects can be very severe.

E.A. described massive bruising over her body for the previous two years. When her platelet count had fallen to 20, she was started on Prednisone 100 mg., which was slowly decreased. Over the next two years she had to be admitted to the hospital seven times. Her spleen was removed in January 1987. When I saw her she was still on Predni-sone 15 mg., with the usual steroid side effects, including weight gain, facial changes, point pain and diarrhea. She had evidence of pyridox-ine/zinc deficiency before she became sick with ITP: many white areas on her nails, many large stretch marks (stria) on her body and severe premenstrual anxiety. She was very depressed.

Initial Treatment: I suspected E.A. had a dairy allergy and ad-vised her to eliminate all dairy products and sugar. (As discussed in Chapter 11, a sugar-free diet also eliminates most of the additives in food.) She supplemented this with ascorbic acid 1 gram and niacinamide 500 mg. three times daily, pyridoxine 250 mg., zinc gluconate 50 mg. and vitamin K 5 mg., all daily. However, she was not able to take the niacinamide because it caused nausea.

Six weeks later she was no longer bruised and was free of diar-rhea, so she was able to decrease the Prednisone to 5 mg. In another six weeks her Prednisone was down to 2.5 mg. Within four months of her first visit, she was normal. I then started her on inositol niacinate 1 gram after each meal and changed the zinc preparation to the citrate.

Continuing Treatment: By September 1988 E.A. was so well and was also fed up with taking so many pills that she decided to dispense with the supplement program. However, by February 1989 her platelet count had dropped to 174, reaching 72 in March. She promptly resumed the Prednisone at 60 mg. and the supplements, increasing her ascorbic acid to 3 to 4 grams daily. Within twelve days of resuming the vitamin program she rebounded, and nineteen days later she decreased the Prednisone to 5 mg. By April 1989 her platelet count was normal. She then decided not to go off the vitamins again.

This is how E.A.'s condition was reported in a daily paper: "She recalled wakening one morning in 1986 bruised from head to toe. The pressure of her body on the bed had been enough to cause this massive bruising. A few months later a morning shower left her covered with tiny blood blisters formed wherever the spray struck. She had her spleen removed and later her gallbladder. One outbreak cost her her job and another her fiancée who could not tolerate her strange behavior induced by Prednisone. She had a remission, which she credited to a vitamin program, but was again battling it with small doses of Prednisone."

In sharp contrast to the toxic drugs which are used as standard treatment—high-dose steroids—the use of orthomolecular treatment is not associated with toxicity. Because nutrient therapy combined with standard treatment is more effective than standard therapy used alone and is associated with minimal side effects, this should be the treatment of choice, but it will not be until the treatment is taught in medical schools.

Chronic Arthritis

K.V. (born 1922) came to A.H. in April 1982. She was in a wheelchair pushed by her husband. He appeared exhausted, depressed and lost, and she was one of the sickest patients I have ever seen, weighing under 90 pounds. She sat in the chair on her ankles, which were crossed beneath her body, because she was not able to straighten them out. Her arms were held in front of her close to her body, and her fingers were permanently deformed and claw-like. She told me she had been deeply depressed for many years because of her severe pain and major impairment.

As she was being wheeled into my office, I saw how ill she was and immediately concluded there was nothing I could do for her. I had to decide how I could let her know without sending her even deeper into despair. However, I changed my mind when she suddenly said, "Dr. Hoffer, I know no one can ever cure me, but if you could only help me with my pain. The pain in my back is unbearable. I just want to get rid of the pain in my back." I realized then that she had a lot of determination and inner strength and that it was worthwhile to try to help her.

She began to suffer from severe pain in her joints in 1952. In 1957 it was diagnosed as arthritis. By 1962 her condition fluctuated and she had to go into a wheelchair some part of the day. By 1973 she was there permanently and soon needed to be pushed. She had gotten some homecare for the three years before she saw me, but most of it at that point was provided by her husband after retirement from his job. He had to carry her to the bathroom, bathe her, cook meals and feed her. He was as exhausted as she was but was somehow able to carry on.

She was severely deformed, especially her hands, and suffered continuous pain, which was worse in her arms, hips and back. Her muscles were also very painful most of the day. Her ankles were badly swollen and she had to wear pressure bandages. She was able to feed herself and to crochet with a few useful fingers, but it must have been extremely difficult. She was not able to write or type, which she use to do with a pencil. A few months earlier she had been suicidal. On top of the severe pain and discomfort she had no appetite, and a full meal nauseated her. Her skin was dry, had patches of eczema, and she had white areas in her nails.

Initial Treatment: I advised her to eliminate sugar, potatoes, tomatoes and peppers (about 10 percent of arthritics have allergic reactions to the nightshade family of plants). She took niacinamide 500 mg. (following the work of W. Kaufman) and ascorbic acid 500 mg. (as an antistress and for subclinical scurvy) four times daily, pyridoxine 250 mg. (found to have antiarthritic properties by Dr. J. Ellis), zinc sulfate 220 mg. (the white areas in her nails indicated she was deficient in zinc), linseed oil 2 tablespoons and cod liver oil 1 tablespoon (her skin condition indicated she had a deficiency of omega 3 essential fatty acids), all daily. [The detailed treatment of arthritis is described in my book *Orthomolecular Medicine for Physicians* (Keats, 1989).]

One month later a new couple came into my office. Her husband was smiling, relaxed and cheerful, and K.V. was sitting with her legs dangling down, smiling as well. When I asked her about her various symptoms, she impatiently broke in with, "Dr. Hoffer, the pain in my back is all gone." The pain in her back and hip were easily controlled with aspirin, she no longer had bruises all over her body and she no longer bled from her bowel. Her heart was regular at last. Much more comfortable, she was cheerful and laughed. I added inositol niacinate 500 mg. four times daily to her program.

She improved even more by June. Now she was able to pull herself up from the prone position on her bed for the first time in fifteen years and she was free of depression. I increased her ascorbic acid to 1 gram four times daily and added vitamin E 800 I.U. Because she had shown such dramatic improvement, I told her she no longer needed to see me.

Continuing Treatment: In October 1983 I wrote to her doctor: "Today Mrs. K.V. reported she had stayed on the whole vitamin program very rigorously for 18 months, but since that time had slacked off somewhat. She is regaining a lot of her muscle strength, can now sit in her wheelchair without difficulty, can also wheel herself around in her wheelchair but, of course, cannot do anything useful with her hands because her fingers are so awful. She would like to become more independent and perhaps could do so if something could be done about her fingers and also about her hip. I am delighted she has arranged to see a plastic surgeon to see if something can be done to get her hand mobilized once more. I have asked her to continue with the vitamins, but because she had difficulty taking so many pills she will take a preparation called Multijet which is available from Portland and contains all the vitamins and minerals and can be dissolved in juice. She will also take inositol niacinate 3 grams daily."

I saw K.V. again in March 1988. She had been taking small amounts of vitamins and was able to use an electric chair. About four of her vertebra had collapsed and she was suffering more pain, which was alleviated by Darvon. It had not been possible to treat her hands surgically. She had been able to eat by herself until six months before this visit, and she had been depressed. I wrote to K.V.'s doctor: "She had gone off the total vitamin program about two or three years ago. It is very difficult for her to swallow and I can understand her reluctance to carry on with this. I have therefore suggested that she take a minimal program which would include inositol niacinate 3 grams daily, ascorbic acid 1 gram three times, linseed oil 2 capsules and cod liver oil 2 capsules. Her spirits are good and I think she is coming along, considering the severe deterioration of her body as a result of the arthritis over the past few decades."

Epidermolysis Bullosa

I was consulted by C.C., a young man, and his mother in December 1989 for help in the treatment of his severe, intractable case of epidermolysis bullosa. The symptoms and signs include severe, chronic diarrhea, muscle wasting, alopecia and rough, thick ulcerated skin about the body orifices and on the extremities.

A few days after C.C. was born in June 1972 his skin, which had been under pressure from a forceps delivery, began to slough off. A few days later lesions developed on his face, mouth, chest and limbs, which later blistered. He did not respond to treatment with topical antibiotics using sterile technique. The lesions in his mouth made it impossible for him to feed, and he became anemic and hypoproteinemic. One month later he was diagnosed with epidermolysis bullosa and started on vitamin E 600 I.U. daily, which was later increased to 800 I.U. At age 4 months 200 mg. of ascorbic acid was added, and at age 6 months he was given iron supplementation and the vitamin E was increased to 1000 I.U. But there was no response.

Two years later C.C. had gastroenteritis and pneumonia. By now he had multiple lesions and denuded areas on his legs, no nails, adhesions between his fingers and his toes, and he was constantly constipated. Every day his mother had to remove his stools manually. In 1980 his parents took him to West Germany for two and one half months to be treated by a biochemist who used special skin salves and other treatment, with some success. He was placed on a vegetarian diet supplemented with a moderate vitamin program (doses unknown). This regimen was helpful, but after one more trip, the family could no longer afford that treatment.

When I first saw C.C., he was 17 but appeared to be about ten years old, very short and immature. Mentally he appeared to be normal. There were no perceptual changes or thought disorder, and his mood was surprisingly cheerful and upbeat. The bulbous lesions continued to erupt, and he had lost all his fingers and toes. An attempt had been made to separate them surgically in Italy with no success. He said food did not taste normal, and he was still severely constipated, having been hospitalized to have stools removed in 1986.

To test his sense of taste for a possible zinc deficiency, I gave C.C. a teaspoon of a special zinc sulfate solution. To him it tasted like stale water, not bitter as it would to normal individuals. I could not order a blood test for zinc since all his superficial veins were gone and it would have required a cut down. Zinc deficiency will cause dwarfism, retarded wound healing and loss of taste. (The classic response to chronic zinc deficiency is acrodermatitis enteropathica.)

Treatment: I had C.C. start on the following supplements: cod liver oil 1/2 teaspoon and linseed oil 1 teaspoon (to increase his intake of omega 3 essential fatty acids) both daily, niacinamide 500 mg., pyridoxine 100 mg. and 10 drops of a solution containing 10% zinc sulfate and 0.5% manganese chloride, all twice a day, and ascorbic acid 500 mg. three times a day. Since his mother informed me that he was very sensitive to any tablets, I had him start one nutrient at a time, and if there was no bad reaction, he was to proceed to the next.

Two weeks later C.C. had had no adverse reactions to any of the supplements and he was much improved. In that brief period he had grown 1/2 inch, his skin was much healthier, and the lesions grew about one third as frequently and those that did develop healed much more quickly. He had gained 2 pounds, was no longer constipated, and was able to have normal bowel movements for the first time in his life. His mood remained normal, and his parents were much more cheerful. I increased his niacinamide to 500 mg. three times daily and the ascorbic acid to 1 gram twice each day.

Two years later after remaining on the total nutrient approach, C.C.'s skin condition was stable, with minor eruptions, he'd grown

about 3 to 4 inches, and he'd gained 15 pounds. He was still constipated, but his mood was level and he was cheerful.

Conclusions: This patient's rapid response to administration of
zinc and the other nutrients raises the possibility that his condition
is a variant of a chronic zinc dependency, but it does not prove it
was due entirely to the administration of zinc. (Harrison describes
an inherited zinc deficiency disease in *Principles of Medicine*.) I
suspect that zinc was the main therapeutic variable, but the other
nutrients must also have played an important part. Since single-
nutrient deficiencies are very rare, I could not in good conscience
withhold the other nutrients since I was not certain that one alone
might help. (This could be determined later on by withdrawing one
at a time to determine which are the most important.) This patient
is probably zinc dependent, though it is possible he has a multiple
nutrient dependency. It is very important that doctors who see
these cases try this nutrient treatment approach with zinc the main
variable but with other supplements as well.

One dramatic, rapid and sustained response to treatment of a
disease for which there is no standard treatment is very significant
and should be compared with the first person with pneumonia who
recovered when given penicillin more than 50 years ago. The response occurred so quickly that there can be no doubt that it was
caused by the nutrients. If this treatment had been known to his
doctors and used when he was first diagnosed, C.C. would have
grown up to be a normal person. As with pneumonia and penicillin,
it is imperative that many more patients with epidermolysis bullosa
be treated using similar nutrients before we can determine what
proportion of the total population will respond. Because this is a
rare condition and because all patients will not respond in the same
way, it is necessary to start treatment in infancy and to run studies
involving many physicians and many hospitals.

Huntington's Disease

A.B. first wrote A.H. about Huntington's Disease (HD) in 1978.
Her mother had had severe HD, as had her grandfather. Because
her husband had recovered from schizophrenia and was well as
long as he took his vitamins—niacin, ascorbic acid and pyridoxine—
A.B. had concluded that a nutritional program might prevent HD's

appearance in her brother and herself. For the past seven years she had been too tired to work and suffered from constant fatigue and fear, a few perceptual problems, which made it impossible for her to drive, and loss of memory.

HD is characterized by progressive movement disorders and intellectual and psychiatric deterioration, which usually begins in middle age. Asocial behavior may be the first behavioral manifestation of the disease, which may precede the movement disorder or develop during its course. Motor manifestations include a lilting gait, movements of the extremities and inability to sustain a motor act. Psychiatric problems range from personality changes of apathy and irritability to full-blown manic-depressive or schizophreniform illness. No treatment is known.

Initial Treatment: I diagnosed A.B. as having latent HD. (HD should be diagnosed early; it is too destructive to wait until the person is hopelessly ill to make the diagnosis.) A.B. had a 50 percent chance of having her mother's gene, and she had all the prodromal symptoms of HD, which were severe enough to prevent her from working for seven years.

A.B. took the following vitamins: vitamin E 800 I.U., niacin 2500 mg., vitamin C 1000 mg. and one multiple vitamin pill. She also took supplements of choline, calcium and magnesium, though I have no records of the amounts. In a short period her symptoms were all gone, she was back at work as an engineer, and she felt normal.

I suggested she prepare a report describing her reaction to the vitamin treatment. She wrote: "Dr. Hoffer advised the quantities to try to 'experiment with' and stressed the importance of a good diet, meaning foods balanced with vitamins—greens, fresh vegetables, meat, little starch, and no sugar or non-natural sweets. Fruits were good, of course, but no artificial additives of any kind. . . . It took me a good year before I started to realize I was getting better. . . . I increased the niacin to 2500 mg. and reduced the C to 1500 mg. . . . With my energy coming back, I started a farm. I wanted to raise healthy food and I have been doing it since. We raise sheep, goats, pigs, poultry, eggs, milk and a huge garden. We bought two large freezers to preserve our food. We completed this diet by honey, health food, soya-flour spaghetti and noodles, whole wheat home-baked bread and nuts. . . .

"While investigating new medical theories my husband came

upon Dr. Frederick's book on breast tumors, for which my oldest daughter and I had to be operated on several times. He read that choline and inositol would be instrumental in bringing back a proper balance or lowering the estrogen levels, which would reduce our breast tumors. With Dr. Hoffer's permission I added 500 mg. each of choline and inositol every day and after six months the result was amazing. I suddenly desired to drive a car and had lost the fear of driving. . . . My daughter tried the choline treatment and we both lost our tumors after about four months of taking it. As my daughter put it, it drives away your fear and your thinking becomes sharp and your memory gets to be so good.

"I am now 47 years old and for the first time in my life I am relaxed and I work more than I ever did. I feel secure and completely unafraid and confident, even about things like making mistakes at work, accidents, diseases or whatever your subconscious would amplify enough to make your life impossible. . . . I attribute this change to a combination of good diet and the mega-vitamin treatment of Dr. Hoffer. I did nothing psychologically to make me get up early with ease or to get rid of the pain in my legs. I always wanted so much to be able to work hard without fatigue and never imagined my legs could be so light. I never lost weight or gained weight either. My feelings about HD are mixed. I feel so good now that I really don't know if I ever had a beginning of this disease and I don't worry as I believe this treatment will take care of me and my three daughters if it ever lurks in the corner."

Continuing Treatment: By 1982 A.B. was taking 8000 mg. niacin in the evening, 1500 mg. vitamin C, 800 I.U. vitamin E, 700 mg. calcium, 300 mg. magnesium in a complex, 2 tablets either Solotron or Nuclix (both B-complexes with minerals, the Solotron the more complete), all daily, 200 mg. inositol alternating every other day with 425 mg. phosphatidylcholine concentrate.

A.B.'s three daughters, aged 22, 21 and 13 respectively, also took supplements, though in lower doses and with less regularity. The eldest has some facial twitching, especially of eyelids, when fatigued and stressed, sporadic involuntary twitching of the foot and great difficulty getting up. The second daughter has never had any twitching, but has had back trouble. The third daughter has a number of symptoms, which increase when she's stressed or fatigued: heavy twitching around the mouth, an involuntary pulling down on the right side of the neck, twitching of the eyelids and rolling her eyes in a way that can be alarming. She has trouble getting up and is terribly affected by sweets. She takes 1500 mg. niacin, 1000 mg. of vitamin C, 800 I.U. of vitamin E, 1400 mg. calcium, 600 mg. of magnesium and 2 tablets of Nuclix daily. Her parents continue to experiment with dosages for her.

In 1986 A.B.'s husband reported that "she is certain she has the disease but feels a great sense of relief that she can control its effects." Of the daughters the youngest "is doing very well, rarely shows any signs of twitching or hand movement, except under stress or after long periods of poor diet when she is away from us. . . . We hold her to a fairly strict discipline concerning the vitamins. Or rather she holds herself. She senses that she has to take them." However, the eldest daughter has been "rather sloppy" about taking vitamins and "generally follows a poor diet by eating out all the time and is showing some effects." He concludes: "As for me I have a lot of notes on mental illness and draft manuscripts concerning my own situation and I'm at the point now in my life where I have to synthesize them into a whole. I would like to explain not only the pit of hell that the megavitamin treatment rescued me from, but also the relation and importance of the creative mind to illness. Or the recovery from illness. I believe this, for reasons of my own, to be so crucial."

Subsequent reports show that the entire family's recovery was maintained as long as they remained on vitamins. A.B. writes about herself: "The vitamins which help me the most are niacin (4 G daily), vitamin E (800 I.U. daily), vitamin C (1 G daily), calcium, magnesium, beta-carotene, trace elements and especially phosphatidyl choline. The last seems to help me the most to get my brain working. . . . I am 58, am free of arthritis, have no fatigue, no depression. . . . I have taken these vitamins for 15 years and I am better and better."

Conclusions: I believe that HD is probably a double dependency on vitamin B3 and E. Vitamin B3 controls the mental portion of this illness, while vitamin E controls the neurological component. Since vitamin B3 also controls schizophrenia, there is indeed a relationship between these two conditions. Perhaps HD is simply schizophrenia with an additional neurological component; it should be noted that schizophrenics on tranquilizers develop tardive dyskinesia.

When one parent has HD, the disease will be passed on to about half of the children. With this family it appears as if all three children have symptoms attributable to this condition. However, by the use of vitamins they have been able to keep these symptoms under control, even though two of them have taken the vitamins only intermittently. The mother, who was the sickest, is now the healthiest, and she is the one who has followed the program most carefully.

Will this type of program be as helpful to other children of parents with HD? We will not know unless they try it. Children of parents with this disease live under a terrible cloud because they do not know if and when the disease will strike them. The ideal treatment for HD is prevention. I would advise every member of the family to be tested for the presence of the genes and go on a good orthomolecular program. However, if they do not wish to be tested, they can determine what the chances are that they have the genes through the proper use of orthomolecular therapy. If they note a rapid improvement over their present condition, this will indicate they probably have the genes. After one year those members who feel they have not benefited probably do not have the genes and need not take the vitamins, while those who are improved probably do have the genes and ought to remain on the program forever to ensure the disease does not strike them later in life. There is no danger in taking nutrients. By starting the treatment early they probably can remain well with a program less intensive than the one required to treat well-established cases. It is likely that once there has been severe psychiatric and neurological impairment, this treatment will not help, and I have not had a chance to treat advanced cases. As there is no effective treatment now, it is imperative that physicians and families try the orthomolecular approach.

Optimal Orthomolecular Treatment: The program should include a diet free of additives including sugar and foods which cause allergic reactions. It should include the following daily supplements: vitamin B3 1 to 6 grams, vitamin C 3 to 12 grams, vitamin E 1600 to 4000 I.U., zinc preparations providing 30 to 50 mg., manganese about 15 mg. and vitamin B-complex 50s. Other vitamins such as folic acid may be required for some. Treatment should be followed at least for one year and perhaps more since improvement may be very slow.

Tic Douloureux

A.E. (born 1915) complained that she had suffered from tic douloureux (trigeminal neuralgia) for 15 years. It is one of the most painful afflictions. It does not kill, but many of the patients who suffer from its intense, lancing pain, which can last seconds or minutes, may wish they were dead. The causes are unknown, but there is some evidence that venous loops compressing the nerve at its entry into the brainstem is a factor. Successive bouts may incapacitate the patient. The only partially effective treatments have included Carbamazepine 200 to 1600 mg. daily, antidepressants and surgery.

A.E. had suffered from recurrent infections from childhood starting with pneumonia when she was five until she was 18. Within the previous few years she had fallen several times with severe fractures. She had discovered she was allergic to chocolate and cheese. Eliminating these foods eased the pain. Mentally she was normal except for her anxiety over the pain. Here's how she describes her onset: "One night out of the blue I woke up screaming with the most devastating pain in my right cheek. I had about 9 bouts that night. It has been a terrible affliction."

Treatment: I advised A.E. to eliminate dairy products and take the following daily supplements: niacin 500 mg. three times a day (to improve her circulation and as an anti-arthritic factor), ascorbic acid 3 grams (as an anti-aging, antistress factor), B-complex 50, cod liver oil 1 capsule, vitamin E 800 I.U., vitamin B12 2 mg. sublingual and folic acid 10 mg. Previously I had found that a combination of ascorbic acid, vitamin B12 and lysine had been very effective in controlling this condition.

One week later A.E. reported that the pain was gone but recurred when she decreased the ascorbic acid. Two weeks later she was free of pain, and she has been well since.

Tic Douloureux (Trigeminal Neuralgia) Complicated by Arthritis

R.A. (born 1931) complained that in addition to arthritis since the age of 16, she had been suffering for the past nine months from severe pain diagnosed as tic douloureux. In 1957 she had rheumatic fever and later rheumatoid arthritis, and in 1964 her arthritis was diagnosed as ankylosing spondylitis, which later became quiescent. By using aspirin and other drugs she was able to work in spite of her pain, but for a few months before she saw A.H., her arthritic pain was worse. She did not have pain in her face but described the feeling as being anesthetized, as if it were frozen and tingling.

Treatment: I advised R.A. to follow a sugar-free diet and avoid nightshade plants. To this I added niacinamide 500 mg. and ascorbic acid 500 mg. four times a day, cod liver oil capsules three times a day, pyridoxine 100 mg. twice a day and zinc sulfate 220 mg. on demand. This is my regular starting program for chronic arthritis. R.A. was also on Prednisone 10 mg. daily, Indocid, Entrophen and a diuretic.

Three weeks later R.A.'s pain was less severe and she was off the Prednisone. I then advised her to go dairy free and eliminate all the drugs. After another month she was much better and had very little pain. Her face had regained its normal color and shape, and she needed very few aspirins.

Six months after starting the nutritional program, R.A. was normal. One year later she went off all the nutrients. However, six months after that she noted a return of pain in her fingers and numbness in the right side and up her left arm. I advised her to resume the nutrients, giving her inositol niacinate instead of niacinamide.

Conclusions: Over the past 16 years I have seen only four patients with tic douloureux, including the two described here. I started the third on vitamin B12 injections, 1-lysine gram daily and ascorbic acid 6 grams daily on a Friday and the following day she was free of pain for the first time since she became ill! The response was so dramatic I have never forgotten it. After that I began to use vitamin B12. The probability that all four patients I have seen would respond so effectively to simple vitamin treatment is so low that it must be significant.

Optimal Orthomolecular Treatment: I have concluded that the treatment of choice for tic douloureux is vitamin B12 by injection (1 mg. intramuscularly several times each week and tapering off depending on progress) or sublingual (1 to 2 mg. each day), ascorbic acid at least 6 grams daily, l-lysine up to 3 to 6 grams daily, plus B-complex or other B vitamins, depending upon other concurrent conditions.

Myelofibrosis, Following Treatment for Polycythemia Rubra Vera

S.E. (born 1915) was admitted to the hospital in 1977 complaining of being clumsy and confused. Her spleen was enlarged, and her hemoglobin was 20 grams. After phlebotomies her mental state improved, and she was also given Myleran; that course of treatment was continued for the next five years. In 1977 S.E.'s hemoglobin was down to 14.1 and the dose of Myleran was lowered and eventually stopped. Her red blood cell (RBC) count was down to 4.0 million. In July 1981 S.E.'s hemoglobin had dropped and she developed leukopenia. Her hematologist suspected she was developing myelofibrosis, a chronic disease characterized by bone marrow fibrosis, splenomegaly and leukoerythroblastic anemia. Its cause is not known, and it has a median survival rate of about 10 years. There is no therapy to reverse or control the underlying process. S.E. was subsequently diagnosed with extensive fibrosis. By early 1982 when her physician referred her to me, her diagnosis of polycythemia had developed into myelofibrosis (hemoglobin 7.2), moderate obesity and mild agitated depression. He added, "She wants to cure this totally nontreatable disease by special diets and vitamin supplements."

I saw S.E. for the first time in March 1982 when she gave me some background on her disease. I did not find any psychiatric problems, but she was very worried and, properly so, about her blood picture. She was also very tired, though she was still able to walk three miles daily.

Initial Treatment: I had no experience treating this condition, but I assumed I might help her with a comprehensive vitamin/mineral program. I advised her to take niacin 100 mg. and ascorbic acid 1 gram three times a day, pyridoxine 100 mg. and zinc sulfate 220 mg. on demand, folic acid 5 mg., vitamin E 400 I.U. and linseed oil one tablespoon daily.

Continuing Treatment: Over the course of the next ten years I checked S.E.'s program every three to six months, adding or varying dosages of vitamins and minerals as her condition changed. For instance, in June 1982 when she was much better (hemoglobin 6.7), more alert, less depressed, and her mind was clear, I increased her vitamin E to 800 I.U. and added magnesium oxide, selenium 200 mcg., dolomite and halibut liver capsules two daily. In August I added vitamin B12 50 mcg. daily. In January 1983 (hemoglobin 6.6) she started to take vitamin B12 injections 1 mg. weekly, and I doubled her folic acid to 10 mg. Later that year I increased her niacin to 500 mg. three times a day. Though she had bouts of phlebitis, bursitis and a fall (when she didn't take B12 injections for a five-week period), S.E. remained basically stable until the fall of 1988 when she was admitted to the hospital after a severe nose-bleed and leukemia was suspected. She felt much better after three transfusions, but I found that her blood copper level was too high. It was 185 and zinc was 88, with a ratio of 2.1 (it should be around 1.0). I increased her intake of zinc and suggested she filter her water to remove copper dissolved from copper plumbing. Later that year I increased her ascorbic acid to 12 grams daily and then in the fall of 1989 I increased it again to 17 grams. This was her best quarter since she first came to see me. Finally, in March 1992 S.E. began to deteriorate, developing pneumonia in the left lung, and died in June 1992.

Conclusions: S.E. was not cured, but she did improve to the level where she was able to live out her life in relative comfort and free of the severe fatigue and depression she had suffered from for so long. Her hemoglobin increased from a low average value of 6.2 to a high level of 10.7, but it was impossible to get it any higher. The myelofibrosis had destroyed enough bone marrow so that recovery was essentially very slow, and we ran out of time. In her weakened condition the pneumonia finally destroyed her. She was happy with the treatment she had received and thanked me in a note in December 1991 "for being always ready to give me very good, helpful advice along all these [ten] years, taking your time to listen carefully to my health problems."

Crohn's Disease

Since 1980 I have seen twelve patients with Crohn's Disease, which is one of the inflammatory bowel diseases, including ulcerative colitis and ulcerative proctitis. It most commonly affects the distal ileum and colon, but it may occur in any part of the GI tract from the mouth to the anus. No specific therapy is known, though it may include antibiotics, especially Sulfasalazine, Prednisone, immunosuppressive drugs and surgery, as well as symptomatic treatment for pain, constipation and anemia.

The treatment I advised has altered over the years, but strenuous efforts must be made to maintain optimum nutrition using nutrients, total foods and elemental foods preparations. It is also essential to eliminate foods which irritate the bowel, and allergic foods such as dairy products and grains are always suspect. It is also necessary to supplement the diet with the optimum mix of nutrients; vitamins E and C plus the B vitamins are very important.

A.P. (born 1948) came to me under severe stress in July 1982 and was very concerned about two conditions: ankylosing spondylitis and Crohn's disease. The arthritis started ten years before when she developed pain in her hips and later in her back. She was treated, responded and had only a residual stiff neck. Four years before I saw her, she had developed severe diarrhea, cramps with bleeding and six months later was diagnosed with Crohn's disease. Medication did not agree with her, and it took her a long time to get used to Salazopyrene and Clineral. After onset, she had two exacerbations, the last a few months before.

Treatment: I advised A.P. to go milk-free over a three-week period (she had consumed 6 glasses of milk daily for many years) and to take niacinamide 500 mg. four times a day, ascorbic acid 1 gram three times a day, pyridoxine 250 mg. on demand and zinc sulfate 220 mg., vitamin E 800 I.U. and selenium 200 mcg. daily. One month later A.P. reported that after a withdrawal of four days she became normal and all her symptoms of Crohn's disease were gone. There was no change in her back pain.

Lupus Erythematosus

I first became interested in systematic lupus erythematosus (SLE) in the late 1970s when I was asked to see a woman, N.K., who was dying from a severe case. Lupus is a very complex inflammatory connective tissue disorder of unknown origin that occurs predominantly in young women. (There are seventeen to nineteen female cases for every male case, and 5,000 women die of it each year in this country.) Not only can it be a vicious disease but also an elusive one. It may start suddenly with fever like an acute infection or may come on slowly for months and years. Any organ can be affected, including the brain (leading to mental changes), kidneys, lymph glands and lungs. Most patients complain of joint symptoms, from intermittent arthralgia to acute polyarthritis. A flush on the cheeks, often in a butterfly shape, or a general reddening of the skin and rashes of various types are characteristic. Treatment includes corticosteroids, nonsteroidal anti-inflammatory drugs and antibiotics against infections.

Because of the prominence of joint pains and arthritis and because I was by then familiar with the use of niacin for treating arthritis, I thought it might help N.K. I started her on niacin about 500 mg. three times a day. I cannot remember what else I gave her, but since it has been my habit to always combine it with ascorbic acid, I probably gave her the same amount of ascorbic acid. To my amazement she was normal in about a week. Her arthritic pain eased, her lesions healed and her depression was less troublesome. I was convinced I had found an answer for this dreadful disease then considered uniformly fatal. However, several months later N.K. was back in the hospital, and this time she no longer responded to any vitamin regimen. Within a few weeks she died. This showed me that there was no simple one-vitamin treatment for this very complicated disease.

Henrietta Aladjem published *The Sun Is My Enemy* about her experiences with lupus in 1972. Her book was a precedent-setting firsthand account of a case of lupus and thus of obvious importance to all doctors and medical students. Although she was fortunate to have access to the resources of the Harvard Medical School, she had to consult many doctors before lupus was diagnosed. Even then the wonder drugs she took didn't help. A few years later, by chance, she heard of a Bulgarian doctor who had been successful in treating lupus with nicotinic acid. Although the doctors in Cambridge were skeptical, her symptoms disappeared in a few months after consulting him and she became strong enough to play tennis. Even her severe kidney damage began to repair itself. The Harvard doctors were totally surprised and are still by no means convinced that it was not a spontaneous remission. Thus Mrs. Aladjem became the first lupus patient in the United States to be treated with nicotinic acid.

A few years later I had lunch with Mrs. Aladjem and heard about her efforts to organize a lupus society in New York that actively promoted further research and newer treatments for lupus. Unfortunately the medical profession ignored these very important first leads, and even today I doubt there are any internists who are familiar with the potential benefit from nicotinic acid in treating patients with lupus. However, Mrs. Aladjem's story makes each and every one of us a little stronger. We are reminded once again what the refusal to admit defeat can do for every individual under stress.

D.R. (born 1971) was diagnosed with lupus in December 1987 and I saw her the following May. As an infant she had suffered with colic for several months, which was followed by constant colds, ear infections and pneumonia when she was 2 1/2. She suffered permanent hearing loss from that and needed a hearing aid. At age 5 she was found positive for nuclear antibody factor. She went into remission on asprin, but two years later required more. At age 12 both knees flared up. For the year before D.R. saw me, she was very tired and developed pain in her fingers, elbows, shoulders, feet, ankles and a churning feeling in her stomach. Eventually she ran a high fever for ten days and had to be admitted to hospital. She was started on Prednisone 90 mg. daily but needed only 10 mg. when I saw her. Her kidney was involved, and her liver was enlarged. She also had the butterfly rash on her face. At times she was depressed.

Initial Treatment: I advised D.R. to eliminate sugar, dairy products and grains. I had her take niacinamide 500 mg. and ascorbic acid 1 gram three times a day and evening primrose oil 3 capsules daily in addition to the Centrum she had been taking.

One month later D.R. was better, though she had not eliminated grains. Her hair was not falling out as fast and new hair was coming in. She still had the rash, but her mood was better. After two months her rash was worse. She had had a flareup and had to increase Prednisone to 20 mg.; I doubled her niacin. After three months all her hair was coming back, her rash began to leave and she had more energy. She was now taking 30 mg. Prednisone. In December 1991 D.R. had a kidney transplant and has been well ever since. She was on Prednisone 15 mg. every other day and was taking only Centrum daily. Her mood was good and she said she felt normal.

Conclusions: This case illustrates how the orthomolecular approach has been helpful but has had to be combined with standard treatment, usually Prednisone. Nutrition and supplements alone have not gotten my patients well nor maintained them. They have always been subject to recurrent episodes, often precipitated by virus infections such as the flu. However, the vitamins and the diet have been helpful in alleviating depression, fatigue and frequency of episodes. Unfortunately, I have not seen very early cases. I think this approach would work even better with them.

14

Benefits of Orthomolecular
Nutritional Therapy

The controversy surrounding orthomolecular treatment goes on un-
abated. It involves the use of megavitamins and minerals; the control of diet, especially the intake of sucrose; and, during the initial
acute phases of health need, all the conventional remedies to con-
front crises. Physical and mental diseases are affected by what we
put into our mouths—or fail to take in as nourishment.

"The vitamins, as nutrients or medicaments," says Linus Pauling,
Ph.D., "pose an interesting question. The question is not, Do we
need them? We know that we do need them, in small amounts to
stay alive. The real question is, What daily amounts of the various
vitamins will lead to the best of health, both physical and mental?
This question has been largely ignored by medical and nutritional
authorities."

Authorities in American medicine have a good thing going in
iatrochemistry, surgery and their powerful union, the AMA. There
is no motivation for medicine to focus on hygiene and prevention
rather than on illness and cure. Why? You have every right to ask.

Unfortunately, many aspects of today's modern medical practice
work against the idea of the healing of the whole person. Current
emphasis by traditionalists in medicine seems to be placed on
assembly-line efficiency, dependence on technology, specialty practice and the treatment of body parts rather than the total human
being. Where formerly the physician served in the multiple roles
of healer, scientist, counselor, friend and sounding board for his
patients, he has now become a victim of our world's increasing
complexity.

There is an increasing trend toward specialization in which the
physician plays a more limited and sharply defined role. The rapid
growth of medical information, both technical and philosophic, has

been overwhelming. This has contributed to medical specialization and superspecialization, with the physician knowing more and more about less and less of his patient. In many cases, he does not know the patient at all—only the patient's particular body part. In unconscious protest, perhaps, one of this book's authors, Morton Walker, changed course after sixteen years of giving treatment to pairs of feet in favor of furnishing information on super good health to the whole person. Individual body parts are not the source of ill health, although medical people frequently forget that.

The result has been that medicine attempts to isolate illness within certain structures or symptoms. Treatment is rendered mostly to the target organ. A specific body part may become the central focus of illness, even when effects of the illness are felt in varying degrees throughout the body and mind.

The medical pendulum seems to have swung radically from a focus on the clinical aspects of practice to scientific investigation. An extreme position of hyperanalysis has been adopted. We need now to return to synthesizing *all* of what we know in order to apply it in clinical terms rather than continuing on our march in the direction of analytical methods alone. Certainly medicine has contributed some significant answers in the past half century, particularly in areas of infectious diseases and infant mortality, but the price paid has been forgetfulness of the patient as a whole person.

It should be recognized that when the body is sick, it is sick throughout. A human being is a unit, an integrated organism in which no part functions independently. Abnormal structure or function in one part of the body creates unfavorable changes in other areas. Therefore, the organism is involved as a whole. Invariably involved components consist of the emotional, psychological, physiological and spiritual influences on illness and health. The entire organism mounts the attack against disorder—not just the body, and certainly not just a *part* of the body. All systems work conjointly to counteract a condition. Recovery comes only when the whole person returns to his normal and harmonious balance.

The practice of medicine that takes into account the entire individual is called *holistic medicine.* A person who seeks fully integrated treatment or follows a lifestyle that furthers living the full human lifespan is applying a program called *holistic health.*

So it is that orthomolecular nutrition holds such importance in everyday life. It offers you holistic health.

H. L. Newbold, M.D., noted neobehavioral orthomolecular psychiatrist and author of *Mega-Nutrients for Your Nerves*, believes that addictions can be precipitated by nutritional deficiencies. Dr. Newbold says that the U.S. has already reached a crisis level in nutrition. "There are a lot of people sick because of what they eat and they are not aware of it. . . . Not only is food a contributing factor to ill health, but environmental pollution, such as air, water, and noise pollution, is contributing to ill health." Dr. Newbold emphatically states that vitamin supplementation, mineral nutrients and a no-junk diet are necessary throughout an individual's life.

HOW BLIND CAN ORTHODOX MEDICINE BE?

Orthodox medicine has closed its eyes to the benefits of orthomolecular medicine. The anti-orthomolecular medical authorities suggest that (1) humans have evolved for a billion years or so and our biochemical equipment is by now adequate to cope with our environment; (2) the essential levels of vitamins are already established by the Public Health Service and other agencies of government; (3) North Americans eat well enough and get sufficient nutrients in their food; (4) orthomolecular physicians are not prominent enough and fail to back their claims with adequate research and double-blind studies.

All these objections are easily answered and have been replied to over and over again. The only real question that remains is: How blind can orthodox medicine be?

First, additives and processed foods are new innovations in the evolutionary process—only about a century old—and people do not as yet have body systems able to cope with what we are forcing our digestive tracts to absorb.

Second, the established recommended daily allowances (RDAs) of vitamins are absolutely wrong. They vary from government agency to government agency and from government to government. Besides, they fail to take into account the individuality of each person. There won't be any excessive levels of vitamins simply because the body gets rid of what it can't use.

Third, the so-called adequate average American diet, nutritionally poverty-stricken though it is, is eaten by only about half our country's citizens, reports the *Journal of Nutrition Education*. The *Jour-*

nal said, "Except for vitamin C, there was a higher percentage of females than males whose intakes were less than two-thirds RDA for all nutrients. Household studies in widely separated areas and covering a spectrum of socioeconomic levels indicate that half were below RDA in calcium, a fifth in iron, a third in vitamin A, a sixth in thiamine, a third in riboflavin, a sixth in niacin, and over a third were below recommended daily allowances (RDA) in vitamin C."

Fourth, as orthomolecular therapy cures more and more people of various diseases, its advocates will undoubtedly grow in stature and acceptability. In the meantime, research is going on. Controlled experiments may or may not be conducted with the use of double-blind techniques, which themselves induce new difficulties and errors. In view of their wide acceptance as an indispensable tool in therapeutic trials, double-blind techniques should be critically reexamined because their value has never been rigorously tested in the laboratory. They are based upon unacceptable mathematical theory; they diminish the effectiveness of two important variables in any therapeutic situation, the faith of the patient and the doctor in the therapy; they are ethically questionable; they cannot be used for comparing small heterogeneous groups; they have not led to the development of any useful new therapies in psychiatry.

In 1973, the American Psychiatric Association published a task force report with the title, "Megavitamins and Orthomolecular Therapy in Psychiatry." However, the chosen committee for such an examination failed to contain anyone who had personal experience with orthomolecular therapy. The committee offered insufficient assurance of objectivity or fairness. Its members did not obtain any evidence from anyone using orthomolecular treatment methods; they accepted double-blind studies only if the study evidence was negative and ignored studies that were positive; the members made false statements, direct and by inference; they took brief sentences out of context from the literature and used them to bolster the committee's preconceived negative view.

The American Psychiatric Association's Task Force on Megavitamin and Orthomolecular Therapy in Psychiatry seemed to look for data in such a way as to support the conclusion they wanted to reach in advance. Scientific dishonesty is a serious matter, especially in this case, to the hundreds of thousands—even millions—of people who will be deprived of a chance to recover from disease with orthomolecular medicine.

The report has had a pernicious effect in dampening interest in orthomolecular psychiatry and orthomolecular therapy in general. While this will not hurt any orthomolecular physicians, it will condemn vast numbers of people to a lifetime of tranquilized chronicity or to health problems labeled as psychosomatic or to quite obvious physical symptoms attributed to no known cause and with no known cure.

Hoffer and Osmond prepared a comprehensive reply to the APA task force report, including a list of scientific reports dealing with orthomolecular therapy and a discussion of the deficiencies inherent in the double-blind design. This is available from the Canadian Schizophrenia Foundation, 16 Florence Ave., Toronto, Ontario, Canada, M2N 1E9; telephone (416) 733-2117.

There is an answer, however, to the false and harmful conclusion the APA task force has foisted on the medical profession. Fortunately, the number of orthomolecular physicians is increasing rapidly, and acceptance of concepts of orthomolecular nutrition is gaining among the populace. Although familiar ways of eating have a kind of "security" attached to them, people are altering bad old habits. They are seeking information about how to help retain good health, and more doctors are disseminating that knowledge.

Controversy is part of the history of medicine and is essential to it if medicine is to continue to advance. There will always be promulgation of new ideas, some of which will eventually be proven wrong. There would be much less emotional controversy, however, if physicians followed the basic rule of science, that of following the same procedures and conditions when attempting to corroborate. If this rule were rigorously followed, it would not fall to a single investigatory task force to rule for or against orthomolecular psychiatry or other medical ideas. Each doctor could make his or her own judgments. Looking at the evidence, that judgment would cause every physician to adapt orthomolecular nutrition as basic armamentarium in medical practice. One can only ask the question over and over again: How blind can orthodox medicine be?

Glossary

ABSORPTION—the process by which nutrients are taken up by the intestines and are passed into the bloodstream.

ACETYLCHOLINE ESTERASE—The enzyme which destroys acetylcholine, and acetic acid ester of choline which causes cardiac inhibition, vasodilation, gastrointestinal peristalsis and other parasympathetic effects. The esterase splits acetylcholine into acetate and choline.

ACUTE—Having a sudden onset, sharp rise and short course.

ADRENOCHROME—A red-colored compound resulting from the oxidation of adrenalin.

ALLERGY—A reaction of body tissue to a specific substance.

ALZHEIMER'S DISEASE—A disease of the brain. Certain parts of the brain atrophy, and there is a gradual deterioration of all brain function leading to psychosis.

AMINO ACIDS—A class of organic compounds known as the "building blocks" of the protein molecule.

ANTIOXIDANT—A substance capable of protecting other substances from oxidation.

BALANCED MEAL—A meal containing all the essential nutrients.

BIOPHYSICAL ENVIRONMENT—Our physical world, including gravity, radiation, atmosphere and every other factor known to impinge upon us.

CATATONIC SCHIZOPHRENIA—One of the subdivisions of schizophrenia characterized by unusual rigidity and posture. Its presence is now quite rare in modern hospitals.

CHOLESTEROL—A fat-like substance found in all animal fats, bile, skin, blood and brain tissue.

CLOROSIS—A term in common use about 100 years ago to indicate a form of anemia.

DEFICIENCY—The lack of a specific nutrient or nutrients.

DEGENERATIVE DISEASES—Diseases which cause permanent deterioration of the tissues such as osteoarthritis, cancer, arteriosclerosis and at least one hundred others.

DIETETICS—The science that deals with food, primarily its preparation. Unfortunately, dietitians spend most of their time blending food for flavor, palatability and color and too little in considering the effect on the consumer of excessive sugar, additives and refined foods.

ECT—Electroconvulsive therapy, also known as "shock therapy."

ESSENTIAL AMINO ACID—An amino acid which cannot be made in the body by the human organism. There are eight essential amino acids (nine for children).

ENZYME—A substance, usually protein in nature and formed in living cells, which brings about chemical changes.

FATTY ACID—One of the components of fats. It is slightly acidic because it has a carboxylic acid group attached to it.

FOOD ADDITIVES—Chemicals added to food to change flavor, palatability, storage properties and so on. In the great majority of cases they do not enhance the nutritional quality of the food.

FOOD ARTIFACTS—Combinations of food components that cause the final product to bear no relationship to any food from which these components were extracted. A perfect example is the doughnut made from refined flour, sugar and cooked in oil.

GENETICS—The study of the inheritance of our bodies and personality.

GLYCOGEN—A substance in which carbohydrates are stored in the body.

HOD TEST—A card sorting test helpful in diagnosing schizophrenia. It is available from Behavior Science Press, 3710 Resource Drive, Tuscaloosa, AL 35401-7059.

HORMONE—A chemical substance that is secreted into body fluids and transported to another organ, where it produces a specific effect on metabolism.

HYDROGENATION—The process of introducing hydrogen into a compound, as when oils are hydrogenated to produce solid fats. This is how margarine is made.

HYPOGLYCEMIA—Blood sugar that is too low.

INSULIN SHOCK—A bad term for insulin coma. This was treatment in which large doses of insulin were given daily. Enough was given to cause a coma.

KRYPTOPYRROLE—The chemical name given to the mauve factor, an abnormal factor excreted in greater frequency in the urine of schizophrenics. It is represented by 2, 4-dimethyl -3 ethylpyrrole.

MALNUTRITION—The condition of a person who does not receive a proper proportion of all essential nutrients.

MEGADOSE—A large dose, often 100 to 1000 times as much as required to prevent deficiency diseases.

MEGAVITAMIN—The term used to describe massive quantities of a specific nutrient when given for therapeutic purposes.

METABOLISM—The chemical changes in living cells by which

energy is produced and new material is assimilated for the repair and replacement of tissues.

METHYL ACCEPTOR—A chemical which accepts and binds with a group called methyl (CH_3).

NAD—Nicotinamide adenine dinucleotide, the enzyme containing vitamin B3.

NORADRENALINE—The precursor of adrenaline or epinephrine, a hormone given off by the adrenal glands, the potent stimulant that increases heart rate and force of contraction and causes vasoconstriction or vasodilation and other physiological effects.

NUTRIENT—A substance needed by a living thing to maintain life, health and reproduction.

NUTRITION—The science that deals with the relationship between food and our needs for all the nutrients required to nourish the cells of the body, covering the biochemical processes from digestion in the gastrointestinal tract to the needs of individual cells.

OPTIDOSE—The most favorable amount of any nutrient.

OPTIMUM DIET—That diet which will provide all the essential nutrients in a form that can be digested and absorbed without disturbing the body's physiology.

ORTHOMOLECULAR MEDICINE—The practice of medicine that takes into account the nutritional needs of patients.

ORTHOMOLECULAR NUTRITION—Nutrition which recognizes the individuality of each person and recognizes that some people require very large amounts of specific nutrients. It takes into account that nutrients are often synergistic and work in harmony together.

POLYUNSATURATED—The state of an organic compound such as a fatty acid in which there is more than one double bond.

PROCESSED FOODS—Any foods in which there is a major separation of food components so that the final product is nutritionally inferior to the foods from which it is made.

PSYCHOSOCIAL ENVIRONMENT—All psychological and social factors which impinge upon every individual including culture, education, training, experience with diseases and health.

PSYCHOTIC DEPRESSION—A deep depression present for no apparent reason. It also is called endogenous depression.

PYROLURIACS—Patients who have more than 20 micrograms of kryptopyrrole in their urine.

RECOMMENDED DIETARY ALLOWANCE—The amount of nutrients suggested by the National Research Council as being necessary to maintain life processes in most healthy persons.

SATURATED FAT—A fat molecule that has no double bonds. It cannot absorb any hydrogen and does not melt at as low a temperature as unsaturated fats. Saturated fats are harder.

SUPPLEMENT—A nutrient taken in addition to regular food in one of many forms, such as pills, powder or liquid.

SYNTHETIC FOODS—This is a misnomer. Man has not yet learned how to make food. Synthetic foods are in reality food artifacts.

TOXICITY—A poisonous effect produced when a person ingests an amount of a substance that is above his or her level of tolerance.

TRACE MINERAL—An element present in minute quantities which is essential to the life of an organism.

TRIGLYCERIDES—Fats containing a three-carbon molecule and three fatty acids.

UNPROCESSED FOODS—Whole foods such as potatoes, apples, oranges, meat, nuts and everything else grown in nature.

UNSATURATED FAT—A fatty acid containing double bonds.

VITAMIN—An organic substance found in foods which performs specific and vital functions in the cells and tissues of the body.

VITAMIN DEPENDENT—A person whose optimum need for a vitamin is much greater than that required by the average person. There is no sharp demarcation between vitamin dependency and deficiency.

Suggested Additional Reading

Abrahamson, E.M., and Pezet, A.W. *Body, Mind and Sugar*. New York: Pyramid, 1971.

Adams, Ruth, and Murray, Frank. *Body, Mind and the B Vitamins*. New York: Pinnacle Books, 1975.

————. *Megavitamin Therapy*. New York: Pinnacle Books, 1975.

Airola, Paavo. *How to Get Well*. Phoenix, Ariz.: Health Plus, 1974.

Altschul, A.M. *Proteins, Their Chemistry and Politics*. New York: Basic Books, 1965.

Aladjem, H. *The Sun Is My Enemy*. Englewood Cliffs, N.J.: Prentice-Hall, 1972.

Bailey, Herbert. *Vitamin E: Your Key to a Healthy Heart*. New York: Arc Books, 1968.

Bieler, Henry G. *Food Is Your Best Medicine*. New York: Random House, 1973.

Blaine, Tom R. *Mental Health through Nutrition*. New York: Citadel Press, 1974.

Bricklin, Mark. *The Practical Encyclopedia of Natural Healing*. Emmaus, Penn.: Rodale Press, 1976.

Cameron, E., & Pauling, L. *Cancer and Vitamin C*. New York: W.W. Norton, 1979.

Cheraskin, E. *The Vitamin C Controversy: Questions and Answers*. Wichita, Kan.: Bio-Communications Press, 1988.

————, Rinsgdorf, W.M., and Brecher, A. *Psychodietetics*. New York: Bantam, 1976.

————, ————, and Clark, J.W.. *Diet and Disease*. New Canaan, Conn.: Keats Publishing, 1977.

————, ————, & Sisley, E.L. *The Vitamin C Connection*. New York: Harper & Row, 1983.

Clark, Linda. *Know Your Nutrition*. New Canaan, Conn.: Keats Publishing, 1977.

Davis, Adelle. *Let's Get Well*. New York: New American Library, 1965.

Di Cyan, E. *Vitamin E and Aging.* New York: Pyramid Books, 1972.

Erasmus, Udo. *Fats and Oils.* Vancouver, B.C.: Alive, 1986.

Finnegan, J. *The Facts about Fats.* Malibu, Calif.: Elysian Arts, 1992.

Foster, D.F. *Health, Disease and the Environment.* Boca Raton, Fla.: CRC Press, 1992.

Fredericks, Carlton, and Goodman, Herman. *Low Blood Sugar and You.* New York: Constellation International, 1976.

Goodhart, Robert S., and Shils, Maurice E. *Modern Nutrition in Health and Disease,* 5th ed. Philadelphia: Lea & Febiger, 1973.

Hawkins, D., and Pauling, L., eds. *Orthomolecular Psychiatry.* San Francisco: W.H. Freeman, 1973.

Hoffer A. *Niacin Therapy in Psychiatry.* Springfield, Ill.: C.C. Thomas, 1962.

————. *Orthomolecular Medicine for Physicians.* New Canaan, Conn.: Keats Publishing, 1989.

————, Kelm, H., and Osmond, H. *The Hoffer-Osmond Diagnostic Test.* Huntington, N.Y.: R.E. Krieger, 1975.

————, and Osmond, H. *The Hallucinogens.* New York: Academic Press, 1967.

————, and ————. *How to Live with Schizophrenia.* New York: University Books, 1966.

Horrobin, D.F. *Clinical Uses for Essential Fatty Acids.* St. Albans, N.Y.: Eden Press, 1983.

Hunter, Beatrice Trum. *The Natural Foods Primer.* New York: Simon & Schuster, 1973.

Kirschmann, John D., Nutrition Search, Inc. *Nutrition Almanac.* New York: McGraw-Hill, 1975.

Lappé, Frances M. *Diet for a Small Planet.* New York: Ballantine Books, 1975.

Lewin, S. *Vitamin C: Its Molecular Biology and Medical Potential.* New York: Academic Press, 1976.

Machlin, L.J. Introduction. *Annals, New York Academy of Sciences.* 669:1–6, 1992.

Null, Gary, and Null, Steve. *The Complete Handbook of Nutrition.* New York: Dell, 1973.

Page, Melvin E., and Abrams, H.L. *Your Body Is Your Best Doctor.* New Canaan, Conn.: Keats Publishing, 1972.

Passwater, Richard A. *Supernutrition.* New York: Pocket Books, 1976.

Pauling, L. *Vitamin C and the Common Cold*. San Francisco: W.H. Freeman, 1971.

————. *How to Live Longer and Feel Better*. New York: W.H. Freeman, 1986.

Petersdorf, R.G. et al. *Harrison's Principles of Internal Medicine*, 10th ed. New York: McGraw-Hill, 1983.

Pfeiffer, C.C. *Mental and Elemental Nutrients*. New Canaan, Conn.: Keats Publishing, 1975.

————. *Zinc and Other Micro-Nutrients*. New Canaan, Conn.: Keats Publishing, 1978.

Prasad, A.S. *Trace Elements in Human Health and Disease*. Vol. 1. *Zinc and Copper*. New York: Academic Press, 1976.

Rath, M. Annual conference, *Journal of Orthomolecular Medicine* and Canadian Schizophrenia Foundation, Toronto, 1993.

Richards, E. *Vitamin C and Cancer: Medicine or Politics?* London: Macmillan Professional and Academic, Ltd., 1991.

Rodale, J.I. *The Complete Book of Vitamins*. Emmaus, Penn.: Rodale Press, 1975.

————. *The Complete Book of Minerals for Health*. Emmaus, Penn.: Rodale Press, 1976.

Rosenberg, Harold, and Feldzaman, A.N. *The Doctor's Book of Vitamin Therapy*. New York: Berkeley, 1975.

Rudin, D.O., and Felix, C. *The Omega-3 Phenomenon*. New York: Rawson Associates, 1987.

Stone, I. *The Healing Factor: Vitamin C against Disease*. New York: Grosset & Dunlap, 1970.

Trivers, E.R. *Zinc: An Essential Trace Element*. Buena Park, Calif.: Committee for World Health, 1991.

Werbach, M.R. *Nutritional Influences on Illness: A Sourcebook of Clinical Research*. 2d ed. Tarzana, Calif.: Third Line Press, 1993.

Williams, S. *You Are Extraordinary*. New York: Random House, 1967.

————. *Nutrition Against Disease*. New York: Bantam, 1973.

————. *Physicians Handbook of Nutritional Science*. Springfield, Ill.: C.C. Thomas, 1975.

Index

Printed in the USA
CPSIA information can be obtained
at www.ICGtesting.com
JSHW011608220224
57758JS00003B/95